THE ORIGINS OF THE COLD WAR

PROBLEMS IN AMERICAN CIVILIZATION

THE ORIGINS OF THE COLD WAR

EDITED WITH AN INTRODUCTION BY

Thomas G. Paterson

UNIVERSITY OF CONNECTICUT

D. C. HEATH AND COMPANY

Lexington, Massachusetts

Printed in the United States of America

Library of Congress Number: 79–129202

CONTENTS

INTRODUCTION

WITH the defeat of Hitler's Germany in 1945, the Big Three alliance of Great Britain, Russia, and the United States began to crumble with alarming speed and impact. The diplomatic impasse and frustrating anxiety that followed were soon labeled the "Cold War," a phrase which Walter Lippmann popularized in 1947 with the publication of a book by that name. To those Americans who nurtured hopes of peaceful postwar international relations, the immediate collapse of the wartime coalition and the increase in Soviet-American tension were shocking and largely unexpected. For others, however, the antagonism was disturbing but anticipated, and for some people, perhaps desired. Indeed, the history of twentieth century Russian-American relations was not comforting to the postwar optimists, for those relations were characterized by coldness and isolation, jilted hopes, and even armed conflict before 1945. And there were two themes running through those relations which were to plague the postwar period as well: national security, and economic development and reconstruction.

The successful Bolshevik Revolution of 1917 precipitated Russia's decision to withdraw its weary people from World War I. To France, Britain, and the United States, the decision to end the war on the eastern front appeared catastrophic. Some observers believed in fact that the Bolsheviks were simply German agents. American and European leaders, considering the Marxist ideology an anathema and the Bolshevik seizure of foreign properties in Russia intolerable, were generally fearful of the success of the Revolution, its possible spread, and its ultimate questioning of and challenge to the capitalist world order. Desirous of keeping Russia in the war and of weakening the Bolsheviks, the United States contributed about 5,000 soldiers to a 1918 Allied interventionist expedition in Northern Russia. Another 10,000 Americans invaded Siberia, and were involved in anti-Bolshevik military ventures until their withdrawal in 1920. American participation in an economic blockade of Russia before 1920 put trade between the two nations on a troubled footing from the beginning. Russia was excluded from the peace conference at Versailles, and in America a Red Scare brought anti-communism to a high fever. Permanent scars were thus early imprinted on Soviet-American relations.

Although Great Britain opened diplomatic relations with Russia in 1924, American recognition was not offered until 1933. Yet recognition did not smooth diplomatic ripples, for soon after, Americans claimed Russia was fomenting international revolution. The two nations failed to reach agreement on the issue of Russian debts owed to the United States government ($193 million), to American nationals ($107 million), and to the American corporations and nationals who lost property after the Bolshevik Revolution ($337 million). Nor did Soviet-American trade improve markedly as anticipated. The diplomacy leading to World War II further embittered relations. Not invited to the Munich conference of 1938, Russia was the only major nation to denounce the appeasement agreement. The Nazi-Soviet pact of 1939 which saw two European dictators carve up helpless Poland, and Russia's seizure of Finnish territory in the "winter war" of 1940–41, confirmed American beliefs that Hitler and Stalin were two of a kind, brutal and aggressive.

After 1941, communist Russia and capitalist America were both at war with Germany, and formed an alliance of convenience for national survival. But the alliance was constantly ridden with strife. The United States and Britain failed to fulfill their 1942 promise of a second front to relieve Russia from carrying the burden of the war. That front finally came at Normandy in June, 1944; the Russians were grateful but also seriously annoyed by the delay. They believed the worst in their desperation: that many in the West were realizing their publicly stated wish that Germany and Russia would annihilate one another while the West watched. Squabbles over Lend-lease shipments, the surrender of Italy to the western front forces, and Soviet liberation of Eastern European countries also divided the Allies. The Big Three wartime conferences at Moscow (1943), Teheran (1943), Dumbarton Oaks (1944), Yalta (1945), and Potsdam (1945), although bringing agreement on the need for a second front, an international organization, the temporary division of Germany, and Russian entry into the war against Japan, left many divisive questions unanswered in statements and declarations that contained a great deal of imprecise language. The administration of Germany and Japan, German boundaries, the status of governments in Eastern Europe—especially Poland, reparations, and the voting procedure in the new United Nations Organization awaited more precise formulation in postwar settlements. In short, a long history of ill will, mutual suspicion, and indecisive conflict lay behind the break-up of the World War II alliance.

But despite the hostilities and tension, Soviet-American relations had experienced times of mutual accommodation and agreement, which suggested to some Americans that the wartime alliance might be perpetuated and that postwar conflict was not inevitable. Shared concerns about economic development and national security had at times brought the two ideologically-opposed nations together. After the removal of American troops from Russia, a period of courtship ensued. The United States encouraged Japan to withdraw its forces from Siberia and to return the island of Northern Sakhalin to Russia. Ideology was shunted aside as trade between the state-controlled economy of Soviet Russia and American businessmen increased. Henry Ford, among others, consummated deals with Soviet industry in the 1920's. And in 1933, the Roosevelt Administration, thinking that Russia might help lift America out of the depression by purchasing American products, and sharing with Russia fear of a strong Japan in the Far East, established diplomatic relations after a hiatus of sixteen years. Following Germany's attack on Russia in 1941, the United States extended valuable Lend-Lease aid to assist the Russian wartime effort, and the Russians hoped economic assistance would be continued into the postwar period. Although the wartime coalition was often rancorous, ideology was played down as Marxists and capitalists merged their common security concerns *vis-à-vis* Germany. Russia sought to eliminate one irritant by disbanding the Communist International in 1943, and on the whole, the American people, temporarily at least, moderated their anti-communist sentiments in order to preserve the alliance with the Russians. Indeed, Americans affectionately called the wartime Russian dictator, "Uncle Joe" Stalin.

As both nations jockeyed for secure international positions and adjusted their economies after the war, troublesome issues broke out in alarming frequency. The dropping of the atomic bomb in August, 1945, introduced a new and dangerous weapon which intruded into diplomacy and frightened Russians and Americans alike. The prospects of postwar American aid to Russia in 1945–46 dwindled as the United States rejected a Soviet request for a large loan. In Eastern Europe, the Soviet Union pressured governments and as American leaders increasingly protested the Soviet presence there, Soviet leaders responded by tightening their grasp on the governments of Poland, Hungary, Rumania, Bulgaria, and Czechoslovakia. The division of Germany became permanent as Russia and America squabbled over reparations and central administration. The Truman Doctrine of 1947 brought American intervention in a Greek civil war, military assistance to Turkey, and a vociferous rhetoric aimed at the containment of Soviet Russia. Developing international blocs were solidified in 1947–48 when the antagonists could not agree on a European recovery program; hence the Marshall Plan developed as an American–Western European scheme of economic reconstruction. And the contours of the European crises were carried to Asia in 1949 with the communist victory in China. That area of the world appeared to be a new battleground between the Soviet Union and the United States.

The leading participants in this series of events disagreed vigorously about the origins of the dissension. Winston Churchill, Clark Clifford, and Harry S Truman strongly blamed an aggressive and obstinate Soviet Union for the coming of the Cold War. Joseph Stalin and V. M. Molotov, in defending and explaining Russian policy, lamented the rise of an uncompromising and expansive Anglo-American bloc which, they argued, refused to recognize legitimate Soviet security fears. Internal critics of American policy like Henry Wallace and Walter Lippmann, in surveying Soviet-American relations through 1946, concluded that guilt must be shared by the United States, because its foreign policy was riddled with rigidities and premises based upon a double standard of international behavior.

Historians have in essence followed the outline of the debate as delineated by the participants. There are two major schools of thought today on the origins of the Cold War, but neither school is monolithic. Those historians who tend to accept the official explanations of the Truman Administration that the United States was largely blameless and helpless and that responsibility for the Cold War rests in Moscow, suggest that there were no workable policy alternatives for America in the face of Soviet intransigence, and hence that conflict was inevitable. This group of "traditionalist" or "orthodox" scholars is represented clearly below by Samuel Flagg Bemis, Joseph Jones, and Robert Ferrell. In addition, Arthur M. Schlesinger, Jr., Adam Ulam, Melvin Croan, Klaus Epstein, and Norman Graebner offer varying themes which fall largely in the traditionalist school, but which have links with the second school.

The other historiographical group on the origins of the Cold War has been labeled "revisionist," because its representatives have questioned the studies which stress Soviet intransigence as the sole or major cause of postwar tension. These scholars find such an explanation too simplistic, one-sided, and negligent in explaining the American role in the coming of the Cold War. Most revisionists deny that the Cold War was inevitable, and stress alternatives. They argue, too, that the United States possessed overwhelming power after the war, wanted to use it to shape an American-oriented world, and that Russia was weak and uncertain in its policy in the crucial 1945–1947 period. The studies by Gar Alperovitz, Thomas G. Paterson, Fred W. Neal, Richard Barnet, William A. Williams, and Walter LaFeber fall within the revisionist category.

It should be emphasized, however, that the two groups are not internally unified nor absolutely opposed in interpretation. The labels will become increasingly less useful, as scholars find new historical sources, refine their generalizations, and bring more sophistication to a relatively new and exciting historical field. Links between the two groups are already being extended. For example, although Arthur Schlesinger lays guilt squarely on Russia, he nevertheless criticizes some aspects of American foreign policy. And, although he sharply disagrees with Gar Alperovitz about the importance of the atomic bomb in the Cold War, Adam Ulam suggests that scholars investigate policy alternatives—and many revisionists have turned their attention to that pursuit.

Yet there are a number of key questions which divided participants and will continue to divide scholars. Which nation or leader was responsible for the Cold War? Was the conflict inevitable? Was postwar Russia aggressive? Was the United States offensive or defensive in its policies? Did Russia have a postwar blueprint for the subjugation of neighboring states? What indeed were the postwar goals of both nations? Were there viable alternative policies which might have been followed by the antagonists? What were the comparative strengths and weaknesses of Russia and America after the war? Did Russia have legitimate security fears? How important was the atomic bomb in Soviet-American relations? Why was the issue of economic reconstruction so significant? Would an American loan to Russia have made any difference? Why were Poland and Eastern Europe centers of dispute between 1945 and 1947? Why was Germany permanently divided? Why did the United States pronounce the Truman Doctrine and intervene in Greece? What role did Russia play in the Greek civil war? Why did not Russia participate in the Marshall Plan? What were the American objectives in that plan? What explains the movement of the Cold War to Asia?

The three sections of readings which follow provide both historical data and provocative interpretations of these questions. The first part develops chronologically the growing debate among contemporaries, and introduces most of the major Cold War issues. The second part chronologically and topically studies these issues in such a way as to intertwine the problems of security and economic reconstruction and to emphasize the continuity of crisis. The last part demonstrates the intensity of the scholars' debate. The chronological chart will help clarify the maze of events, and the bibliographical essay should assist the curious in reading further on the origins of the Cold War. Footnotes have been deleted for reasons of space; the original works should be consulted by those people intending further study. Abbreviations which appear below include Cominform (Communist Information Bureau), Comintern (Third Communist International), EAM (Greek National Liberation Front), ECA (Economic Cooperation Administration), ECE (Economic Commission for Europe), EDES (National Republican Greek League), ELAS (Greek National Army of Liberation), ERP (European Recovery Program), FDR (Franklin D. Roosevelt), JCS (Joint Chiefs of Staff), NATO (North Atlantic Treaty Organization), NEP (New Economic Policy), UK (United Kingdom), UNRRA (United Nations Relief and Rehabilitation Administration), and USSR (Union of Soviet Socialist Republics).

CHRONOLOGY

1945

FEBRUARY: Yalta Conference. APRIL: Jacques Duclos letter. MAY: German surrender. JUNE: UN Charter signed. JULY: US recognition of Communist-dominated Polish government. JULY 17–AUGUST 2: Potsdam Conference. AUGUST 6: Atomic bomb on Hiroshima. SEPTEMBER 11–OCTOBER 2: London Foreign Ministers meeting. NOVEMBER: Communists defeated in Hungarian national elections. DECEMBER: Moscow Foreign Ministers meeting.

1946

JANUARY: United Nations Atomic Energy Commission established; Iran charged Russia with interference in internal affairs; USSR charged Britain with interference in Greek affairs. FEBRUARY: Stalin announced new Five Year Plan and military preparations. MARCH 1: US found "lost" Russian loan request. MARCH 5: Churchill's Fulton speech. APRIL: Soviet troops left Iran and Paris Foreign Ministers meeting began. MAY: Greek civil war began again; Clay halted German reparations to USSR. JUNE: Baruch Plan presented by Truman. JULY–DECEMBER: Paris Peace Conference wrote peace treaties for Italy, Hungary, Rumania, Bulgaria, and Finland. AUGUST: USSR demanded from Turkey base in Dardanelles; US charged Poland with failure to create democracy. SEPTEMBER: Wallace speech against "get tough" policy; Wallace forced to resign. NOVEMBER: US-China treaty of friendship, commerce, and navigation; New York Foreign Ministers meeting. DECEMBER: Anglo-American agreement on economic fusion of their German zones.

1947

JANUARY: US charged Poland with violation of pledge for free elections; George C. Marshall sworn in as Secretary of State. MARCH: Communists began subversion of Hungarian government; Truman Doctrine. MARCH–APRIL: Moscow Foreign Ministers meeting. MAY: Aid to Greece-Turkey bill signed by Truman. JUNE 5: Marshall Plan speech at Harvard. JULY 2: USSR rejected Anglo-French plan for European recovery and left Paris talks. AUGUST: Polish-Russian trade agreement. OCTOBER: Cominform established by USSR. NOVEMBER–DECEMBER: London Foreign Ministers meeting. DECEMBER: Truman signed Interim Aid to Europe bill; Greek regime outlawed EAM and Communist Party.

1948

FEBRUARY: Communist coup in Czechoslovakia. MARCH: Marshall Plan passed Senate, 67–17; USSR walked out of Allied Control Council in Germany charging destruction by other three powers; House passed Marshall Plan, 329–74. APRIL: Truman signed European Recovery Act of $5.3 billion; Committee of European Economic Cooperation (16 nations and western German zones) formed. JUNE: Currency reform announced in western zones of Germany; Berlin blockade by USSR; Yugoslavia expelled from Cominform.

1949

JANUARY: Truman suggested idea of Point Four program. APRIL: NATO signed by 12 countries. MAY: Berlin blockade lifted. AUGUST: US White Paper on China announcing no more aid to Chiang Kai-Shek. SEPTEMBER: USSR exploded atomic bomb. OCTOBER: People's Republic of China (Communist) proclaimed. DECEMBER: National Chinese government of Chiang completed evacuation of mainland for Formosa.

1950

JANUARY: Hydrogen bomb development authorized by Truman. FEBRUARY: Senator Joseph McCarthy opened attacks upon alleged subversives in government. JUNE: Outbreak of Korean War.

THE CONFLICT OF OPINION

From Stettin in the Baltic to Trieste in the Adriatic, an iron curtain has descended across the continent. . . . Police governments are prevailing in nearly every case, and so far, except in Czechoslovakia, there is no true democracy.

WINSTON S. CHURCHILL

In substance, Mr. Churchill now stands in the position of a firebrand of war. And Mr. Churchill is not alone here. He has friends not only in England but also in the United States of America. . . . One cannot forget the following fact: the Germans carried out an invasion of the U.S.S.R. through Finland, Poland, Rumania, Bulgaria and Hungary. . . . One can ask, therefore, what can be surprising in the fact that the Soviet Union, in a desire to ensure its security for the future, tries to achieve that these countries should have governments whose relations to the Soviet Union are loyal?

JOSEPH STALIN

The Soviet government will never be easy to "get along with." The American people must accustom themselves to this thought, not as a cause for despair, but as a fact to be faced objectively and courageously. If we find it impossible to enlist Soviet cooperation in the solution of world problems, we should be prepared to join with the British and other Western countries in an attempt to build up a world of our own. . . . As long as the Soviet government maintains its present foreign policy, based upon the theory of an ultimate struggle between communism and capitalism, the United States must assume that the U.S.S.R. might fight at any time for the two-fold purpose of expanding the territory under Communist control and weakening its potential capitalist opponents.

CLARK CLIFFORD

How do American actions since V-J Day appear to other nations? I mean by actions the concrete things like $13 billion for the War and Navy Departments, the Bikini tests of the atomic bomb and continued production of bombs, the plan to arm Latin America with our weapons, production of B-29's and planned production of B-36's, and the effort to secure air bases spread over half the globe. . . . How would it look to us if Russia had the atomic bomb and we did not, if Russia had 10,000 bombers and air bases within a thousand miles of our coast lines and we did not? . . . Most of us are firmly convinced of the soundness of our position when we suggested the internationalization and defortification of the Danube or of the Dardanelles, but we would be horrified and angered by any Russian counter-proposal that would involve also the internationalizing and disarming of Suez or Panama. We must recognize that to the Russians these seem to be identical situations.

HENRY A. WALLACE

The Big Three chose to begin the settlement of the world war in the eastern half of Europe. This was a gigantic blunder, made by men who had had no part in the strategic conduct of the war, and failed to take into account its strategic consequences. For it narrowed the issue between Russia and the West to the very region where the conflict was sharpest and a settlement the most difficult. . . . Mr. Byrnes and Mr. Bevin have spent their energies assaulting the strongest position of Russia's vital interests. Thus they have furnished the Soviet Union with reasons, with pretexts, for an iron rule behind the iron curtain, and with ground for believing what Russians are conditioned to believe: that a coalition is being organized to destroy them.

WALTER LIPPMANN

Today the ruling circles of the U.S.A. and Great Britain head one international grouping, which has as its aim the consolidation of capitalism and the achievement of the dominations of these countries over other peoples. These countries are headed by imperialist and anti-democratic forces in international affairs, with the active participation of certain Socialist leaders in several European states.

V. M. MOLOTOV

Whether it be the control of atomic energy, aggression against small nations, the German or the Austrian peace settlements, or any of the other questions, the majority of nations concerned have found a common basis for action. But in every case the majority agreement has been rejected, denounced, and openly attacked by the Soviet Union and her satellites whose policy she controls. . . . What the world needs in order to regain a sense of security is an end to Soviet obstruction and aggression.

HARRY S TRUMAN

I. THE PARTICIPANTS DEBATE THE ORIGINS

Winston S. Churchill

THE IRON CURTAIN DROPPED BY RUSSIA

Winston S. Churchill was no longer Prime Minister of Britain when he startled many Americans by his frank but polite "Iron Curtain" speech delivered in Fulton, Missouri on March 5, 1946. He called for Anglo-American unity against a threatening, expansionistic Soviet Union and continuation of America's monopoly of the atomic bomb. Ignoring British predominance in Greece and the British Empire, the former World War II leader chastised Russia for its influence in Eastern Europe. For some observers, President Harry S Truman's presence on the platform signified American endorsement of Churchill's remarks. Indeed, Churchill stated publicly what some American officials had been uttering quietly. Exactly two months earlier, Truman had lectured Secretary of State James F. Byrnes, saying, "I'm tired of babying the Soviets."

THE United States stands at this time at the pinnacle of world power. It is a solemn moment for the American democracy. With primacy in power is also joined an awe-inspiring accountability to the future. As you look around you, you feel not only the sense of duty done but also feel anxiety lest you fall below the level of achievement. Opportunity is here now, clear and shining, for both our countries. To reject it or ignore it or fritter it away will bring upon us all the long reproaches of the after-time. It is necessary that constancy of mind, persistency of purpose, and the grand simplicity of decision shall guide and rule the conduct of the English-speaking peoples in peace as they did in war. We must and I believe we shall prove ourselves equal to this severe requirement. . . .

Before we cast away the solid assurances of national armaments for self-preservation, we must be certain that our temple is built, not upon shifting sands or quagmires, but upon the rock. Anyone with his eyes open can see that our path will be difficult and also long, but if we persevere together as we did in the two World Wars—though not, alas, in the interval between them—I cannot doubt that we shall achieve our common purpose in the end.

I have, however, a definite and practical proposal to make for action. Courts and magistrates cannot function without sheriffs and constables. The United Nations Organization must immediately begin to be equipped with an international armed force. In such a matter we can only go step by step; but we must begin now. I propose that each of the powers and states should be invited to dedicate a certain number of air squadrons to the service of the world organization. These squadrons would be trained and prepared in their own countries but would move around in rotation from one country to another. They would wear the uniform of their own countries with different badges. They would not be required to act against their own nation but in other respects they would be directed by the world organization. This might be

From the *Congressional Record,* 79th Congress, 2nd Session, pp. A1145–A1147.

started on a modest scale and a grow [sic] as confidence grew. I wished to see this done after the First World War and trust it may be done forthwith.

It would nevertheless be wrong and imprudent to entrust the secret knowledge or experience of the atomic bomb, which the United States, Great Britain, and Canada now share, to the world organization, while it is still in its infancy. It would be criminal madness to cast it adrift in this still agitated and un-united world. No one in any country has slept less well in their beds because this knowledge and the method and the raw materials to apply it are at present largely retained in American hands. I do not believe we should all have slept so soundly had the positions been reversed and some Communist or neo-Fascist state monopolized, for the time being, these dread agencies. The fear of them alone might easily have been used to enforce totalitarian systems upon the free democratic world, with consequences appalling to human imagination.

God has willed that this shall not be, and we have at least a breathing space before this peril has to be encountered, and even then, if no effort is spared, we should still possess so formidable a superiority as to impose effective deterrents upon its employment or threat of employment by others. Ultimately when the essential brother of man is truly embodied and expressed in a world organization, these powers may be confided to it. . . .

There is . . . an important question we must ask ourselves. Would a special relationship between the United States and the British Commonwealth be inconsistent with our overriding loyalties to the world organization? I reply that on the contrary, it is probably the only means by which that organization will achieve its full stature and strength. There are already the special United States relations with Canada and between the United States and the South American republics. We also have our 20 years' treaty of collaboration and mutual assistance with Soviet Russia. I agree with Mr. Bevin that it might well be a 50-year treaty. We have an alliance with Portugal unbroken since 1384. None of these clash with the general interest of a world agreement. On the contrary they help it. "In my Father's house are many mansions." Special associations between members of the United Nations which have no aggressive point against any other country, which harbor no design incompatible with the Charter of the United Nations, far from being harmful, are beneficial and, as I believe, indispensable. . . .

A shadow has fallen upon the scenes so lately lighted by the Allied victory. Nobody knows what Soviet Russia and its Communist international organization intends to do in the immediate future, or what are the limits, if any, to their expansive and proselytizing tendencies. I have a strong admiration and regard for the valiant Russian people and for my wartime comrade, Marshal Stalin. There is sympathy and good will in Britain—and I doubt not here also—toward the peoples of all the Russias and a resolve to persevere through many differences and rebuffs in establishing lasting friendships.

We understand the Russian need to be secure on her western frontiers from all renewal of German aggression. We welcome her to her rightful place among the leading nations of the world. Above all, we welcome constant, frequent, and growing contacts between the Russian people and our own people on both sides of the Atlantic. It is my duty, however, to place before you certain facts about the present position in Europe.

From Stettin in the Baltic to Trieste in the Adriatic, an iron curtain has descended across the continent. Behind that line lie all the capitals of the ancient states of central and eastern Europe. Warsaw, Berlin, Prague, Vienna, Budapest, Belgrade, Bucharest, and Sofia, all these famous cities and the populations around them lie in the Soviet sphere and all are subject, in one form or another, not only to Soviet influence but to a very high and increasing measure of control from Moscow. Athens alone, with its immortal glories, is free to decide its future at an election under British, American, and French observation.

The Russian-dominated Polish Government has been encouraged to make enormous and wrongful inroads upon Germany, and mass expulsions of millions of Germans on a scale grievous and undreamed of are now taking place. The Communist parties, which were very small in all these eastern states of Europe, have been raised to preeminence and power far beyond their numbers and are seeking everywhere to obtain totalitarian control. Police governments are prevailing in nearly every case, and so far, except in Czechoslovakia, there is no true democracy.

Turkey and Persia are both profoundly alarmed and disturbed at the claims which are made upon them and at the pressure being exerted by the Moscow government. An attempt is being made by the Russians in Berlin to build up a quasi-Communist party in their zone of occupied Germany by showing special favors to groups of left-wing German leaders. At the end of the fighting last June, the American and British Armies withdrew westward, in accordance with an earlier agreement, to a depth at some points of 150 miles on a front of nearly 400 miles, to allow the Russians to occupy this vast expanse of territory which the western democracies had conquered.

If now the Soviet Government tries, by separate action, to build up a pro-Communist Germany in their areas, this will cause new serious difficulties in the British and American zones, and will give the defeated Germans the power of putting themselves up to auction between the Soviets and the western democracies. Whatever conclusions may be drawn from these facts—and facts they are—this is certainly not the liberated Europe we fought to build up. Nor is it one which contains the essentials of permanent peace.

In front of the iron curtain which lies across Europe are other causes for anxiety. In Italy the Communist Party is seriously hampered by having to support the Communist-trained Marshal Tito's claims to former Italian territory at the head of the Adriatic. Nevertheless, the future of Italy hangs in the balance. Again, one cannot imagine a regenerated Europe without a strong France. . . .

However, in a great number of countries, far from the Russian frontiers and throughout the world, Communist fifth columns are established and work in complete unity and absolute obedience to the directions they receive from the Communist center. Except in the British Commonwealth, and in the United States, where communism is in its infancy, the Communist parties or fifth columns constitute a growing challenge and peril to Christian civilization. These are somber facts for anyone to have to recite on the morrow of a victory gained by so much splendid comradeship in arms and in the cause of freedom and democracy, and we should be most unwise not to face them squarely while time remains.

The outlook is also anxious in the Far East and especially in Manchuria. The agreement which was made at Yalta, to which I was a party, was extremely favorable to Soviet Russia, but it was made at a time when no one could say that the German war might not extend all through the summer and autumn of 1945 and when the Japanese war was expected to last for a further 18 months from the end of the German war. In this country you are all so well informed about the Far East and such devoted friends of China that I do not need to expatiate on the situation there.

I have felt bound to portray the shadow which, alike in the West and in the East, falls upon the world. I was a minister at the time of the Versailles Treaty and a close friend of Mr. Lloyd George. I did not myself agree with many things that were done, but I have a very strong impression in my mind of that situation, and I find it painful to contrast it with that which prevails now. In those days there were high hopes and unbounded confidence that the wars were over, and that the League of Nations would become all-powerful. I do not see or feel the same confidence or even the same hopes in the haggard world at this time.

On the other hand, I repulse the idea that a new war is inevitable, still more that it is imminent. It is because I am so sure that our fortunes are in our own hands and that we hold the power to save the future, that I feel the duty to speak out now that I have an occasion to do so.

I do not believe that Soviet Russia desires war. What they desire is the fruits of war and the indefinite expansion of their power and doctrines. But what we have to consider here today while time remains, is the permanent prevention of war and the establishment of conditions of freedom and democracy as rapidly as possible in all countries.

Our difficulties and dangers will not be removed by closing our eyes to them; they will not be removed by mere waiting to see what happens; nor will they be relieved by a policy of appeasement. What is needed is a settlement, and the longer this is delayed, the more difficult it will be and the greater our dangers will become. From what I have seen of our Russian friends and allies during the war, I am convinced that there is nothing they admire so much as strength, and there is nothing for which they have less respect than for military weakness. For that reason the old doctrine of a balance of power is unsound. We cannot afford, if we can help it, to work on narrow margins, offering temptations to a trial of strength. If the western democracies stand together in strict adherence to the principles of the United Nations Charter, their influence for furthering these principles will be immense and no one is likely to molest them. If, however, they become divided or falter in their duty, and if these all-important years are allowed to slip away, then indeed catastrophe may overwhelm us all.

Last time I saw it all coming, and cried aloud to my own fellow countrymen and to the world, but no one paid any attention. Up till the year 1933 or even 1935, Germany might have been saved from the awful fate which has overtaken her and we might all have been spared the miseries Hitler let loose upon mankind.

There never was a war in all history easier to prevent by timely action than the one which has just desolated such great areas of the globe. It could have been prevented without the firing of a single shot, and Germany might be powerful, prosperous, and honored today, but no one would listen and one by one we were all sucked into the awful whirlpool.

We surely must not let that happen again. This can only be achieved by reaching now, in 1946, a good understanding on all points with Russia under the general authority of the United Nations and by the maintenance of that good understanding through many peaceful years, by the world instrument, supported by the whole strength of the English-speaking world and all its connections.

Let no man underrate the abiding power of the British Empire and Commonwealth. Because you see the 46,000,000 in our island harassed about their food supply, of which they only grow one-half, even in wartime, or because we have difficulty in restarting our industries and export trade after 6 years of passionate war effort, do not suppose that we shall not come through these dark years of privations as we have come through the glorious years of agony, or that half a century from now, you will not see seventy or eighty millions of Britons spread about the world and united in defense of our traditions, our way of life, and of the world causes we and you espouse. If the population of the English-speaking Commonwealth be added to that of the United States, with all that such cooperation implies in the air, on the sea, and in science and industry, there will be no quivering, precarious balance of power to offer its temptation to ambition or adventure. On the contrary there will be an overwhelming assurance of security. If we adhere faithfully to the Charter of the United Nations and walk forward in sedate and sober strength, seeking no one's land or treasure, or seeking to lay no arbitrary control on the thoughts of men, if all British moral and material forces and convictions are joined with your own in fraternal association, the high roads of the future will be clear, not only for us but for all, not only for our time but for a century to come.

Joseph Stalin

THE HOSTILE ANGLO-AMERICAN ALLIANCE

Shortly after Churchill's Fulton speech, the Russian newspaper *Pravda* interviewed Joseph Stalin, the ruler of Russia since the 1920's. Extremely irritated by Churchill's charges, Stalin bluntly labeled them warlike and libelous. Denying that democracy had been snuffed out in Eastern Europe, he also emphasized the crucial importance of that area to Soviet security. Stalin assumed that Churchill's "friends"—the United States—accepted Churchill's conclusions.

Q. How do you assess the last speech of Mr. Churchill which was made in the United States?

A. I assess it as a dangerous act calculated to sow the seed of discord among the Allied governments and hamper their cooperation.

Q. Can one consider that the speech of Mr. Churchill is damaging to the cause of peace and security?

A. Undoubtedly, yes. In substance, Mr. Churchill now stands in the position of a firebrand of war. And Mr. Churchill is not alone here. He has friends not only in England but also in the United States of America.

In this respect, one is reminded remarkably of Hitler and his friends. Hitler began to set war loose by announcing his racial theory, declaring that only people speaking the German language represent a fully valuable nation. Mr. Churchill begins to set war loose also by a racial theory, maintaining that only nations speaking the English language are fully valuable nations, called upon to decide the destinies of the entire world.

The German racial theory brought Hitler and his friends to the conclusion that the Germans, as the only fully valuable nation, must rule over other nations. The English racial theory brings Mr. Churchill and his friends to the conclusion that nations speaking the English language, being the only fully valuable nations, should rule over the remaining nations of the world.

In substance, Mr. Churchill and his friends in England and the United States present nations not speaking the English language with something like an ultimatum: "Recognize our lordship voluntarily and then all will be well. In the contrary case, war is inevitable."

But the nations have shed their blood during five years of cruel war for the sake of liberty and the independence of their countries, and not for the sake of exchanging the lordship of Hitler for the lordship of Churchill.

It is, therefore, highly probable that the nations not speaking English and which, however, make up an enormous majority of the world's population, will not consent to go into a new slavery. The tragedy of Mr. Churchill lies in the fact that he, as a deep-rooted Tory, cannot understand this simple and obvious truth.

There is no doubt that the set-up of Mr. Churchill is a set-up for war, a call to war with the Soviet Union. . . .

Q. How do you assess that part of Mr. Churchill's speech in which he attacks the democratic regime of the European countries which are our neighbors and in which he criticizes the good neighborly relations established between these countries and the Soviet Union?

A. This part of Mr. Churchill's speech is a mixture of the elements of the libel with the elements of rudeness and lack of tact. Mr. Churchill maintains that Warsaw, Berlin, Prague, Vienna, Budapest, Belgrade, Bucharest and Sofia, all these famous cities and the populations of those areas, are within the Soviet sphere and are all subjected to Soviet influence and to the increasing control of Moscow.

Mr. Churchill qualifies this as the "boundless expansionist tendencies of the Soviet Union." It requires no special effort to show that Mr. Churchill rudely and shamelessly libels not only Moscow but also the above-mentioned States neighborly to the U.S.S.R.

To begin with, it is quite absurd to speak of the exclusive control of the U.S.S.R. in Vienna and Berlin, where there are Allied control councils with representatives of four States, where the U.S.S.R. has only one-fourth of the voices.

It happens sometimes that some people are unable to refrain from libel, but still they should know a limit.

Secondly, one cannot forget the following fact: the Germans carried out an invasion of the U.S.S.R. through Finland, Poland, Rumania, Bulgaria and Hungary. The Germans were able to carry out the invasion through these countries by reason of the fact that these countries had governments inimical to the Soviet Union.

As a result of the German invasion, the Soviet Union has irrevocably lost in battles with the Germans, and also during the German occupation and through the expulsion of Soviet citizens to German slave labor camps, about 7,000,000 people. In other words, the Soviet Union has lost in men several times more than Britain and the United States together.

It may be that some quarters are trying to push into oblivion these sacrifices of the Soviet people which insured the liberation of Europe from the Hitlerite yoke.

But the Soviet Union cannot forget them. One can ask, therefore, what can be surprising in the fact that the Soviet Union, in a desire to ensure its security for the future, tries to achieve that these countries should have governments whose relations to the Soviet Union are loyal? How can one, without having lost one's reason, qualify these peaceful aspirations of the Soviet Union as "expansionist tendencies" of our Government?

Mr. Churchill further maintains that the Polish Government under Russian lordship has been spurred to an unjust and criminal spoliation against Germany. Here, every word is a rude and offensive libel. Contemporary democratic Poland is led by outstanding men. They have shown in deeds that they know how to defend the interests and worth of their homeland, as their predecessors failed to do.

What reason has Mr. Churchill to maintain that the leaders of contemporary Poland can submit their country to a lordship by representatives of any country whatever? Does Mr. Churchill here libel the Russians because he has intentions of sowing the seeds of discord between Poland and the Soviet Union?

Mr. Churchill is not pleased that Poland should have turned her policy toward friendship and alliance with the U.S.S.R. There was a time when in the mutual relations between Poland and the U.S.S.R. there prevailed an element of conflict and contradiction. This gave a possibility to statesmen, of the kind of Mr. Churchill, to play on these contradictions, to take Poland in hand under the guise of protection from the Russians, to frighten Russia by specters of a war between Poland and herself, and to take for themselves the role of arbiters.

But this time is past. For enmity between Poland and Russia has given place to friendship between them, and Poland, present democratic Poland, does not wish any longer to be a playing-ball in the hands of foreigners. It seems to be that this is just what annoys Mr. Churchill and urges him to rude, tactless outbursts against Poland. After all, it is no laughing matter for him. He is not allowed to play for other people's stakes.

As for Mr. Churchill's attack on the Soviet Union in connection with the extending of the western boundaries of Poland, as compensation for the territories seized by the Germans in the past, there it seems to me that he quite blatantly distorts the facts.

As is known, the western frontiers of

Poland were decided upon at the Berlin conference of the three powers, on the basis of Poland's demands.

The Soviet Union repeatedly declared that it considered Poland's demands just and correct. It may well be that Mr. Churchill is not pleased with this decision. But why does Mr. Churchill, not sparing his darts against the Russians in the matter, conceal from his readers the fact that the decision was taken at the Berlin conference unanimously, that not only the Russians voted for this decision but also the English and Americans?

Why did Mr. Churchill have to delude people? Mr. Churchill further maintains that the Communist parties were very insignificant in all these Eastern European countries but reached exceptional strength, exceeding their numbers by far, and are attempting to establish totalitarian control everywhere; that police-government prevailed in almost all these countries, even up to now, with the exception of Czechoslovakia, and that there exists in them no real democracy.

As is known in Britain at present there is one party which rules the country—the Labor party. The rest of the parties are barred from the Government of the country. This is called by Churchill a true democracy, meanwhile Poland, Rumania, Yugoslavia, Bulgaria and Hungary are governed by several parties—from four to six parties. And besides, the opposition, if it is loyal, is guaranteed the right to participate in the Government. This, Churchill calls totalitarian and the Government of police.

On what grounds? Do you expect an answer from Churchill? Does he not understand the ridiculous situation he is putting himself in by such speeches on the basis of totalitarianism and police rule? Churchill would have liked Poland to be ruled by Sosnkowski and Anders, Yugoslavia by Mikhailovitch, Rumania by Prince Stirbey and Radescu, Hungary and Austria by some king from the House of Habsburg, and so on.

Mr. Churchill wants to assure us that these gentlemen from the Fascist servants' hall can ensure true democracy. Such is the Democracy of Mr. Churchill. Mr. Churchill wanders around the truth when he speaks of the growth of the influence of the Communist parties in eastern Europe. It should, however, be noted that he is not quite accurate. The influence of Communist parties grew not only in Eastern Europe but in almost every country of Europe where fascism has ruled before: Italy, Germany, Hungary, Bulgaria, Rumania, Finland, and in countries which have suffered German, Italian or Hungarian occupation. France, Belgium, Holland, Norway, Denmark, Poland, Czechoslovakia, Yugoslavia, Greece, the Soviet Union and so on.

The growth of the influence of communism cannot be considered accidental. It is a normal function. The influence of the Communists grew because during the hard years of the mastery of fascism in Europe, Communists showed themselves to be reliable, daring and self-sacrificing fighters against fascist regimes for the liberty of peoples.

Mr. Churchill sometimes recalls in his speeches the common people from small houses, patting them on the shoulder in a lordly manner and pretending to be their friend. But these people are not so simple-minded as it might appear at first sight. Common people, too, have their opinions and their own politics. And they know how to stand up for themselves.

It is they, millions of these common people, who voted Mr. Churchill and his party out in England, giving their votes to the Labor party. It is they, millions of these common people, who isolated reactionaries in Europe, collaborators with fascism, and gave preference to Left democratic parties.

It is they, millions of these common people, having tried the Communists in the fire of struggle and resistance to fascism, who decided that the Communists deserve completely the confidence of the people. Thus grew the Communists' influence in Europe. Such is the law of historical development.

Of course, Mr. Churchill does not like such a development of events. And he raised the alarm, appealing to force. But he also did not like the appearance of the Soviet regime in Russia after the First World War. Then, too, he raised the alarm and organized an armed expedition of fourteen states against Russia with the aim of turning back the wheel of history.

But history turned out to be stronger than Churchill's intervention and the quixotic antics of Churchill resulted in his complete defeat. I do not know whether Mr. Churchill and his friends will succeed in organizing after the Second World War a new military expedition against eastern Europe. But if they succeed in this, which is not very probable, since millions of common people stand on guard over the peace, then one man confidently says that they will be beaten, just as they were beaten twenty-six years ago.

Clark Clifford

AMERICAN MILITARY FIRMNESS VS. SOVIET AGGRESSION

In 1946, President Harry S Truman asked his Special Counsel, Clark Clifford, to prepare a report on American relations with Russia. After consulting the Secretary of State, the Secretary of War, the Joint Chiefs of Staff, and other high level officials, Clifford summarized their views and his own in a lengthy memorandum of September, 1946. It was a thorough indictment of postwar Soviet foreign policy, dismissing as mere rhetoric Stalin's complaints about security. The report urged the President to arm America for possible war, to enter negotiations reluctantly, and to avoid diplomatic compromises which might be interpreted as American weakness. He also emphasized the importance of American economic power as a potential means of forcing Soviet concessions.

IT IS perhaps the greatest paradox of the present day that the leaders of a nation, now stronger than it has ever been before, should embark on so aggressive a course because their nation is "weak." And yet Stalin and his cohorts proclaim that "monopoly capitalism" threatens the world with war and that Russia must strengthen her defenses against the danger of foreign attacks. The U.S.S.R., according to Kremlin propaganda, is imperilled so long as it remains within a "capitalistic encirclement." This idea is absurd when adopted by so vast a country with such great natural wealth, a population of almost 200 million and no powerful or aggressive neighbors. But the process of injecting this propaganda into the minds of the Soviet people goes on with increasing intensity.

The concept of danger from the outside is deeply rooted in the Russian people's haunting sense of insecurity inherited from their past. It is maintained by their present leaders as a justification for the oppressive nature of the Soviet police state. The thesis, that the capitalist world is conspiring to attack the Soviet Union, is not based on any objective analysis of the situation beyond Russia's borders. It has little to do, indeed, with conditions outside the Soviet Union, and it has arisen mainly from basic inner-Russian necessities which existed before the second World War and which exist today. . . .

The Soviet Government, in developing the theme of "encirclement," maintains continuous propaganda for domestic consumption regarding the dangerously aggressive intentions of American "atom diplomacy" and British imperialism, designed to arouse in the Soviet people fear and suspicion of all capitalistic nations.

Despite the fact that the Soviet Government believes in the inevitability of a conflict with the capitalist world and prepares for that conflict by building up its own strength and undermining that of other nations, its leaders want to postpone the conflict for many years. The western powers are still too strong, the U.S.S.R. is still too weak. Soviet officials must therefore not provoke, by their policies of expansion and aggression, too strong a reaction by other powers.

The Kremlin acknowledges no limit to the eventual power of the Soviet Union, but it is practical enough to be concerned with the actual position of the U.S.S.R. today. In any matter deemed essential to the security of the Soviet Union, Soviet leaders will prove adamant in their claims and demands. In other matters they will prove grasping and opportunistic, but flexible in proportion to the degree and nature of the resistance encountered.

Recognition of the need to postpone the "inevitable" conflict is in no sense a betrayal of the Communist faith. Marx and Lenin encouraged compromise and collaboration with non-communists for the accomplishment of ultimate communistic purposes. The U.S.S.R. has followed such a course in the past. In 1939 the Kremlin signed a non-aggression pact with Germany and in 1941 a neutrality pact with Japan. Soviet leaders will continue to collaborate whenever it seems expedient, for time is needed to build up Soviet strength and weaken the opposition. Time is on the side of the Soviet Union, since population growth and economic development will, in the Soviet view, bring an increase in its relative strength. . . .

A direct threat to American security is implicit in Soviet foreign policy which is designed to prepare the Soviet Union for war with the leading capitalistic nations of the world. Soviet leaders recognize that the United States will be the Soviet Union's most powerful enemy if such a war as that predicted by Communist theory ever comes about and therefore the United States is the chief target of Soviet foreign and military policy.

A recent Soviet shift of emphasis from Great Britain to the United States as the principle "enemy" has been made known to the world by harsh and strident propaganda attacks upon the United States and upon American activities and interests around the globe. The United States, as seen by radio Moscow and the Soviet press, is the principle architect of the "capitalistic encirclement" which now "menaces the liberty and welfare of the great Soviet masses." These verbal assaults on the United States are designed to justify to the Russian people the expense and hardships of maintaining a powerful military establishment and to insure the support of the Russian people for the aggressive actions of the Soviet Government.

The most obvious Soviet threat to American security is the growing ability of the U.S.S.R. to wage an offensive war against the United States. This has not hitherto been possible, in the absence of Soviet long-range strategic air power and an almost total lack of sea power. Now, however, the U.S.S.R. is rapidly developing elements of her military strength which she hitherto lacked and which will give the Soviet Union great offensive capabilities. Stalin has declared his intention of sparing no effort to build up the military strength of the Soviet Union. Development of atomic weapons, guided missiles, materials for biological warfare, a strategic air force, submarines of great cruising range, naval mines and mine craft, to name the most important, are extending the effective range of Soviet military power well into areas which the United States regards as vital to its security. . . .

Although the Soviet Union at the present moment is precluded from military aggression beyond the land mass of Eurasia, the acquisition of a strategic air force, naval forces and atomic bombs in quantity would give the U.S.S.R. the capability of striking anywhere on the globe. Ability to wage aggressive warfare in any area of the world is the ultimate goal of Soviet military policy.

* * *

The primary objective of United States policy toward the Soviet Union is to convince Soviet leaders that it is in their interest to participate in a system of world cooperation, that there are no fundamental causes for war between our two nations, and that the security and prosperity of the Soviet Union, and that of the rest of the world as well, is being jeopardized by the aggressive militaristic imperialism such as that in which the Soviet Union is now engaged.

However, these same leaders with whom we hope to achieve an understanding on the principles of international peace appear to believe that a war with the United States and the other leading capitalistic nations is inevitable. They are increasing their military power and the sphere of Soviet influence in preparation for the "inevitable" conflict, and they are trying to weaken and subvert their potential opponents by every means at their disposal. So long as these men adhere to these beliefs, it is highly dangerous to conclude that hope of international peace lies only in "accord," "mutual understanding," or "solidarity" with the Soviet Union.

Adoption of such a policy would impel the United States to make sacrifices for the sake of Soviet-U.S. relations, which would only have the effect of raising Soviet hopes and increasing Soviet demands, and to ignore alternative lines of policy, which might be much more compatible with our own national and international interests.

The Soviet Government will never be easy to "get along with." The American people must accustom themselves to this thought, not as a cause for despair, but as a fact to be faced objectively and courageously. If we find it impossible to enlist Soviet cooperation in the solution of world problems, we should be prepared to join with the British and other Western countries in an attempt to build up a world of our own which will pursue its own objectives and will recognize the Soviet orbit as a distinct entity with which conflict is not predestined but with which we cannot pursue common aims.

As long as the Soviet Government maintains its present foreign policy, based upon the theory of an ultimate struggle between communism and capitalism, the United States must assume that the U.S.S.R. might fight at any time for the two-fold purpose of expanding the territory under communist control and weakening its potential capitalist opponents. The Soviet Union was able to flow into the political vacuum of the Balkans, Eastern Europe, the Near East, Manchuria and Korea because no other nation was both willing and able to prevent it. Soviet leaders were encouraged by easy success and they are now preparing to take over new areas in the same way. The Soviet Union, as Stalin euphemistically phrased it, is preparing "for any eventuality."

Unless the United States is willing to sacrifice its future security for the sake of "accord" with the U.S.S.R. now, this government must, as a first step toward world stabilization, seek to prevent additional Soviet aggression. The greater the area controlled by the Soviet Union, the greater the military requirements of this country will be. Our present military plans are based on the assumption that, for the next few years at least, Western Europe, the Middle East, China and Japan will remain outside the Soviet sphere. If the Soviet Union acquires control of one or more of these areas, the military forces required to hold in check those of the U.S.S.R. and prevent still further acquisitions will be substantially enlarged. That will also be true if any of the naval and air bases in the Atlantic and Pacific, upon which our present plans rest, are given up. This government should be prepared, while scrupulously avoiding any act which would be an excuse for the Soviets to begin a war, to resist vigorously and successfully any efforts of the U.S.S.R. to expand into areas vital to American security.

The language of military power is the only language which disciples of power politics understand. The United States must use that language in order that Soviet leaders will realize that our government is determined to uphold the interests of its citizens and the rights of small nations. Compromise and concessions are considered, by the Soviets, to be evidences of weakness and they are encouraged by our "retreats" to make new and greater demands.

The main deterrent to Soviet attack on the United States, or to attack on areas of the world which are vital to our security, will be the military power of this country. It must be made apparent to the Soviet Government that our strength will be sufficient to repel any attack and sufficient to defeat the U.S.S.R. decisively if a war should start. The prospect of defeat is the only sure means of deterring the Soviet Union.

The Soviet Union's vulnerability is limited due to the vast area over which its key industries and natural resources are widely dispersed, but it is vulnerable to atomic weapons, biological warfare, and long-range power. Therefore, in order to maintain our strength at a level which will be effective in restraining the Soviet Union, the United States must be prepared to wage atomic and biological warfare. A highly mechanized army, which can be moved either by sea or by air, capable of seizing and holding strategic areas, must be supported by powerful naval and air forces. A war with the U.S.S.R. would be "total" in a more horrible sense than any previous war and there must be constant research for both offensive and defensive weapons.

Whether it would actually be in this country's interest to employ atomic and biological weapons against the Soviet Union in the event of hostilities is a question which would require careful consideration in the light of the circumstances prevailing at the time. The decision would probably be influenced by a number of factors, such as the Soviet Union's capacity to employ similar weapons, which can not now be estimated. But the important point is that the United States must be prepared to wage atomic and biological warfare if necessary. The mere fact of preparedness may be the only powerful deterrent to Soviet aggressive action and in this sense the only sure guaranty of peace.

The United States, with a military potential composed primarily of high effective technical weapons, should entertain no proposal for disarmament or limitation of armament as long as the possibility of Soviet aggression exists. Any discussion on the limitation of armaments should be pursued slowly and carefully with the knowledge constantly in mind that proposals on outlawing atomic warfare and long-range offensive weapons would greatly limit United States strength, while only moderately affecting the Soviet Union. The Soviet Union relies primarily on a large infantry and artillery force and the result of such arms limitation would be to deprive the United States of its most effective weapons without impairing the Soviet Union's ability to wage a quick war of aggression in Western Europe, the Middle East or the Far East.

The Soviet Government's rigid controls on travellers, and its internal security measures, enable it to develop military weapons and build up military forces without our knowledge. The United States should not agree to arms limitations until adequate intelligence of events in the U.S.S.R. is available and, as long as this situation prevails, no effort should be spared to make our forces adequate and strong. Unification of the services and the adoption of universal military training would be strong aids in carrying out a forthright United States policy. In addition to increasing the efficiency of our armed forces, this program would have a salutary psychological effect upon Soviet ambitions.

Comparable to our caution in agreeing to arms limitation, the United States should avoid premature disclosure of scientific and technological information relating to war material until we are assured of either a change in Soviet policies or workable international controls. Any disclosure would decrease the advantage the United States now has in technological fields and diminish our strength in relation to that of the U.S.S.R.

In addition to maintaining our own strength, the United States should support and assist all democratic countries which are in any way menaced or endangered by the U.S.S.R. Providing military support in case of attack is a last resort; a more effective barrier to communism is strong economic support. Trade agreements, loans and technical missions strengthen our ties with friendly nations and are effective demonstrations that capitalism is at least the equal of communism. The United States can do much to ensure that economic opportunities, personal freedom and social equality are made possible in countries outside the Soviet sphere by generous financial assistance. Our policy on reparations should be directed toward strengthening the areas we are endeavoring to keep outside the Soviet sphere. Our efforts to break down trade barriers, open up rivers and international waterways, and bring about economic unification of countries, now divided by occupation armies, are also directed toward the re-establishment of vigorous and healthy non-communist economies.

The Soviet Union recognizes the effectiveness of American economic assistance to small nations and denounces it bitterly by constant propaganda. The United States should realize that Soviet propaganda is dangerous (especially when American "imperialism" is emphasized) and should avoid any actions which give an appearance of truth to the Soviet charges. A determined effort should be made to expose the fallacies of such propaganda.

*   *   *

In conclusion, as long as the Soviet Government adheres to its present policy, the United States should maintain military forces powerful enough to restrain the Soviet Union and to confine Soviet influence to its present area. All nations not now within the Soviet sphere should be given generous economic assistance and political support in their opposition to Soviet penetration. Economic aid may also be given to the Soviet Government and private trade with the U.S.S.R. permitted provided the results are beneficial to our interests and do not simply strengthen the Soviet program. We should continue to work for cultural and intellectual understanding between the United States and the Soviet Union but that does not mean that, under the guise of an exchange program, communist subversion and infiltration in the United States will be tolerated. In order to carry out an effective policy toward the Soviet Union, the United States Government should coordinate its own activities, inform and instruct the American people about the Soviet Union, and enlist their support based upon knowledge and confidence. These actions by the United States are necessary before we shall ever be able to achieve understanding and accord with the Soviet Government on any terms other than its own.

Even though Soviet leaders profess to believe that the conflict between Capitalism and Communism is irreconcilable and must eventually be resolved by the triumph of the latter, it is our hope that they will change their minds and work out with us a fair and equitable settlement when they realize that we are too strong to be beaten and too determined to be frightened.

Henry A. Wallace

THE AMERICAN DOUBLE STANDARD

Disturbed by what he believed was growing American militancy and hostility toward Russia, Secretary of Commerce Henry Wallace wrote the following letter to the President in July, 1946. It was made public in September after Wallace was ousted from the Cabinet for his dissenting foreign policy views. He criticized American policy for applying a double standard to American actions and to those of other nations. Wallace held that American influence in Latin America was similar to Soviet influence in Eastern Europe, and since the United States was in no position to remove the Soviet presence from Eastern Europe, recognition of the *fait accompli* would reduce real Soviet security fears. In essence refuting Churchill and Clifford, Wallace told the President that the awesome American monopoly of atomic power and superior economic power were major contributors to Soviet-American tension. In 1948, Wallace took his ideas unsuccessfully into the political campaign as a presidential candidate for the Progressive Party.

HOW DO American actions since V-J Day appear to other nations? I mean by actions the concrete things like $13 billion for the War and Navy Departments, the Bikini tests of the atomic bomb and continued production of bombs, the plan to arm Latin America with our weapons, production of B-29's and planned production of B-36's, and the effort to secure air bases spread over half the globe from which the other half of the globe can be bombed. I cannot but feel that these actions must make it look to the rest of the world as if we were only paying lip-service to peace at the conference table. These facts rather make it appear either (1) that we are preparing ourselves to win the war which we regard as inevitable or (2) that we are trying to build up a predominance of force to intimidate the rest of mankind. How would it look to us if Russia had the atomic bomb and we did not, if Russia had 10,000-mile bombers and air bases within a thousand miles of our coast lines and we did not?

Some of the military men and self-styled "realists" are saying: "What's wrong with trying to build up a predominance of force? The only way to preserve peace is for this country to be so well armed that no one will dare attack us. We know that America will never start a war."

The flaw in this policy is simply that it will not work. In a world of atomic bombs and other revolutionary new weapons, such as radioactive poison gases and biological warfare, a peace maintained by a predominance of force is no longer possible.

Why is this so? The reasons are clear:

First. Atomic warfare is cheap and easy compared with old-fashioned war. Within a very few years several countries can have atomic bombs and other atomic weapons. Compared with the cost of large armies and the manufacture of old-fashioned weapons, atomic bombs cost very little and require only a relatively small part of a nation's production plant and labor force.

Second. So far as winning a war is concerned, having more bombs—even many more bombs—than the other fellow is no longer a decisive advantage. If another nation had enough bombs to eliminate all of our principal cities and our heavy industry, it wouldn't help us very much if we had ten times as many

From Henry A. Wallace, "The Path to Peace with Russia," *New Republic*, 115 (September 30, 1946), pp. 401–406.

bombs as we needed to do the same to them.

Third. The most important, the very fact that several nations have atomic bombs will inevitably result in a neurotic, fear-ridden, itching-trigger psychology in all the peoples of the world, and because of our wealth and vulnerability we would be among the most seriously affected. Atomic war will not require vast and time-consuming preparations, the mobilization of large armies, the conversion of a large proportion of a country's industrial plants to the manufacture of weapons. In a world armed with atomic weapons, some incident will lead to the use of those weapons.

There is a school of military thinking which recognizes these facts, recognizes that when several nations have atomic bombs, a war which will destroy modern civilization will result and that no nation or combination of nations can win such a war. This school of thought therefore advocates a "preventive war," an attack on Russia now, before Russia has atomic bombs. This scheme is not only immoral but stupid. If we should attempt to destroy all the principal Russian cities and her heavy industry, we might well succeed. But the immediate counter-measure which such an attack would call forth is the prompt occupation of all continental Europe by the Red Army. Would we be prepared to destroy the cities of all Europe in trying to finish what we had started? This idea is so contrary to all the basic instincts and principles of the American people that any such action would be possible only under a dictatorship at home.

Thus the "predominance of force" idea and the notion of a "defensive attack" are both unworkable. The only solution is the one which you have so wisely advanced and which forms the basis of the Moscow statement on atomic energy. That solution consists of mutual trust and confidence among nations, atomic disarmament and an effective system of enforcing that disarmament.

There is, however, a fatal defect in the Moscow statement, in the Acheson report, and in the American plan recently presented to the United Nations Atomic Energy Commission. That defect is the scheme, as it is generally understood, of arriving at international agreements by "easy stages," of requiring other nations to enter into binding commitments not to conduct research into the military uses of atomic energy and to disclose their uranium and thorium resources while the United States retains the right to withhold its technical knowledge of atomic energy until the international control and inspection system is working to our satisfaction. In other words, we are telling the Russians that if they are "good boys" we may eventually turn over our knowledge of atomic energy to them and to the other nations. But there is no objective standard of what will qualify them as being "good" nor any specified time for sharing our knowledge.

Is it any wonder that the Russians did not show any great enthusiasm for our plan? Would we have been enthusiastic if the Russians had a monopoly of atomic energy, and offered to share the information with us at some indefinite time in the future at their discretion if we agreed now not to try to make a bomb and give them information on our secret resources of uranium and thorium? I think we should react as the Russians appear to have done. We would have put up counter-proposal for the record, but our real effort would go into trying to make a bomb so that our bargaining position would be equalized. . . .

Insistence on our part that the game must be played our way will only lead to a deadlock. The Russians will redouble their efforts to manufacture bombs, and they may also decide to expand their "security zone" in a serious way. Up to now, despite all our outcries against it, their efforts to develop a security zone in Eastern Europe and in the Middle East are small change from the point of view of military power as compared with our air bases in Greenland, Okinawa and many other places thousands of miles from our shores. We may feel very self-righteous if we refuse to budge on our plan and the Russians refuse to accept it, but that means only one thing—the atomic-armament race is on in deadly earnest.

I am convinced therefore that if we

are to achieve our hopes of negotiating a treaty which will result in effective international atomic disarmament we must abandon the impractical form of the "step-by-step" idea which was presented to the United Nations Atomic Energy Commission. We must be prepared to reach an agreement which will commit us to disclosing information and destroying our bombs at a specific time or in terms of specified actions by other countries, rather than at our unfettered discretion. If we are willing to negotiate on this basis, I believe the Russians will also negotiate seriously with a view to reaching an agreement.

There can be, of course, no absolute assurance the Russians will finally agree to a workable plan if we adopt this view. They may prefer to stall until they also have bombs and can negotiate on a more equal basis, not realizing the danger to themselves as well as the rest of the world in a situation in which several nations have atomic bombs. But we must make the effort to head off the atomic-bomb race. We have everything to gain by doing so, and do not give up anything by adopting this policy as the fundamental basis for our negotiation. During the transition period toward full-scale international control we retain our technical know-how, and the only existing production plants for fissionable materials and bombs remain within our borders. . . .

Our basic distrust of the Russians, which has been greatly intensified in recent months by the playing up of conflict in the press, stems from differences in political and economic organizations. For the first time in our history defeatists among us have raised the fear of another system as a successful rival to democracy and free enterprise in other countries and perhaps even our own. I am convinced that we can meet that challenge as we have in the past by demonstrating that economic abundance can be achieved without sacrificing personal, political and religious liberties. We cannot meet it, as Hitler tried to, by an anti-Comintern alliance.

It is perhaps too easy to forget that despite the deep-seated differences in our culture and intensive anti-Russian propaganda of some twenty-five years' standing, the American people reversed their attitudes during the crisis of war. Today, under the pressure of seemingly insoluble international problems and continuing deadlocks, the tide of American public opinion is again turning against Russia. In this reaction lies one of the dangers to which this letter is addressed.

I should list the factors which make for Russian distrust of the United States and of the Western world as follows: The first is Russian history, which we must take into account because it is the setting in which Russians see all actions and policies of the rest of the world. Russian history for over a thousand years has been a succession of attempts, often unsuccessful, to resist invasion and conquest—by the Mongols, the Turks, the Swedes, the Germans and the Poles. The scant thirty years of the existence of the Soviet government has in Russian eyes been a continuation of their historical struggle for national existence. The first four years of the new regime, from 1917 through 1921, were spent in resisting attempts at destruction by the Japanese, British and French, with some American assistance, and by the several White Russian armies encouraged and financed by the Western powers. Then, in 1941, the Soviet state was almost conquered by the Germans after a period during which the Western European powers had apparently acquiesced in the rearming of Germany in the belief that the Nazis would seek to expand eastward rather than westward. The Russians, therefore, obviously see themselves as fighting for their existence in a hostile world.

Second, it follows that to the Russians all of the defense and security measures of the Western powers seem to have an aggressive intent. Our actions to expand our military security system—such steps as extending the Monroe Doctrine to include the arming of the Western Hemisphere nations, our present monopoly of the atomic bomb, our interest in outlying bases and our general support of the British Empire—appear to them as going far beyond the requirements of defense. I think we might feel the same if the

United States were the only capitalistic country in the world and the principal socialistic countries were creating a level of armed strength far exceeding anything in their previous history. From the Russian point of view, also, the granting of a loan to Britain and the lack of tangible results on their request to borrow for rehabilitation purposes may be regarded as another evidence of strengthening of an anti-Soviet bloc.

Finally, our resistance to her attempts to obtain warm-water ports and her own security system in the form of "friendly" neighboring states seems, from the Russian point of view, to clinch the case. After twenty-five years of isolation and after having achieved the status of a major power, Russia believes that she is entitled to recognition of her new status. Our interest in establishing democracy in Eastern Europe, where democracy by and large has never existed, seems to her an attempt to reëstablish the encirclement of unfriendly neighbors which was created after the last war and which might serve as a springboard of still another effort to destroy her.

If this analysis is correct, and there is ample evidence to support it, the action to improve the situation is clearly indicated. The fundamental objective of such action should be to allay any reasonable Russian grounds for fear, suspicions and distrust. We must recognize that the world has changed and that today there can be no "one world" unless the United States and Russia can find some way of living together. For example, most of us are firmly convinced of the soundness of our position when we suggest the internationalization and defortification of the Danube or of the Dardanelles, but we would be horrified and angered by any Russian counter-proposal that would involve also the internationalizing and disarming of Suez or Panama. We must recognize that to the Russians these seem to be identical situations.

We should ascertain from a fresh point of view what Russia believes to be essential to her own security as a prerequisite to the writing of the peace and to coöperation in the construction of a world order. We should be prepared to judge her requirements against the background of what we ourselves and the British have insisted upon as essential to our respective security. We should be prepared, even at the expense of risking epithets of appeasement, to agree to reasonable Russian guarantees of security....

We should also be prepared to enter into economic discussions without demanding that the Russians agree in advance to discussion of a series of what are to them difficult and somewhat unrelated political and economic concessions. Although this is the field in which my department is most directly concerned, I must say that in my opinion this aspect of the problem is not as critical as some of the others, and certainly is far less important than the question of atomic-energy control. But successful negotiation in this field might help considerably to bridge the chasm that separates us. The question of a loan should be approached on economic and commercial grounds and should be dissociated as much as possible from the current misunderstandings which flow from the basic differences between their system and ours. You have already clearly dissociated yourself and the American people from the expressions of anti-Soviet support for the British loan. If we could have followed up your statement on signing the British-loan bill with a loan to the USSR on a commercial basis and on similar financial terms, I believe that it would have clearly demonstrated that this country is not attempting to use its economic resources in the game of power politics. In the light of the present Export-Import Bank situation it is now of the greatest importance that we undertake general economic discussions at an early date.

It is of the greatest importance that we should discuss with the Russians in a friendly way their long-range economic problems and the future of our coöperation in matters of trade. The reconstruction program of the USSR and the plans for the full development of the Soviet Union offer tremendous opportunities for American goods and American technicians.

American products, especially machines of all kinds, are well established in the Soviet Union. For example, American equipment, practices and methods are standard in coal mining, iron and steel, oil and non-ferrous metals.

Nor would this trade be one-sided. Although the Soviet Union has been an excellent credit risk in the past, eventually the goods and services exported from this country must be paid for by the Russians by exports to us and to other countries. Russian products which are either definitely needed or which are non-competitive in this country are various non-ferrous metal ores, furs, linen products, lumber products, vegetable drugs, paper and pulp and native handicrafts. . . .

Many of the problems relating to the countries bordering on Russia could more readily be solved once an atmosphere of mutual trust and confidence is established and some form of economic arrangements is worked out with Russia. These problems also might be helped by discussions of an economic nature. Russian economic penetration of the Danube area, for example, might be countered by concrete proposals for economic collaboration in the development of the resources of this area, rather than by insisting that the Russians should cease their unilateral penetration and offering no solution to the present economic chaos there.

This proposal admittedly calls for a shift in some of our thinking about international matters. It is imperative that we make this shift. We have little time to lose. Our post-war actions have not yet been adjusted to the lessons to be gained from experience of Allied coöperation during the war and the facts of the atomic age.

It is certainly desirable that, as far as possible, we achieve unity on the home front with respect to our international relations; but unity on the basis of building up conflict abroad would prove to be not only unsound but disastrous. I think there is some reason to fear that in our earnest efforts to achieve bipartisan unity in this country we may have given way too much to isolationism masquerading as tough realism in international affairs.

Walter Lippmann

THE FAILURE OF THE PEACEMAKERS

Walter Lippmann had been commenting on foreign policy questions for over thirty years when he wrote an assessment of postwar disunity in late 1946. His essay invited the great powers to shift their attention from the insoluble Eastern European area or face repeated conflict. He held, too, that Western leadership was somewhat ill-equipped to handle postwar issues, and he lamented the diplomatic stalemate which impeded European reconstruction. With the publication of *The Cold War* in 1947, Lippmann established himself as a vociferous critic of the doctrine of containment of Russia made famous by George F. Kennan's "The Sources of Soviet Conduct" in *Foreign Affairs* magazine (1947).

FIFTEEN months have elapsed, as this article goes to press, since Potsdam, where the Big Three decided to approach the settlement of the world war by negotiating treaties for the European satellite states. A phase of this first chapter of the peacemaking ended with the adjournment in Paris on October 15 of the conference of the twenty-one nations. The Big Four, France having been admitted after Potsdam, are now at work in New York trying to conclude these treaties. They have fixed on the end of November as the time to begin to discuss a settlement with Germany. They have no agreement about when they will discuss Austria. They have not yet begun to discuss when they will begin to discuss the settlement with Japan.

The calendar and the agenda of the peacemaking are extraordinary, indeed astonishing. After no great war of modern times have the victors allowed so much time to pass before treating with their principal enemies. And though this is supposed to be the global settlement of a war that made this "one world," we have thus far confined our peacemaking to one region of the world.

If we ask why there has been this unusually long delay in coming to grips with the main issues of a settlement, why instead there has been this prolonged preoccupation with the satellites, the explanation would, I suppose, be that it is inordinately difficult to deal with Soviet Russia. Now there is no doubt that Mr. Truman and Mr. Byrnes, Mr. Attlee and Mr. Bevin, have found it inordinately difficult to deal with Soviet Russia. But this is not a sufficient explanation. For while it might explain a failure to reach agreement for a general settlement, which would require a settlement for Germany and Japan, it does not explain the fact that fifteen months have passed without a serious attempt to begin to negotiate a general settlement.

We must look for the explanation by asking how it happened, and why, contrary to all precedents in the making of peace, the Allies decided to postpone the settlements with the chief enemy states and to deal instead with the satellites of Germany. They took this decision at Potsdam. They took it, I believe, as the consequence of three considerations which at the time seemed of paramount importance to the Soviet Union, to Britain, and to the United States. The first was that Russia insisted on fixing *de facto* a new eastern frontier for Germany on the line of the Oder and the western Neisse. The second was that Britain had been given the sole control of Northwestern Germany, which contains 70 per cent of the pre-war German heavy industry, and is the most important economic region of Europe. The third was that the United States insisted that we should have the sole control and the deciding voice in the occupation of Japan. By these three decisions each of the Big Three powers got what each of them most wanted immediately. After that a general settlement of the war, which would have had to deal with Germany and Japan, was postponed indefinitely.

Had Germany been put first on the agenda for Europe, the concession to the Soviet Union on the eastern frontier would have been reopened at once. The British control of the Ruhr and of German heavy industry would have had to be re-examined. There would have had to be negotiations about all the frontiers of Germany, not merely about the eastern. Silesia would have had to be examined along with the Ruhr, and East Prussia along with the Rhineland, and instead of the simple decision conceding the claims of Poland and the Soviet Union, there would have had to be an equal consideration of the claims of France, the Netherlands, and Belgium. It would have been necessary to strike a balance that took into account the security of all of Germany's victims, and their right to reparations, and the future of Germany itself as a viable state. It would have been necessary, in short, to negotiate, and not to postpone, a European settlement.

But the United States was inhibited from insisting upon a European settlement around Germany because the Russians would have countered by asking for a simultaneous settlement in Eastern Asia around Japan. We were as little anxious to negotiate immediately about Japan as the Russians or the British were about Germany. Russia and Britain and America would each have had to surrender the special and peculiar position it had obtained—Russia because she had played the main part in defeating Germany and was at the Elbe, Britain because Mr. Churchill had persuaded President Roosevelt to let him have the Ruhr, we because we had conquered Japan and were in possession of it.

When the Potsdam Conference had confirmed the Russian position in Eastern Germany, the British position in the Ruhr, and our position in Japan, the Allies had left on their agenda only the European satellites. And so, contrary to all precedents in settling wars, they chose to begin their peacemaking with the satellites of their principal enemy.

This meant that they would attempt to govern the moon in order to regulate the sun. For a satellite is by definition a secondary planet which revolves around a larger one. Italy, Rumania, Bulgaria, Finland, Hungary, and also Austria, were, are, and are destined to remain, secondary powers. What becomes of them, what should be done with them and for them, and what can be done, depend on the structure of Europe as a whole. Europe cannot be reconstructed around the satellites: the satellites have to be fitted into the reconstruction of Europe. For this reason no statesmen interested in a general world settlement would have considered it possible or wise to deal with the satellites until there had been a settlement among the great powers. But after Potsdam the Allied statesmen had foreclosed a general settlement.

They were confirmed in their choice of the satellites as the subject of their labors by two opposite but complementary purposes. The Soviet Union was interested in dealing with the satellites first. For this meant that the settlements would be made while the Red Army was still near its maximum power and prestige. Excepting Italy, all the satellites were under Russian military occupation, and, therefore, Russia would have the first word and the last in the negotiations. In the case of Italy the Russian and the Yugoslav claims had a better chance if they were pressed before a settlement with Germany had removed the reason for maintaining huge armies in the heart of Europe.

The British and Americans were also preoccupied with the satellites. Mr. Churchill was most particularly concerned about the strength of the Red Army and its advance to the Elbe River. Now Mr. Bevin and Mr. Byrnes were unable to force the Red Army to retire from Central Europe. But they undertook to make the Red Army retire by concentrating on the satellites. The Russians were as far west as they were because they were occupying the satellites. Mr. Byrnes and Mr. Bevin thought that if they could conclude treaties of peace with the satellites, the Russians would then have to evacuate Central and Eastern Europe. This would, they told themselves, arrest the spread of communism, would reestablish democracy and liberty behind the iron curtain, and would restore the balance of power in Germany and in Europe, which had been so radically upset by the advance of the Red Army to the Elbe River.

From the London Conference of September, 1945, through the Paris Conference which closed in October, 1946, they worked on this particular project to the exclusion of all other projects for the settlement of the world war.

The Big Three chose to begin the settlement of the world war in the eastern half of Europe. This was a gigantic blunder, made by men who had had no part in the strategic conduct of the war, and failed to take into account its strategic consequences. For it narrowed the issue between Russia and the West to the very region where the conflict was sharpest and a settlement the most difficult.

Rumania, Bulgaria, Hungary, and Finland had been occupied by the Red Army. The greater part of Venezia Giulia to the suburbs of Gorizia and Trieste was occupied by the Yugoslav Army. The Italian peninsula, up to the line to which Tito's troops were pushed back, was occupied by British and American troops. The Italian colonial empire was occupied by British troops. Given the military position at the end of the war, it would not have been possible to choose a worse theater of diplomatic negotiation in which to initiate a world settlement.

Mr. Byrnes and Mr. Bevin had set themselves an impossible task. While they held firmly for the Western powers the whole position in Africa and the Mediterranean—which they had won by defeating Italy—and the whole of Western Germany containing 46 million Germans to 18 million in the Russian zone, containing the greater part of the demobilized and disbanded veterans of the Wehrmacht and 70 per cent of Germany's pre-war heavy industry, they undertook by negotiation and diplomatic pressure to reduce the position in Eastern Europe—which the Soviet Union had won because the Red Army had defeated two thirds of the German Army.

I am not saying that it was not a desirable and a necessary thing to reduce the military expansion of Russia. I have no doubt that it is. But I am saying that it was an impossible thing to do immediately, and as our prime object, in the first few months after the war. Mr. Byrnes and Mr. Bevin, armed only with the Atlantic Charter and the Yalta Declaration, were attempting to take by frontal assault the main positions held by the Red Army. These positions are looked upon by all Russians as the British look upon the Low Countries, as we look upon the Caribbean region—as vital to the security of Russia against invasion. Mr. Byrnes and Mr. Bevin picked the one region of the globe where the Soviet Union was the strongest, and we most nearly impotent. In this region the Russians were in possession and could act; Mr. Byrnes and Mr. Bevin could only argue and protest.

In any other region they had power, influence, and possessions with which to bargain. They had two thirds of Germany, much the best part of Germany. They had Japan. They had the leading position in China. They had as their close partners France and the highly civilized nations of Western and Northern and Southern Europe. They had the Mediterranean. They had the Middle East. They had the whole of Africa. They had Southern Asia. They had the whole colonial world. They had the whole democratic world. They had the whole capitalist system. They were preponderant in the organization of the United Nations. They had command of all the seas. They had command of the air. They had the atomic bomb.

The one thing they did not have was ground armies to match the Red Army in the region which the Red Army had just conquered triumphantly, and at a terrible cost of blood and treasure. Yet that was the region where they elected to put to the test their relations with the Soviet Union and the whole great business of a world settlement.

Was it not certain that here they must fail, as in fact they have failed, and in the failure to reach a settlement where it was most difficult to reach it, that they must make it infinitely difficult to make any general settlement? Let no one seek to explain away the failure by pointing out how brutal, how stubborn, how faithless, how aggressive the Russians have proved themselves to be. The worse one thinks of the Russians, the greater must be deemed the error of having elected to challenge the Russians first of all on the ground where they were most able to be, and were most certain to be, brutal, stubborn, faithless, and aggressive.

When Mr. Byrnes and Mr. Bevin decided to concentrate their efforts on Eastern Europe, they may have believed that they could not deal with Germany, with Europe as a whole, with the Mediterranean, the Middle East, the Far East, and the colonies unless they could first reduce the power of the Soviet Union. But they had no way of compelling the Soviet Union to relax its grip on Eastern Europe. There may have been as many as 200 Soviet divisions within reach of that region of the world, whereas the British and American forces were being withdrawn and demobilized rapidly.

If, as many of Mr. Byrnes's advisers believed, the Russians wished to keep the non-Soviet world unsettled while they consolidated their own conquests behind the iron curtain, then Machiavelli himself could not have devised a plan which served better this Russian purpose. Mr. Byrnes and Mr. Bevin have spent their energies assaulting the strongest position of Russia's vital interests. Thus they have furnished the Soviet Union with reasons, with pretexts, for an iron rule behind the iron curtain, and with ground for believing what Russians are conditioned to believe: that a coalition is being organized to destroy them.

At the same time Mr. Bevin and Mr. Byrnes have subjected the small nations, which they meant to befriend, to the cruel ordeal of having to stand up publicly every day and, in the presence of Messrs. Molotov and Vishinsky, to say whether they are with the Soviet Union or with the Anglo-Americans. As a result we have compromised the political leaders and parties in Poland and elsewhere who wished to be independent of Moscow. We have sponsored them without in fact being able to support them. . . .

Poland is no more independent than it was—though we have pounded on the iron curtain for more than a year. For Poland cannot be made an independent state simply by detaching Poland from Russian domination. The fact is that Poland cannot live independently in a political vacuum. Poland can be independent only if she is attached to a European system which has settled with Germany. The same holds for Austria, for Hungary, and for Czechoslovakia. They cannot, they will not, they dare not, detach themselves from Russia unless there is something else to which they can attach themselves. That something else cannot be the waning power of Britain or the distant power of the United States. It can be only a framework for continental Europe. . . .

The answer to Russian domination in Eastern Europe was to confront them with the solidarity of the West, as an accomplished fact. Then, instead of our pushing against and picking at the Russian orbit, we should have been pulling the people of Europe away from it, pulling them not into a British-American orbit but into the orbit of Europe itself. The peoples of Eastern Europe would have had another place to go. They would have had reason for going there. But now, as we have managed the matter, we have invited them to quarrel with the Russians though we can give them only our moral support. We have not offered them the prospect of the solidarity of Europe but a choice between the Russians and ourselves—with the Continent as the appointed theater of another war.

It is most significant, I think, that in this country and in Great Britain, the men who have been trying to settle the war are a different set of men from those who conducted the war. This is most unusual. The leading figures at the Congress of Vienna and at the Paris Conference of 1919 were the leading figures of the war. But this time they have not been. Roosevelt was dead, Churchill was out of office, and Stalin had withdrawn into the recesses of the Kremlin. . . .

As the war was concluded and before it could be settled, Roosevelt and Churchill were replaced by Truman and Attlee, Byrnes and Bevin. The peacemakers for the Western world were men to whom the problems of war and the settlement of war were novel. They had experience only in the internal politics of the two democracies, where the consideration of high strategy and high diplomacy plays no part. The settlement of the war, which was integral with the conduct of the war, was abruptly transferred from the commanders-in-chief to civilian politicians.

Mr. Attlee and Mr. Bevin had, to be sure, been members of the War Cabinet, and had no doubt been kept reasonably well-informed by Mr. Churchill and Mr. Eden about the course of the war. But they had been immersed in domestic affairs and neither of them had, I believe, ever participated in any of the international councils of war before they took over at Potsdam. Mr. Truman had been a Senator who investigated aspects of our own mobilization. He had had no part in the direction of the war. Mr. Byrnes had been at the White House, and therefore much closer to the center of things. But until he attended the Yalta Conference, his task was to act for the President on matters that were not in the field of high policy, so that the President would be free to devote his main attention to the strategy and diplomacy of the war.

The civilian politicians, suddenly and unexpectedly charged with the settlement of the war, were unable to learn quickly the vocabulary and the grammar of diplomacy. Thus they mistook the strategical realities, and committed themselves to the task of negotiating the Soviet Union out of the sphere of its maximum interest and influence. When they found that they could not do this by arguing with M. Molotov, they fell back on the procedure and the tactics which they had learned to use against their opponents in domestic politics. . . .

But to apply the methods of domestic politics to international politics is like using the rules of checkers in a game of chess. Within a democratic state, conflicts are decided by an actual or a potential count of votes—as the saying goes, by ballots rather than bullets. But in a world of sovereign states conflicts are decided by power, actual or potential, for the ultimate arbiter is not an election but war.

To apply among sovereign states the procedures of a democratic state is, therefore, to invite trouble. The voting cannot decide the issue. But the issues are sharply defined by the voting. This causes everyone to speculate on the chances of war. Mr. Byrnes came home from Paris and deplored the amount of talk about war. But if day after day the use of public votes has advertised—the apologists say "clarified"—a conflict among armed states, and if it is demonstrated day after day that a majority of votes does not decide the issue, it is inevitable that men should think about war, which is the only arbiter that can decide an irreconcilable issue among great powers.

So what the world has seen is not the triumph of democracy but a failure of diplomacy. Yet it is only by diplomacy that the interests of sovereign nations can be modified, adjusted, and reconciled.

This failure of diplomacy is not necessarily fatal and irreparable. The first year of peacemaking may prove to have been the hardest and the worst. For while the peacemakers have not advanced towards a settlement, or even conceived in outline the form and structure of a settlement, their peoples realize it. They themselves may realize it. What they have come to is a deadlock and a stalemate. But since everywhere the hatred of war is much stronger than the willingness to fight a war, there is a margin of safety in the diplomatic failure.

V. M. Molotov

THE IMPERIALISM OF AMERICA AND BRITAIN

On the thirtieth anniversary of the Bolshevik Revolution in 1947, Russian Foreign Minister V. M. Molotov complained of aggressive Anglo-American capitalism and militarism. In a rhetorical style very similar to that evident in American Independence Day orations, Molotov blamed the United States for postwar tension and made his case for a history of Russian anti-imperialism. Molotov held his post from 1939 to 1949, and again from 1953 to 1956.

THE Soviet Union has invariably carried out, and is carrying out, the policy of peace and international collaboration. Such are the relations of the Soviet Union with all the countries which evince a desire to collaborate.

The policy outlined by Comrade Stalin is opposed at present by another policy, based on quite different principles. Here we can talk first and foremost of the foreign policy of the United States, as well as that of Great Britain. Possibly there exists in the United States a program of economic development of the country for some period ahead. However, the press has not yet announced anything about this, although press conferences take place there quite frequently. On the other hand, much noise is being spread about various American projects, connected now with the Truman Doctrine, now with the Marshall plan.

Reading of all these American plans for aid to Europe, aid to China, and so on, one might think that the domestic problems of the United States have long ago been solved, and that now it is only a question of America's putting the affairs of other states in order, dictating its policy to them and even the composition of their governments.

In reality, matters are not like that. If the ruling circles of the U.S.A. had no cause for anxiety concerning domestic affairs, especially in connection with an approaching economic crisis, there would not be such a superfluity of economic projects of U.S.A. expansion, which in their turn are based on the aggressive military-political plans of American imperialism.

Now they no longer hide the fact that the United States of America, not infrequently together with Great Britain, is acquiring ever new naval and air bases in all parts of the globe, and even adapts whole states for such like aims, especially if closely situated to the Soviet Union.

Who does not complain about the pressure of American imperialism in that respect? Even if the governments of certain big states of Europe, Asia and America preserve a kind of solid silence in regard to this matter, it is clear that certain small states are faced by an absolutely intolerable position. Denmark, for instance, cannot achieve the restoration of her national sovereignty over Greenland, which the Americans do not want to leave after the end of the war. Egypt legitimately demands the withdrawal of British troops from her territory. Britain refuses to do that, and America supports the British imperialists in these matters also.

It is, however, clear that the creation of military bases in various parts of the world is not designed for defense purposes, but as a preparation for aggression. It is also clear that if, up to now, the combined British-American General Staff, created during the second World War, has been maintained, this is not

"Excerpts from Molotov's speech on 30th Anniversary of Revolution of November 7, 1947," from the *New York Times*, November 7, 1947, p. 3.

being done for peace-loving purposes, but for the purpose of intimidating with the possibility of new aggression.

It would be a good thing for all this to be known to the American people, for under the so-called Western freedom of the press, when almost all newspapers and radio stations are in the hands of small cliques, the aggressive cliques of the capitalists and their servitors, it is difficult for the people to know the real truth.

It is interesting that in expansionist circles of the U.S.A. a new, peculiar sort of illusion is widespread—while having no faith in their internal strength—faith is placed in the secret of the atom bomb, although this secret has long ceased to exist.

Evidently the imperialists need this faith in the atom bomb which, as is known, is not a means of defense but a weapon of aggression. . . .

It is well known that the industry of the United States of America in the period between the two world wars has grown, although its development proceeded extremely unevenly and twice fell considerably below the level of 1913. For all that, during the second World War American industry grew rapidly, became inflated and began to yield enormous profits to the capitalists and state revenues, which American state monopoly capitalism is putting into circulation and applying to exert pressure everywhere in Europe and China, in Greece and Turkey, in South America and in the Middle East.

Certainly there are not a few who like to make use of a war situation. . . .

Today the ruling circles of the U.S.A. and Great Britain head one international grouping, which has as its aim the consolidation of capitalism and the achievement of the dominations of these countries over other peoples. These countries are headed by imperialist and anti-democratic forces in international affairs, with the active participation of certain Socialist leaders in several European states. . . .

As a result of post-war Anglo-American policy the British and American zones of occupation of Germany were united into a jointly administered bizonal territory—which has been given the name of "Bi-zonia" in the press—so that an Anglo-American policy could be unilaterally carried out there independently of the Control Council, in which representatives of all four occupying powers participate.

Our representatives in Germany are today virtually concerned only with the Soviet zone. A situation has arisen which cannot but produce alarm among the German people also, since, as the result of the Anglo-American policy, there exists the joint zone and other zones, but there is no Germany, no single German state.

The Soviet Union considers it necessary that the decisions of the Yalta and Potsdam conferences on the German question, decisions which provided for the restoration of Germany as a single, democratic state, should be put into effect. Moreover, in the Soviet Union it is entirely understood that the joint zone is not Germany and that the German people has a right to the existence of its own state which, it goes without saying, must be a democratic state and must not create the threat of new aggression for other peace-loving states.

At the present time there exists the Anglo-American plan—by giving some aims to calm the population of the Anglo-American zone of Germany—for basing themselves here on the former capitalists who were recently the Hitlerite support, and for utilizing with their aid the joint zone with its Ruhr industrial basin as a threat against those countries which do not display slavish submissiveness with regard to the Anglo-American plans for domination in Europe.

But these adventurists' plans, based on Germany, will lead to nothing good and it goes without saying, will be rejected by democratic Europe.

From the example of the German question, one can see how widely present day Anglo-American principles diverge from the principles of the Soviet state, how Anglo-American principles are steeped in open imperialism, while the Soviet stands firmly on democratic positions.

The Soviet Union, in common with other democratic states, stands for peace and international collaboration on democratic principles. Under present conditions, this demands the uniting of all forces of the anti-imperialist and democratic camp in Europe and beyond the boundaries of Europe, so that an insurmountable barrier shall be created against imperialism, which is becoming more active, and against its new policy of aggression.

The rallying of democratic forces and courageous struggle against imperialism in its new plans for war adventures will unite the peoples into a powerful army, the equal of which cannot be possessed by imperialism, which denies the democratic rights of the people, infringing on the sovereignty of the nations and basing its plans on threats and adventures.

Uneasiness and alarm are growing in the imperialist ranks, since everybody sees that the ground is shaking under the feet of imperialism, while the forces of democracy and socialism are daily growing and consolidating.

What can the policy of imperialism offer people? Nothing but strengthening of oppression, the rebirth of the vestiges of hated fascism and imperialistic adventures.

It is necessary to open the peoples' eyes and to unite all the democratic and anti-imperialistic forces in order to foil any plans for the economic enslavement of nations and any new adventures on the part of the imperialists.

The historic experience of the Soviet Union has confirmed the justice of the great Lenin's words on the invincibility of the people which took power into their hands. Lenin said: "One can never conquer a people where the majority of workers and peasants have realized, sensed and seen that they are upholding their own sovereign power, the power of the working people, the victory of whose cause, if upheld, will secure for them and their children the possibility of enjoying all the benefits of culture, all the achievements of human labor."

The task of our time is to unite all the anti-imperialistic and democratic forces of the nations into one mighty camp, welded together by the unity of their vital interests against the imperialist and anti-democratic camp and its policy of enslavement of the peoples and new adventures.

A sober attitude to the matter shows simultaneously that in our time new imperialistic adventures constitute a dangerous game with destinies of capitalism.

Harry S Truman

THE PEACEFUL COURSE OF THE UNITED STATES

When Vice-President Truman assumed the presidential office in April, 1945, he had had little experience with the formulation of foreign policy. But he quickly took command, and through a number of forceful but sometimes halting actions, his administration hammered out policies which led eventually to the March, 1947 Truman Doctrine of containing Soviet Communism. A few months after the Marshall Plan for European economic recovery was launched, the President addressed an audience in Berkeley, California (June 12, 1948). In language strikingly similar to that of Molotov, Truman issued the American defense of its record for peace since 1945.

THE United States has consistently done its part in meeting the requirements for a peaceful world.

We fought through World War II with only one purpose: to destroy the tyrants who tried to impose their rule on the world and enslave the people. We sought no territories; we asked for only token reparations. At the end of the war, we quickly dismantled the greatest military machine ever built by any nation. We withdrew and demobilized the American armies that had swept across Europe and the Pacific, leaving only minimum occupation forces in Germany, Austria, Japan, and Korea. The nations which our army had helped to liberate were left free to work out their postwar problems without interference from us.

That was not the course of a nation that sought to impose its will upon others. It was not the course of an aggressor.

Long before the fighting had ended, our Government began planning for a world organization which could provide security for all nations. At Dumbarton Oaks, at Yalta, at San Francisco, the United States led the way in preparing for a strong and useful United Nations. In the past 3 years we have taken a leading part in establishing the United Nations, and the related agencies—such as the World Bank and the Food and Agriculture Organization—which are fundamental to world peace and prosperity.

No action by the United States has revealed more clearly our sincere desire for peace than our proposal in the United Nations for the international control of atomic energy. In a step without precedent, we have voluntarily offered to share with others the secrets of atomic power. We ask only for conditions that will guarantee its use for the benefit of humanity—and not for the destruction of humanity.

To assist world economic recovery, we have contributed nearly $20 billion in loans and grants to other nations. American dollars have been invested generously in the cause of peace because we know what peace is worth.

This is a record of action in behalf of peace without parallel in history.

Many other nations have joined wholeheartedly with us in our work for peace. They share our desire for international control of atomic energy, for the early conclusion of peace treaties, for world economic recovery, and for the effective development of the United Nations.

Why then, after such great exertions and huge expenditures, do we live today in a twilight period, between war so dearly won and a peace that still eludes our grasp?

From the *Public Papers of the Presidents of the United States: Harry S Truman, 1948* (Washington, 1964), pp. 336–340.

The answer is not hard to find.

It lies largely in the attitude of one nation—the Soviet Union.

Long before the war the United States established normal diplomatic and commercial relations with the Soviet Union. In doing so we demonstrated our belief that it was possible to get along with a nation whose economic and political system differs sharply from ours.

During the war we worked with the Soviet Union wholeheartedly in defeating the common enemy. In every way we could we tried to convince the Soviet Government that it was possible and necessary for allied unity to continue in the great task of establishing the peace. We hoped that the Soviet Union, secure in her own strength and doubly secure in respect of her allies, would accept full partnership in a peaceful world community.

The record, however, is clear for all to read. The Soviet Government has rejected the invitation to participate, freely and on equal terms, in a great cooperative program for reconstruction of Europe. It has constantly maneuvered for delay and for propaganda effect in every international conference. It has used the veto excessively and unreasonably in the Security Council of the United Nations. It has boycotted the "Little Assembly" and several special United Nations commissions. It has used indirect aggression against a number of nations in Eastern Europe and extreme pressure against others in the Middle East. It has intervened in the internal affairs of many other countries by means of Communist parties directed from Moscow.

The refusal of the Soviet Union to work with its wartime allies for world recovery and world peace is the most bitter disappointment of our time.

The great issues of world peace and world recovery are sometimes portrayed as disputes solely between the United States and the Soviet Union. This is not the case. The fact is that not a single one of the major unsettled questions of the postwar world is primarily a disagreement between this country and the Soviet Union. We are not engaged in a struggle with the Soviet Union for any territory or for any economic gain. We have no hostile or aggressive designs against the Soviet Union or any other country. We are not waging a "cold war."

The cleavage that exists is not between the Soviet Union and the United States. It is between the Soviet Union and the rest of the world.

The great questions at stake today affect not only the United States and the Soviet Union; they affect all nations.

Whether it be the control of atomic energy, aggression against small nations, the German or the Austrian peace settlements, or any of the other questions, the majority of nations concerned have found a common basis for action. But in every case the majority agreement has been rejected, denounced, and openly attacked by the Soviet Union and her satellites whose policy she controls.

Let me repeat: the division has not been between the United States and the Soviet Union, but between the Soviet Union and the free nations of the world.

The United States is strongly devoted to the principle of discussion and negotiation in settling international differences. We do not believe in settling differences by force. There are certain types of disputes in international affairs which can and must be settled by negotiation and agreement.

But there are others which are not susceptible to negotiation.

There is nothing to negotiate when one nation disregards the principles of international conduct to which all the members of the United Nations have subscribed. There is nothing to negotiate when one nation habitually uses coercion and open aggression in international affairs.

What the world needs in order to regain a sense of security is an end to Soviet obstruction and aggression. . . .

I stated our American policy for peace at the end of the war. It has been restated many times, but I shall repeat the essential elements of our policy again so that there can be no misunderstanding anywhere by anyone.

"We seek no territorial expansion or selfish advantage.

"We have no plans for aggression

against any other state, large or small.

"We have no objective which need clash with the peaceful aims of any other nation."

The United States has been conscientious and consistent in its devotion to those principles.

II. THE TROUBLESOME ISSUES: SECURITY AND ECONOMIC RECOVERY

Gar Alperovitz

THE ATOMIC BOMB AS A DIPLOMATIC WEAPON

In 1965, Gar Alperovitz published his controversial *Atomic Diplomacy: Hiroshima and Potsdam.* Then an American Fellow of King's College (Cambridge, England), he challenged the official story of the dropping of the atomic bomb on Hiroshima on August 6, 1945. In his book and in the article below, Alperovitz argues that the atomic weapon was closely linked to American diplomacy, that its use was unnecessary to end the war with Japan, and that the bomb was exploded to frighten the Soviets into diplomatic concessions. His interpretation has stimulated considerable debate, including Adam Ulam's critique of revisionism and Alperovitz in Part III.

Dear Mr. President,

I think it is very important that I should have a talk with you as soon as possible on a highly secret matter. I mentioned it to you shortly after you took office, but have not urged it since on account of the pressure you have been under. It, however, has such a bearing on our present foreign relations and has such an important effect upon all my thinking in this field that I think you ought to know about it without much further delay.

—SECRETARY OF WAR HENRY L. STIMSON TO PRESIDENT TRUMAN, APRIL 24, 1945

This note was written twelve days after Franklin Delano Roosevelt's death and two weeks before World War II ended in Europe. The following day Secretary Stimson advised President Truman that the "highly secret matter" would have a "decisive" effect upon America's postwar foreign policy. Stimson then outlined the role the atomic bomb would play in America's relations with other countries. In diplomacy, he confided to his diary, the weapon would be a "master card."

In the spring of 1945, postwar problems unfolded as rapidly as the Allied armies converged in Central Europe. During the fighting which preceded Nazi surrender the Red Army conquered a great belt of territory bordering the Soviet Union. Debating the consequences of this fact, American policy-makers defined a series of interrelated problems: What political and economic pattern was likely to emerge in Eastern and Central Europe? Would Soviet influence predominate? Most important, what power—if any—did the United States have to effect the ultimate settlement on the very borders of Russia?

Roosevelt, Churchill, and Stalin had attempted to resolve these issues of East-West influence at the February, 1945, Yalta Conference. With the Red Army clearly in control of Eastern Europe, the West was in a weak bargaining position.

From Gar Alperovitz, "Why We Dropped the Bomb," *The Progressive,* 29 (August, 1965), pp. 11–14. Reprinted by permission of *The Progressive.*

It was important to reach an understanding with Stalin before American troops began their planned withdrawal from the European continent. Poland, the first major country intensely discussed by the Big Three, took on unusual significance; the balance of influence struck between Soviet-oriented and Western-oriented politicians in the government of this one country could set a pattern for big-power relationships in the rest of Eastern Europe.

Although the Yalta Conference ended with a signed accord covering Poland, within a few weeks it was clear that Allied understanding was more apparent than real. None of the heads of government interpreted the somewhat vague agreement in the same way. Churchill began to press for more Western influence; Stalin urged less. True to his well-known policy of cooperation and conciliation, Roosevelt attempted to achieve a more definite understanding for Poland and a pattern for East-West relations in Europe. Caught for much of the last of his life between the determination of Churchill and the stubbornness of Stalin, Roosevelt at times fired off angry cables to Moscow, and at others warned London against an "attempt to evade the fact that we placed, as clearly shown in the agreement, somewhat more emphasis . . . [on Soviet-oriented Polish politicians in the government]."

President Roosevelt died on April 12, 1945, only two months after Yalta. When President Truman met with Secretary Stimson to discuss the "bearing" of the atomic bomb upon foreign relations, the powers were deeply ensnarled in a tense public struggle over the meaning of the Yalta agreement. Poland had come to symbolize *all* East-West relations. Truman was forced to pick up the tangled threads of policy with little knowledge of the broader, more complex issues involved.

Herbert Feis, a noted expert on the period, has written that "Truman made up his mind that he would not depart from Roosevelt's course or renounce his ways." Others have argued that "we tried to work out the problems of the peace in close cooperation with the Russians." It is often believed that American policy followed a conciliatory course, changing —in reaction to Soviet intransigence— only in 1947 with the Truman Doctrine and the Marshall Plan. My own belief is somewhat different. It derives from the comment of Mr. Truman's Secretary of State, James F. Byrnes, that by early autumn of 1945 it was "understandable" that Soviet leaders should feel American policy had shifted radically after Roosevelt's death: It is now evident that, far from following his predecessor's policy of cooperation, shortly after taking office President Truman launched a powerful foreign policy initiative aimed at reducing or eliminating Soviet influence in Europe.

The ultimate point of this study is not, however, that America's approach to Russia changed after Roosevelt. Rather it is that the atomic bomb played a role in the formulation of policy, particularly in connection with President Truman's only meeting with Stalin, the Potsdam Conference of late July and early August, 1945. Again, my judgment differs from Feis's conclusion that "the light of the explosion 'brighter than a thousand suns' filtered into the conference rooms at Potsdam only as a distant gleam." I believe new evidence proves not only that the atomic bomb influenced diplomacy, but that it determined much of Mr. Truman's shift to a tough policy aimed at forcing Soviet acquiescence to American plans for Eastern and Central Europe.

The weapon "gave him an entirely new feeling of confidence," the President told his Secretary of War, Henry L. Stimson. By the time of Potsdam, Mr. Truman had been advised on the role of the atomic bomb by both Secretary Stimson and Secretary of State Byrnes. Though the two men differed as to tactics, each urged a tough line. Part of my study attempts to define how closely Truman followed a subtle policy outlined by Stimson, and to what extent he followed the straightforward advice of Byrnes that the bomb (in Mr. Truman's words) "put us in a position to dictate our own terms at the end of the war."

Stalin's approach seems to have been

cautiously moderate during the brief few months here described. It is perhaps symbolized by the Soviet-sponsored free elections which routed the Communist Party in Hungary in the autumn of 1945. I do not attempt to interpret this moderation, nor to explain how or why Soviet policy changed to the harsh totalitarian controls characteristic of the period after 1946.

The judgment that Truman radically altered Roosevelt's policy in mid-1945 nevertheless obviously suggests a new point of departure for interpretations of the cold war. In late 1945, General Dwight D. Eisenhower observed in Moscow that "before the atom bomb was used, I would have said, yes, I was sure we could keep the peace with Russia. Now I don't know. . . . People are frightened and disturbed all over. Everyone feels insecure again." To what extent did postwar Soviet policies derive from insecurity based upon a fear of America's atom bomb and changed policy? I stop short of this fundamental question, concluding that further research is needed to test Secretary Stimson's judgment that "the problem of our satisfactory relations with Russia [was] not merely connected with but [was] virtually dominated by the problem of the atomic bomb."

Similarly, I believe more research and more information are needed to reach a conclusive understanding of why the atomic bomb was used. The common belief is that the question is closed, and that President Truman's explanation is correct: "The dropping of the bombs stopped the war, saved millions of lives." My own view is that available evidence shows the atomic bomb was not needed to end the war or to save lives—and that this was understood by American leaders at the time.

General Eisenhower recently recalled that in mid-1945 he expressed a similar opinion to the Secretary of War: "I told him I was against it on two counts. First, the Japanese were ready to surrender and it wasn't necessary to hit them with that awful thing. Second, I hated to see our country be the first to use such a weapon. . . ." To go beyond the limited conclusion that the bomb was unnecessary is not possible at present.

Perhaps the most remarkable aspect of the decision to use the atomic bomb is that the President and his senior political advisers do not seem ever to have shared Eisenhower's "grave misgivings." They simply assumed that they would use the bomb, never really giving serious consideration to not using it. Hence, to state in a precise way the question, "Why was the atomic bomb used?" is to ask why senior political officials did *not* seriously question its use, as General Eisenhower did.

The first point to note is that the decision to use the weapon did not derive from overriding military considerations. Despite Mr. Truman's subsequent statement that the weapon "saved millions of lives," Eisenhower's judgment that it was "completely unnecessary" as a measure to save lives was almost certainly correct. This is not a matter of hindsight; *before the atomic bomb was dropped each of the joint Chiefs of Staff advised that it was highly likely that Japan could be forced to surrender "unconditionally," without use of the bomb and without an invasion.* Indeed, this characterization of the position taken by the senior military advisers is a conservative one.

General George C. Marshall's June 18 appraisal was the most cautiously phrased advice offered by any of the Joint Chiefs: "The impact of Russian entry on the already hopeless Japanese may well be the decisive action levering them into capitulation. . . ." Admiral William D. Leahy was absolutely certain there was no need for the bombing to obviate the necessity of an invasion. His judgment after the fact was the same as his view before the bombing: "It is my opinion that the use of this barbarous weapon at Hiroshima and Nagasaki was of no material assistance in our war against Japan. The Japanese were already defeated and ready to surrender. . . ." Similarly, through most of 1945, Admiral Ernest J. King believed the bomb unnecessary, and Generals Henry H. Arnold and Curtis E. LeMay defined the official Air Force position in this way: Whether or not the atomic bomb should be dropped was not for the Air Force to decide, but explosion of the bomb was not necessary to win the war or make an invasion unnecessary.

Similar views prevailed in Britain long before the bombs were used. General Hastings Ismay recalls that by the time of Potsdam, "for some time past it had been firmly fixed in my mind that the Japanese were tottering." Ismay's reaction to the suggestion of the bombing was, like Eisenhower's and Leahy's, one of "revulsion." And Churchill, who as early as September, 1944, felt that Russian entry into the war with Japan was likely to force capitulation, has written: "It would be a mistake to suppose that the fate of Japan was settled by the atomic bomb. Her defeat was certain before the first bomb fell. . . ."

The military appraisals made before the weapons were used have been confirmed by numerous post-surrender studies. The best known is that of the United States Strategic Bombing Survey. The Survey's conclusion is unequivocal: "Japan would have surrendered even if the atomic bombs had not been dropped, even if Russia had not entered the war, and even if no invasion had been planned or contemplated."

That military considerations were not decisive is confirmed—and illuminated—by the fact that the President did not even ask the opinion of the military adviser most directly concerned. General Douglas MacArthur, Supreme Commander of Allied Forces in the Pacific, was simply informed of the weapon shortly before it was used at Hiroshima. Before his death he stated on numerous occasions that, like Eisenhower, he believed the atomic bomb was completely unnecessary from a military point of view.

Although military considerations were not primary, unquestionably political considerations related to Russia played a major role in the decision; from at least mid-May in 1945, American policy-makers hoped to end the hostilities before the Red Army entered Manchuria. For this reason they had no wish to test whether Russian entry into the war would force capitulation—as most thought likely—long before the scheduled November Allied invasion of Japan. Indeed, they actively attempted to delay Stalin's declaration of war.

Nevertheless, it would be wrong to conclude that the atomic bomb was used simply to keep the Red Army out of Manchuria. Given the desperate efforts of the Japanese to surrender, and President Truman's willingness to offer assurances to the Emperor, it is entirely possible that the war could have been ended by negotiation before the Red Army had begun its attack. But after history's first atomic explosion at Alamogordo neither the President nor his senior political advisers were interested in exploring this possibility.

One reason may have been their fear that if time-consuming negotiations were once initiated, the Red Army might attack in order to seize Manchurian objectives. But, if this explanation is accepted, once more one must conclude that the bomb was used primarily because it was felt to be politically important to prevent Soviet domination of the area.

Such a conclusion is difficult to accept, for American interests in Manchuria, although historically important to the State Department, were not of great significance. The further question therefore arises: Were there other political reasons for using the atomic bomb? In approaching this question, it is important to note that most of the men involved at the time who since have made their views public always mention *two* considerations which dominated discussions. The first was the desire to end the Japanese war quickly, which was not primarily a military consideration, but a political one. The second is always referred to indirectly.

In June, for example, a leading member of President Truman's Advisory Interim Committee's scientific panel, A. H. Compton, advised against the Franck report's suggestion of a technical demonstration of the new weapon: Not only was there a possibility that this might not end the war promptly, but failure to make a combat demonstration would mean the "loss of the opportunity to impress the world with the national sacrifices that enduring security demanded." The general phrasing that the bomb was needed "to impress the world" has been made more specific by J. Robert Oppenheimer. Testifying on this matter some years later he stated that the second of the two "overriding considerations" in discussions regarding the bomb was "the effect of our actions on the stability, on our strength, and the stability of the postwar world." And the problem of postwar stability was inevitably the problem of Russia. Oppenheimer has put it this way: "Much of the discussion revolved around the question raised by Secretary Stimson as to whether there was any hope at all of using this development to get less barbarous relations with the Russians."

Vannevar Bush, Stimson's chief aide for atomic matters, has been quite explicit: "That bomb was developed on time. . . ." Not only did it mean a quick end to the Japanese war, but "it was also delivered on time so that there was no necessity for any concessions to Russia at the end of the war."

In essence, the second of the two overriding considerations seems to have been that a combat demonstration was needed to convince the Russians to accept the American plan for a stable peace. And the crucial point of this effort was the need to force agreement on the main questions in dispute: the American proposals for Central and Eastern Europe. President Truman may well have expressed the key consideration in October, 1945; publicly urging the necessity of a more conventional form of military power (his proposal for universal military training), in a personal appearance before Congress, the President declared: "It is only by strength that we can impress the fact upon possible future aggressors that we will tolerate no threat to peace. . . ."

If indeed the "second consideration" involved in the bombing of Hiroshima and Nagasaki was the desire to impress the Russians, it might explain the strangely ambiguous statement by Mr. Truman that not only did the bomb end the war, but it gave the world "a chance to face the facts." It would also accord with Stimson's private advice to Assistant Secretary of War John J. McCloy: "We have got to regain the lead and perhaps do it in a pretty rough and realistic way. . . . We have coming into action a weapon which will be unique. Now the thing [to do is] . . . let our actions speak for themselves."

Again, it would accord with Stimson's statement to Mr. Truman that the "greatest complication" would occur if the President negotiated with Stalin before the bomb had been "laid on Japan." It would tie in with the fact that from mid-May, strategy toward all major diplomatic problems was based upon the assumption the bomb would be demonstrated. Finally, it might explain why none of the highest civilian officials seriously questioned the use of the bomb as Eisenhower did; for, having reversed the basic direction of diplomatic strategy *because* of the atomic bomb, it would have been difficult indeed for anyone subsequently to challenge an idea which had come to dominate all calculations of high policy.

It might also explain why the sober and self-controlled Stimson reacted so strongly when General Eisenhower objected to the bombing: "The Secretary was deeply perturbed by my attitude, almost angrily refuting the reasons I gave. . . ." Stimson's post-Hiroshima reversal, and his repeated references to the gravity of the moral issues raised by the new weapon, are evidence of his own doubts. General Eisenhower's searching criticism may well have touched upon a tender point—namely, Stimson's undoubted awareness that Hiroshima and Nagasaki were to be sacrificed primarily for political, not military, reasons.

At present no final conclusion can be reached on this question. But the problem can be defined with some precision: Why did the American government refuse to attempt to exploit Japanese efforts to surrender? Or, alternatively, why did it refuse to test whether a Russian declaration of war would force capitulation? Were Hiroshima and Nagasaki bombed primarily to impress the world with the need to accept America's plan for a stable and lasting peace—that is, primarily, America's plan for Europe? The evidence strongly suggests that the view which the President's personal representative offered to one of the atomic scientists in May, 1945, was an accurate statement of policy: "Mr. Byrnes did not argue that it was necessary to use the bomb against the cities of Japan in order to win the war . . . Mr. Byrnes's . . . view [was] that our possessing and demonstrating the bomb would make Russia more manageable in Europe. . . ."

Walter LaFeber

THE CONTINUED TENSION OF ATOMIC DIPLOMACY

In his well-received *The New Empire: An Interpretation of American Expansion* (1963) and *America, Russia, and the Cold War* (1967), Walter LaFeber of Cornell University has distinguished himself as a careful student of foreign relations. In the following selection from the latter book, LaFeber surveys the friction between Russia and the United States in their discussions of the postwar control of atomic weapons, and indicates the American determination to retain supremacy. With the failure of atomic negotiations in 1946, the atomic arms race was launched with the United States continuing to test and stockpile weapons and with Soviet development of the destructive bomb in 1949.

AMERICAN officials responded to the crisis in Germany and Eastern Europe by devising . . . tactics which, they believed, would draw back the enveloping curtain. First, throughout the summer of 1945, the Truman Administration hoped that the American possession of atomic bombs would, in the words of Secretary of War Henry Stimson, result in "less barbarous relations with the Russians." Stimson believed that world peace was unobtainable until "Russia's secret police state" opened itself to the fresh winds from the West. More to the point, James F. Byrnes, soon to be Secretary of State, informed scientists Leo Szilard and Harold Urey in June 1945 that the bomb "would make Russia more manageable in Europe." Eastern Europe remained sealed off, however, even after Hiroshima and Nagasaki endured the terrible birth agonies of a new era in world history.

Stimson now advised changing tactics. In a memorandum of September 11 to President Truman, the retiring Secretary of War prophesied "that it would not be possible to use our possession of the atomic bomb as a direct lever to produce the change" desired inside Eastern Europe and Russia. If Soviet-American negotiations continue with "this weapon rather ostentatiously on our hip, their suspicions and their distrust of our purposes and motives will increase." Stimson urged direct, bilateral discussions with the Soviets to formulate control of atomic energy and write a general peace settlement. . . .

Since Hiroshima, the terrible specter of atomic energy had overhung every diplomatic exchange. In December 1945, the Big Three Foreign Ministers attempted to deal with this horror by establishing an Atomic Energy Commission tied to the Security Council of the United Nations. On March 16, 1946, the United States released its own plan for the control of atomic energy, the so-called Acheson-Lilienthal proposal. This report suggested a series of stages through which the world could pass to international control of atomic weapons; throughout this transition period the United States, possessing the only atomic bombs, would remain in a favored position while other nations agreed to be inspected by international agencies. A month later Bernard Baruch was named by the President to be the first American delegate to the United Nations Commission. American policy soon began to assume new forms. Deeply suspicious by nature, Baruch distrusted the Acheson-Lilienthal Report, partly because he had not sat on the committee, and partly because it said nothing about the Russian veto on the Security Council.

From Walter LaFeber, *America, Russia, and the Cold War, 1945–1966* (New York, 1967), pp. 21–22, 34–36. Permission granted by John Wiley & Sons, Inc.

Baruch determined to eliminate any Russian power to veto inspections or sanctions. The Acheson-Lilienthal Report, on the other hand, said nothing about the veto; it planned to obtain Russian agreement to general principles and then discuss the veto problem. Top American military officials supported Baruch. Admiral Chester Nimitz, Chief of Naval Operations, and Admiral William D. Leahy, Truman's chief military adviser, urged, in Nimitz's words, that little be done on atomic energy until a "satisfactory peace" could be established. Baruch became increasingly bitter about Acheson (whom he mistakenly accused of recording their telephone conversations), and those "One Worlders" like Joseph Alsop and Walter Lippmann, "whom I can't understand any more"; all of these men criticized Baruch's insistence on immediately removing the veto power. But he finally triumphed by convincing Truman that the United States must be tough with the Russians earlier rather than later. After recalling the dismantling of the American Navy in the 1920's and Stimson's troubles in Manchuria in 1931, the President agreed: "we should not under any circumstances throw away our gun until we are sure the rest of the world can't arm against us." Military and political advisers bolstered this view by avowing that Russia could not build A-bombs for at least five to fifteen years. Only a few scientists warned that the period might be considerably shorter.

In a dramatic speech at the United Nations on June 14, Baruch presented his plan: atomic energy would be controlled through international management of the necessary raw materials and inspection by international agencies; no vetoes of these controls and inspections would be allowed; majority vote would rule. In the realm of peaceful uses of atomic energy, an Atomic Development Authority, again free of the veto, would establish atomic plants not according to need (as in underdeveloped areas or in large stretches of Russia), but according to strategic and geographical criteria; this criteria would allow more plants in Europe and the United States. Furthermore, by controlling a majority within the Authority, the United States could also control the development of the industrial uses of nuclear energy *within* the Soviet Union. The Soviets countered by demanding destruction of all atomic weapons, the cessation of their production, agreement of all powers not to use these weapons, and then a discussion of controls. Negotiations stalled until October when the Russians agreed to international inspection and eliminating the veto on day-to-day inspections, although not eliminating it on punishment of violations. Baruch retorted that either the Russians must accept the entire American plan or there would be no plan. There was no plan. Instead, Congress established a United States Atomic Energy Commission under the Atomic Energy Act of 1946. Under strong military pressure, the act prohibited any exchange of information on the use of atomic energy with any nation until Congress should decide by joint resolution that "effective" international controls were in force. . . .

American policy had radically changed since Stimson's memorandum to Truman of September 11, 1945 had suggested direct, bilateral talks on a give-and-take basis with the Soviets. Exactly one year later to the day, James Forrestal flew to New York to counsel with the retired Stimson. "He said," Forrestal recorded in his diary that night, "the way things had now developed he thought we should not delay in going forward with the manufacture of all the atomic missiles we could make." Such was the inheritance left by the first year of the continued, although cold, war.

Thomas G. Paterson

THE USE OF ECONOMIC POWER IN DIPLOMACY

If atomic diplomacy offered one of the first stumbling blocks to peaceful postwar relations, so too did the question of Soviet economic reconstruction and an American loan, a subject that has received little attention from historians. In the following essay, Thomas G. Paterson of the University of Connecticut presents a segment of his forthcoming study of American economic foreign policy in the early Cold War. He argues that economic recovery was a major postwar goal of Russia, and that the United States employed its economic power in such a way as to embitter Soviet-American relations. The essay explores the possibility of a postwar loan to Russia as peacemaker in the immediate postwar period. Arthur Schlesinger disagrees that the loan would have had any effect at all in Part III of this volume. Paterson is also the editor of and a contributor to: *Cold War Critics: Alternatives to American Foreign Policy in the Truman Period* (1971).

THE American ambassador to Moscow, W. Averell Harriman, cabled the Department of State in January 1945 that the Soviet Union placed "high importance on a large postwar credit as a basis for the development of 'Soviet-American relations.' From his [V. M. Molotov's] statement I sensed an implication that the development of our friendly relations would depend upon a generous credit." In October 1945, a diplomat at the Foreign Ministers Council meeting in London noted the issues which he thought were impeding amicable Russian-American relations—the atomic bomb and an American loan to Russia. A few years later, an associate of Donald M. Nelson, War Production Board chairman, wrote: "Although little publicized, the possibility of this loan for a time almost certainly influenced Soviet policy toward the United States, and its refusal coincided significantly with the increasing aggressiveness of the Kremlin."

In the 1943–1945 period, a postwar American loan to the Soviet Union might have served as peacemaker; but by the early part of 1946 both nations had become increasingly uncompromising on the major international issues, and the usefulness of a loan to the United States, to Russia, and to amicable and productive relations had been called into serious doubt. "Whether such a loan," Secretary of State Edward R. Stettinius, Jr., later wrote, "would have made the Soviet Union a more reasonable and cooperative nation in the postwar world will be one of the great 'if' questions of history." The recent availability of historical sources provides material for a suggestive answer to Stettinius' question. The evidence suggests that America's refusal to aid Russia through a loan similar to that granted to the British in early 1946, perhaps contributed to a continuation of a low standard of living for the Russian people with detrimental international effects, to a less conciliatory and harsher Russian policy toward Germany and Eastern Europe, and to unsettled and inimical postwar Soviet-American relations.

World War II had been cruel to the Soviet Union. Coupled with the deaths of millions was the devastation of most of Western Russia. Over 30,000 industrial factories and 40,000 miles of railroad line had been destroyed. In 1945, Soviet

From Thomas G. Paterson, "The Abortive American Loan to Russia and the Origins of the Cold War, 1943–1946," *Journal of American History*, LVI (June, 1969), pp. 70–92. Reprinted by permission.

agricultural output was about half the 1940 level. One state department study reported that the Soviet Union had lost sixteen billion dollars in fixed capital, or one quarter of the prewar total. Secretary of War Henry L. Stimson recorded that the "completeness of the destruction was absolute" in the Ukraine. To help repair the massive war damage, the Russians looked eagerly to the United States. . . .

On January 3, 1945, Molotov handed Harriman the first formal Russian request for a postwar loan. Harriman considered the Russian proposal a "curiously worded document." Three days later he reported: "I have recovered from my surprise at Molotov's strange procedure in initiating discussions regarding a postwar credit in such a detailed *aide-mémoire*. . . ." What surprised and obviously upset Harriman was the nature of Molotov's proposal:

> The Soviet Government accordingly wishes to state the following: Having in mind the repeated statements of American public figures concerning the desirability of receiving extensive large Soviet orders for the postwar and transition period, the Soviet Government considers it possible to place orders on the basis of long-term credits to the amount of 6 billion dollars. Such orders would be for manufactured goods (oil pipes, rails, railroad cars, locomotives and other products) and industrial equipment. The credit would also cover orders for locomotives, railroad cars, rails and trucks and industrial equipment placed under Lend-Lease but not delivered to the Soviet Union before the end of the war. The credits should run for 30 years, amortization to begin on the last day of the 9th year and to end on the last day of the 30th year. . . .

Harriman urged Washington officials to "disregard the unconventional character of the document and the unreasonableness of its terms and chalk it up to ignorance of normal business procedures and the strange ideas of the Russians on how to get the best trade." He chided the Russians for starting "negotiations on the basis of 'twice as much for half the price.' . . ." Any loan, he argued, should be dependent upon Russian behavior in overall international relations—that is, the Russians must conduct their diplomatic affairs according to American wishes and standards. "I feel strongly," he added, "that the sooner the Soviet Union can develop a decent life for its people the more tolerant they will become." But such a concern was secondary, and he demanded complete American control of the funds "in order that the political advantages may be retained and that we may be satisfied that the equipment purchased is for purposes that meet our general approval."

Harriman's response was curious and, certainly from the Russians' point of view, unreasonable. Certainly, the United States had been approached before by foreign governments with detailed requests for aid. Later, the United States was to insist that the Marshall Plan recipients do the same. Indeed, Harriman had earlier asked the Russians to be precise. And it is diplomatic practice to ask for more than one expects to get. Harriman should not have been surprised that Russia was aware of the repeated statements of American public figures concerning the desirability of receiving extensive, large Soviet orders. What perhaps disturbed him most was the boldness, thoroughness, and the attitude of independence expressed in the Russian request. He seemed fearful that the United States would fail to make political gain from the loan—that diplomatic leverage would be lost.

Assistant Secretary of State William Clayton staunchly agreed with Harriman: "From a tactical point of view, it would seem harmful to us to offer such a large credit at this time and thus lose what appears to be the only concrete bargaining lever for use in connection with the many other political and economic problems which will arise between our two countries." The Department of State soon lined up behind Harriman. A department study, probably based upon a report by the Office of Strategic Services, concluded that Russia could recover without American aid. Without foreign assistance, but with the help of reparations, Russia could regain her prewar level of capital investment by 1948; and a loan of two billion dollars would only speed up reconstruction by three to four months. The study went on to deemphasize American-Russian trade potential by citing comparatively low prewar figures and argued cynically that "she will repay unless she feels it politically desirable not to do so." Again conscious of bargaining power, the state department memorandum stated what both Harriman and Clayton feared—that "the U.S.S.R. will be in a position to take a highly independent position in negotiations regarding foreign credits." Joseph C. Grew and Clayton insisted that the time was "harmful" to offer such a large credit to Russia because the United States would lose a "bargaining" position. . . .

In an important message to the state department, in April [1945], Harriman was pessimistic about any postwar economic cooperation with Russia. Although the Russians were "keen" to obtain a six billion dollar credit, he believed that "It certainly should be borne in mind that our basic interests might better be served by increasing our trade with other parts of the world rather than giving preference to the Soviet Union as a source of supply." The United States should undertake a domestic conservation program and end its dependence upon Soviet imports by seeking supplies in Brazil, Africa, and India. He also suggested that the President ask Congress for a blanket foreign loan program which would leave the administration the flexibility to name the recipient countries, including the Soviet Union, if agreement were possible on American terms. No credits should be extended to Russia unless the United States retained "the power to restrict or reduce them as we may see fit," he wrote, because "it is not possible to bank general goodwill in Moscow. . . ." But he cautioned: "It would be inadvisable to give the Soviets the idea that we were cooling off on our desire to help, although we should at all times make it plain that our cooperation is dependent upon a reciprocal cooperative attitude of the Soviet Government on other matters." Indeed, Harriman and Clayton both argued that the post-war loan to Russia "was the greatest element in our leverage" in Soviet-American diplomatic questions which centered on Eastern Europe, China, and Turkey. The "other matters" referred to by Harriman dealt largely with Eastern European countries, especially Poland, which were entering a Russian sphere of influence.

President Truman, generally unprepared to handle the difficult and growing foreign policy problems facing the country, relied heavily upon subordinates. On the subject of the Russian loan, the state department (Grew and Clayton in particular) and Harriman were ready to advise the President. On April 22, Truman met with Molotov in Washington to discuss the Polish question. The exchange was acrimonious, and Truman addressed Molotov as if he were a rebellious Missouri ward politician. He warned Molotov that the Russian government's international behavior would affect American decisions; "legislative appropriations were required for any economic measures in the foreign field, and I had no hope of getting such measures through Congress unless there was public support for them."

Truman's scruples about congressional impediments are not convincing. The new administration and the state department had not prepared either the public or Congress for a loan to Russia. In fact, public discussion had been discouraged. The administration had neither sought to inform public opinion nor demonstrate to the Soviet Union that the United States was willing to undertake serious negotiations on the loan question. And the state department was lethargic in recommending that the Johnson Act be repealed and that the funds of the Export-Import Bank be expanded. Over a year and a half after the Russians first [in 1943] approached the United States for postwar help, the state department had still not acted effectively to remove legislative impediments. Not until July 1945 did Truman ask Congress to increase the lending authority of the Export-Import Bank from 700 million dollars to three and one-half billion dollars with the idea that one billion of it would be earmarked for Russia, should a loan agreement be worked out. The administration did not have to apologize for suggesting that funds might go to Russia, a full-scale public congressional debate never occurred, and Truman got the increase as well as repeal of the Johnson Act insofar as it related to the Export-Import Bank. The legislative considerations that state department officials and Truman thought so imposing were quickly and painlessly swept away. . . .

One of the items the Americans intended to discuss bilaterally with the Russians at Potsdam was "Credits to the USSR." But the subject did not come up, even though Truman later contended that he had gone there planning to offer help for Russian reconstruction. Truman said that all Stalin wanted to talk about was the ending of lend-lease. The Potsdam records do not reveal that Stalin pushed the lend-lease issue. But why did the United States fail to push the Russian loan if Truman was as prepared as he said he was to do so?

When Truman was at Potsdam, Nelson sent the President a memorandum which encouraged him to foster Russian-American trade relations. He explained that Roosevelt had wanted to reach agreement on a trade program, that Stalin had shown considerable interest in the establishment of a business delegation to handle economic relations between the two countries, and that Harriman had insisted that the question be placed in the hands of the state department, in conjunction with other agencies. Nelson summed up his frustration: "I could find no way to get the proposal out of the State Department pigeonhole." He went on to observe: "Postwar trade relations between America and Russia still remain unsettled—a factor which I am convinced militates against satisfactory political relations between the two countries."

With the legislative hurdles overcome and with hope that some bargaining power still rested in a loan to Russia, Harriman informed the Russians on August 9, 1945, that the Export-Import Bank was prepared to consider in Washington Soviet proposals for a credit. On August 28, the Russians presented the Bank with a request for a one billion dollar credit at two and three-eighths percent interest. The drop from a six billion dollar figure to one billion was necessitated by the limited lending power of the Export-Import Bank, and the administration chose not to seek larger funds for the Bank or to approach Congress for a special appropriation, as it did later for the British loan. But the Bank rejected the Russian-proposed interest rate as too low. The Bank's comparatively high and inflexible interest rate of three percent thus impeded negotiations. . . .

In November the administration received some support from the Colmer congressional committee in its policy of using the loan as a diplomatic weapon. Its eighth report on *Economic Reconstruction in Europe* acknowledged that the Russian economy was in massive disarray and that the German "scorched earth" policy had left much of Russia in ruins. Economic cooperation with Russia should be effected, but certain points, the committee argued, should be clarified before a "sound relationship" could develop. First, the United States must be assured that any aid would not go into armaments buildup. Second, the Russians should make "a full and frank disclosure" of their production statistics. Third, Russia must withdraw its occupation forces from Eastern Europe; and, fourth, the Soviets must disclose the terms of their trade treaties with Eastern Europe. Fifth, relief should be administered on nonpolitical grounds, with no siphoning of relief supplies to Russia from Eastern Europe. And, last, before any loans were made to Eastern European countries, there must be protection for American property there. Other items mentioned also centered on the "open door": "free entry" of American planes flying ordinary Russian air routes; willingness to protect American copyrights; and the granting of visas in "adequate quantities."

Shortly after the Colmer committee report, Harriman assessed the status of the loan question. He wrote significantly and inquisitively that American economic policy toward the U.S.S.R. had "so far added to our misunderstanding and increased the Soviets [sic] recent tendency to take unilateral action." Moreover, the American loan policy "has no doubt caused them to tighten their belts as regards improvement of the living conditions of their people and *may have contributed to their avaricious policies in the countries occupied or liberated by the Red Army.*" He added that Russia worked on long-range plans and by November had probably formulated its program leaving aside American credits. Hence, any help the United States extends, he wrote, would be over and above the Soviet program. He called for a review of Soviet-American economic relations, apparently with the idea of denying Russia any further United Nations Relief and Rehabilitation Administration aid, which he thought did the United States little good, and from lend-lease, and an Export-Import Bank loan. His assessment indicated that the use of economic power as a diplomatic weapon had failed. Russia had not been swayed by such power. But, more importantly, Harriman's memorandum suggested that, had the United States earlier granted a loan to Russia, tension between the two nations might have been reduced. If he was right in his overall assessment, the United States, in its desire to use its economic power as a diplomatic weapon to gain American solutions to world issues, rather than as a negotiating tool, contributed to the schism in international relations. . . .

On February 21, [1946] the Russian chargé in Washington was handed a note drafted by Harriman which explained that the one billion dollar credit was "one among a number of outstanding economic questions" between the United States and the Soviet Union. The note suggested negotiations and invited the Soviet Union to send observers to the first meeting of the International Monetary Fund and the International Bank scheduled for March 1946. In early March 1946, the Department of State made the false and bizarre announcement that the Russian loan request had been "lost" since August; it had been misplaced during the transference of the papers of the Foreign Economic Administration (overseer of the Export-Import Bank during and shortly after the war) to the state department. As Arthur Schlesinger, Jr., recently wrote, this "only strengthened Soviet suspicions of American purposes." What is the scholar to make of this strange announcement? The evidence is clear that the loan question was not "lost." Did the United States, because it needed a public excuse for not having pursued the loan with the Soviet Union from August to February, feign administrative clumsiness and incompetence? This question raises an even more crucial one: Why did not the Truman administration take up the matter with the Soviet Union in that period? Did the United States believe that the bargaining power of the loan was slipping and seek time to retrieve it? With the first meeting of the Bretton Woods institutions forthcoming, and with the necessity of deciding where the limited funds of the Export-Import Bank would be distributed, the administration may have considered late February the most propitious time for reviving the loan question.

The American conditions for a loan—multilateral trade policy, membership in the International Bank and the International Monetary Fund, and the open door in Eastern Europe—conflicted with Soviet policies. The Russians were not eager to assume American trade principles and to reject the state-trading practices that its economic and social system required that had been in use since the early years of the Soviet government. They were also wary of joining the International Bank and Fund, both dominated by American dollars, voting power, and leadership. Russia would have derived little economic benefit from membership and would have had to reverse a long-time reluctance to divulge details about its economy to the institutions. Nor were the Soviets willing to accept the American position that the open door—especially Russian trade treaties with the Eastern European countries—be discussed in the loan negotiations. Predictably, Russia replied to the February 21 note with a refusal to discuss her economic links with Eastern Europe;

but, apparently, it left the question of Bretton Woods membership in abeyance.

A few days before the Russian reply, Secretary of Commerce Henry Wallace, an advocate of a loan, urged Truman to make "a new approach along economic and trade lines." Critical of the current American handling of economic relations with Russia and conscious of the state department's laxity in pursuing the loan question, he advised that a "new group" be appointed to undertake the discussions. And he summarized the issue:

> We know that much of the recent Soviet behavior which has caused us concern has been the result of their dire economic needs and their disturbed sense of security. The events of the past few months have thrown the Soviets back to their pre-1939 fears of "capitalist encirclement" and to their erroneous belief that the western world, including the USA, is invariably and unanimously hostile.

Truman later wrote: "I ignored this letter of Wallace's."

In late April 1946, the United States sent Russia another note and offered to begin talks in May on a loan. This note was very similar to the first, but apparently milder in its demands on Eastern Europe. Yet, one news correspondent commented, ". . . the conditions laid down by the United States are still regarded as so rugged from the Soviet point of view that there was little expectation among informed officials that the Russians would accept them." The note raised the questions of trade policy, Bretton Woods, and political and commercial policy in Eastern Europe.

At this point, American domestic politics influenced the status of the loan. A troublesome dilemma faced the administration. If the Export-Import Bank earmarked one billion dollars for Russia, the administration would have to go to Congress for an additional one and one quarter billion dollars needed for France. If it did not earmark the one billion, it would have to go to Congress specifically for a Russian loan. In either case, Truman would have to face open debate on the Russian loan. Such a debate would inflame Russian-American relations and embarrass the administration. First, since the administration had never prepared the public or Congress for a Russian loan and Russian-American relations were increasingly divisive, it seemed improbable that the loan could pass (the vote on the British loan was very close). Second, Congress at that time was not in a spending mood. And third, the administration was reluctant to place another controversial issue in the political arena on the eve of congressional elections.

The loan issue was not dead, however, for in May the Soviet Union, in a note to Washington, again demonstrated its interest. The American response firmly insisted that Eastern Europe be included on the agenda for negotiations and specifically protested Russian five-year trade treaties with Hungary and Rumania. With only 300 to 400 million dollars remaining in the Export-Import Bank in July, and with Congress leaving Washington to prepare for elections, there was little likelihood that the United States would grant Russia's requested loan. Clayton confirmed that the loan was virtually shelved when, a few days later, he told a Senate committee that discussions had never gone beyond "a preliminary stage." Indeed, "We've had an application but we have never agreed even on an agenda for negotiations." By October, Harriman could tell the National Press Club that the loan was no longer a "current issue." Wallace, in November, continued to call for a nonpolitical loan to Russia; and Stalin indicated in the fall of 1946 that he still hoped for economic aid from the United States. But the general question of American assistance to Russian reconstruction was seldom heard again until June of 1947, when Secretary of State George C. Marshall offered American dollars to a European recovery program. By that time the Cold War was tense, and it was clear that the Marshall Plan was to be closely supervised by Americans. Russia at first considered membership, but later summarily rejected the offer and began to tighten its grip on Eastern Europe through new trade treaties, the Molotov

Plan, fixed elections, and political *coups*. . . .

The history of the abortive Russian loan posits some provocative questions. Would the Soviet Union have sought such heavy reparations from former Axis countries in Eastern Europe had a loan been granted? Harriman suggested that the Russians would not have been so "avaricious." Would there have been so much tension arising from Eastern European issues? Harriman stated that the Russians might not have followed a "unilateral" course had a loan been granted. [Henry] Morgenthau argued, according to biographer John Blum, that a postwar credit to Russia would "soften the Soviet Mood on all outstanding political questions." And in June 1945, Grenville Clark asked President Truman: "Now that Russia has regained self-confidence and military strength, is it surprising that without firm promises of aid from the United States . . . she should seek other methods of self-protection? I do not think so. On the contrary, it is inevitable and natural. This might have been mitigated if months ago we had made a treaty with Russia. . . ."

Would the Soviets have been so demanding *vis-à-vis* Germany had a loan been offered? Would they have eased up on reparation demands and have agreed early to unite the German zones if the United States had acted with speed to aid Russia, as it was later to do for Britain? One scholar writes that a loan might have taken "the acrimony out of the Russian attitude on reparations." Albert Carr concludes that "It seems altogether probable that these two matters, an American credit and German reparations, were closely linked in Soviet political thinking, for our attitude toward both questions profoundly affected the rate of Russia's postwar recovery." Indeed, as early as 1944, the American ambassador to Great Britain, John G. Winant, linked the two issues and urged Washington to assist Russian recovery. According to one of his former staff members, Winant argued "that the Russian need for material aid in repairing the vast destruction in the Soviet Union was bound to make the Soviet government particularly eager to receive reparations deliveries from Germany on a large scale." American leaders did not doubt that there was a direct connection between Russia's reparation demands and her postwar reconstruction crisis. Edwin Pauley, American reparations ambassador, wrote in 1947 that "It can be assumed . . . that Russia's intransigent position on unification and reparations is due to a desire to obtain the maximum amount of industrial and consumer goods from Germany, to meet internal political prestige needs and to help rebuild the Soviet industrial machine." Reporter Edgar Snow noted in the same year that "Ivan" was asking: "Did America offer Russia a serious alternative to reparations?" Finally, what effect would a loan have had upon the internal severities of the Russian nation? Recent indications suggest, as did Harriman earlier, that the more prosperous Russia becomes, the more attention Russian officials give to popular preferences.

At the close of World War II, Stalin told Harriman: "I will not tolerate a new *cordon sanitaire*." The American use of the loan as a diplomatic weapon, at the same time that Great Britain was granted a handsome loan at below two percent interest, fed exaggerated Soviet fears, but fears nevertheless, that the United States was creating an international bloc and repeating post-World War I experience. As Wallace put it in a July 1946 letter to Truman:

> From the Russian point of view, also, the granting of a loan to Britain and the lack of tangible results on their request to borrow for rehabilitation purposes may be regarded as another evidence of strengthening of an anti-Soviet bloc.

The proposed American loan to Russia was never given the opportunity to demonstrate if it could serve as a peace potion for easing increasingly bitter Soviet-American relations in the 1945–1946 period. From the Soviet point of view, the American insistent requests for both a politically and economically "open door" in Eastern Europe, for Soviet acceptance of American multilateral most-favored-nation trade principles, and for Soviet membership in the Bretton Woods institutions, seemed to require capitulation of national interest and security concerns. From the American point of view, Soviet failure to concede these issues endangered the American conception of postwar peace and prosperity. In order to fulfill that conception, the Truman administration—over the objections of Morgenthau, Nelson, White, and Wallace, among others—decided to employ the loan as a diplomatic *weapon before* negotiations began rather than as a diplomatic *tool at* the conference table. Few nations or individuals are eager to enter negotiations when the attitude of the other party is simplistically "Our way or not at all." The diplomatic use of economic power by any nation possessing it is to be expected and can conceivably be helpful in achieving fruitful and mutually beneficial negotiations. But if that power thwarts negotiations or is employed to buttress demands which alone are held to be the *sine qua non* for peaceful settlement, the result is schism and conflict.

Samuel Flagg Bemis

THE CREATION OF THE SOVIET SATELLITES

Towards the end of World War II, Soviet armies marched into Eastern Europe on the heels of the retreating Germans. The Soviet occupation and degree of influence in the countries of that area varied. Rumania and Bulgaria, as former Axis nations, were firmly controlled, as was Japan by the United States in the Far East. Poland was influenced greatly by Russia, but non-Communists were allowed to participate in the government before 1947. Soviet troops were withdrawn from both Czechoslovakia and Yugoslavia in late 1945, and a free election in Hungary in the fall of 1945 routed the Communists. Finland enjoyed a considerable degree of independence. Many Americans believed with Churchill that an "iron curtain" had sealed Eastern Europe off from the West. The seizure of power by Communists in Czechoslovakia in early 1948 confirmed popular American sentiment. In his survey of American foreign relations, Samuel Flagg Bemis, one of the most prominent American diplomatic historians, accounts for Soviet incursions into Eastern Europe. Depicting Soviet foreign policy as a world revolutionary movement, he suggests that Russia possessed a well-formulated postwar plan of expansion. Bemis is also the author of *Jay's Treaty* (1923), *The Latin American Policy of the United States* (1943), and *John Quincy Adams and the Foundations of American Policy* (1949).

THE Yalta Conference (February 4–11, 1945) was one of the most dramatic personal parleys in modern history, rivaling in that respect the memorable meeting of Napoleon and Alexander I on a raft in the middle of the Niemen River. There, amidst the soft airs of the ravaged Crimea, on the seats of the mighty in the old Livadia palace of the Czars, sat in joyful situation Joseph Stalin, the man of steel, dictator of the Russian proletariat, father of a new Pan-Slavism, implacable *Realpolitiker* of the Revolution, sponsor of a future WUSSR. On the other end of the row of three sat Winston Churchill, dauntless leader of large enterprises, greatest statesman of English history, somber man of blood and tears and toil and sweat, and now of smiling victory, striving for a peace that would make the world safe for a disintegrating British Empire. Between them sat the amiable Roosevelt, civilian Commander in Chief of the armies and navies and airfleets of the United States, new dealer of good will and promises to the common man and voter, would-be good neighbor to all the world, preacher of the four freedoms to all the men in all the lands. Graven on his anxious visage were the ravages of fatigue and fatal illness. The last task of his life was to wean Stalin away from the inexorable revolutionary goal of a World Union of Soviet Socialist Republics into a peaceful World Family of Democratic Nations.

The joint public announcement of the results of the Yalta Conference masked the secret agreements of the three Chiefs of State. Publicly they announced that they had agreed on the timing, scope, and co-ordination of military plans for the defeat and unconditional surrender of Germany and enforcement by military occupation by the United States, Great Britain, Russia, and France, in separate zones, with a joint Allied Control Commission of their respective commanders in that field. They declared that they would root out all vestiges of Nazism in order to give hope for a future decent life for Germans and a place for them in the comity of nations. They made known that they would call a conference of the signatories of the United Nations Declaration to meet at San Francisco April 25, 1945, to agree upon a world peace organization on the basis of the proposals of Dumbarton Oaks. They revealed that they had reached an agreement, to be announced in due course, on the voting formula of the big powers within the Security Council of such an organization. They broadcast their resolution to endow the liberated nations of Europe with provisional governments representative of all the democratic elements in the population pledged to free elections of *de jure* governments responsible to the will of the people. They did not define democracy, any more than they had done at Teheran, but they reaffirmed their faith in the principles of the Atlantic Charter.

They conceded that a new situation had been created in Poland, as a result of her complete liberation by the Red Army, that called for the establishment of a more broadly based Provisional Government, to include democratic leaders from Poland itself and from Poles abroad; this government would be pledged to hold free and unfettered elections as soon as possible on the basis of universal suffrage and secret ballot to be participated in by all democratic and anti-Nazi parties. They recognized that the eastern boundary of Poland "should" follow the Curzon Line, with minor deviations in favor of Poland, and that Poland "must" receive substantial accessions of territory in the north and west—as compensation for her losses in the east. They agreed to the establishment of a new government in Yugoslavia under Marshal Tito—the Soviet protégé—but with a broader basis including former members of parliament who had not compromised themselves by collaboration with the enemy. They provided for periodic meetings of the foreign secretaries of their respective governments, by rotation in the three capitals, to follow after the United Nations Conference on World Organization.

Most important products of Yalta were the three secret supplementary agreements, not included in the public declaration of February 11, 1945, but of the same date: (1) an agreement on the repatriation of citizens of the USA and the USSR, and on prisoners of war and civilians liberated by American and Soviet forces respectively; (2) on the voting formula for the Big Four in the Security Council kept secret only until cleared with France and China; and (3) conditions agreed upon for the entrance of Russia into the war with Japan "in two or three months after Germany has surrendered."

The latter agreement pledged the United States and Great Britain "unquestionably" to fulfill for Russia, after Japan's defeat: (1) the *status quo* of outer-Mongolia—named as The Mongolian Peoples' Republic—which had severed itself from China and accepted Russian protection; (2) restoration to Russia of her former status in Manchuria before the Russo-Japanese War of 1904–1905, with specific safeguarding of the "pre-eminent interests" of Soviet Russia in the internationalized free port of Dairen, in a naval base (by lease) at Port Arthur, and in joint Sino-Russian control and operation of the Chinese-Eastern and South Manchurian Railroads; (3) the Kurile Islands and the southern half of the island of Sakhalin to be handed over to the USSR.

The pledges at Yalta to Stalin, which the Russian leader was careful to have written down explicitly over the signatures of the Big Three, ran directly counter to the promises which Roosevelt and Churchill had made to Chiang Kai-shek in the Cairo Declaration. They placed the President under the "unquestionable" requirement of obtaining from the Generalissimo his consent, a most mortifying function for the United States, but which Chiang accepted with satisfaction. Further, by failing to stipulate in writing an unquestionable guaranty of the Open Door for the USA along with the "pre-eminent interests" of the USSR in Manchuria, Roosevelt overlooked a fundamental of American foreign policy in the very region that originally called forth that doctrine and led to its pronouncement for all of China in 1899.

Roosevelt signed the last, secret pact of Yalta—relating to Russia's entry into the war with Japan—while personally closeted with Stalin and Churchill. It was this agreement which provoked the most severe animadversions among the President's countrymen when the text became known. Roosevelt had led the United States into a double war in order to preserve a global balance of power. At Yalta, on the eve of certain victory, he made concessions to Stalin at the expense of China which unhinged the balance of power in both Asia and Europe. Yet it is difficult to see how, short of turning on the ally Russia in actual war, either the United States or Great Britain could have prevented in fact the flow of Russian power into the vacuums east and west that were being created by the defeat of Germany and Japan. To be sure, in return for these concessions Stalin pledged support to the Chinese Nationalist Government and to uphold democratic principles in the liberated states in Eastern Europe and elsewhere—just as Chamberlain received guaranties from Hitler at Munich not to advance any farther in Europe after taking part of Czechoslovakia. Placing this promise of Stalin's on record for these principles was a most important factor in the great issues that were to follow. Nevertheless, in its aftermath of deception, Yalta was in a sense another Munich. It was Stalin who called the tune.

* * *

Hostilities had ceased with the surrender and occupation of the enemy countries, but peace could not come to the world until the final treaties of peace were signed and ratified. Even then it would not be possible without the sincere desire and common collaboration of the remaining superpowers, particularly of the USA and the USSR. The Council of Foreign Ministers in one meeting after another wrangled over the provisions of the minor peace treaties until December, 1946, with the Soviet representative trying to secure heavy reparations from Italy (to be pumped out of that prostrate state as expected American relief money poured in), to get the port of Trieste for Yugoslavia, to obtain for Russia a trusteeship over Italian colonies in North Africa, and to keep the Western Allies from any free navigation of the Danube River. The five peace treaties finally concluded with Bulgaria, Finland, Hungary, Italy, and Roumania, made relatively small territorial changes in the map of Europe, already vastly altered *de facto* by Russian absorption of the Baltic states, the coast of East Prussia, eastern Poland, northern Bucovina, and Bessarabia. The former satellites of Germany were laid under heavy indemnities to Russia, Yugoslavia, and Greece, with token indemnities to Albania and Ethiopia. Trieste became a provisional Free Territory under the guaranty of the United Nations, occupied by American, British and Yugoslav troops until a neutral (i.e., not Yugoslav or Italian or Triestine) governor, to be appointed by the Security Council, should decide upon their withdrawal. The Italian treaty left the disposition of Italian colonies in Africa to the Council of Foreign Ministers the more to dispute about, with the provision that if it was not settled by September 1, 1948, it should be determined by the General Assembly of the United Nations. (On November 22, 1949, the Assembly voted to establish Libya as an independent state not later than January 1, 1952; to give independence to Somaliland after ten years under Italian trusteeship; and deferred the disposition of Eritrea pending further study.) It was agreed to call a conference of the Big Four plus the riparian states to regulate freedom of navigation on the Danube River. (It assembled at Belgrade in the summer of 1948, where seven of the eleven states signed a convention excluding nonriparian states from the International Danubian Commission, which was equivalent to excluding them from navigation.)

The minor treaties disarmed the Balkan states and Italy and thus left Yugoslavia a heavily preponderant military power in southeastern Europe. They were far from satisfactory to the United States, but the Senate ratified them and the President proclaimed them, obstinately hoping thereby to introduce some element of stability into European affairs and to make way for peace treaties with Austria and Germany.

What appealed most to the people and Government of the United States was the article common to all the minor treaties by which the former enemy state solemnly guaranteed to "take all measures necessary to secure to all persons under [its] jurisdiction, without distinction as to race, language, or religion, the enjoyment of human rights and of the fundamental freedoms, including freedom of expression, of press and of publication, of religious worship, of political opinion and of public meeting."

Trustful Americans hoped that the minor peace treaties would be the forerunner of a general peace, first in Europe and then in the Far East, protected and administered by a World Family of Democratic Nations. This hope crumbled slowly in the following months and years. Soviet Russia carried forward her revolutionary program, first in contiguous states, next in remoter regions, finally through fifth columns of communists all over the world. Russian power flowed irresistibly into the vacuums left by the collapse of German and Japanese authority in Europe and Asia. The USSR clenched its hold on the territorial occupations in Eastern Europe. Then it intervened with the force of revolution, syphoned out of Soviet military might, to overturn the principles of real democracy and free and unfettered elections agreed to at Teheran and Yalta. One by one it installed communist governments in the satellite states to the west and southwest and imposed upon them a structure of alliances and political and economic control in the form of "co-operation" and "collaboration" for cultural and economic purposes: with Czechoslovakia, Roumania, Yugoslavia, Hungary, Albania, Poland, Bulgaria. In Eastern Europe the *Comintern* (Communist international, politely suspended during the Strange Alliance) reappeared in the shape of the *Cominform* to implement these Soviet alliances. It invoked the solidarity of the several states in their forthcoming struggle against "Anglo-American imperialism." In Northern Europe, Finland, and behind Finland the Scandinavian countries, Sweden, Norway and Denmark trembled before the aggressive advances of the revolutionary colossus.

To the Far East, Soviet expansion thrust rapidly into the great continent of Asia. A mutual-assistance treaty (February 27, 1946) brought the "Mongolian People's Republic" into the Russian power system; communistic revolutionary governments were installed in Manchuria, Inner Mongolia, Northern Korea, and for all practical purposes in Sinkiang. The tiny territory of Tannu Tuva, on the border between Outer Mongolia and Russia—tiny by Asiatic standards, but with a thinly populated area as large as Great Britain—went through the whole cycle of Red imperialism: from Chinese province to autonomy, from autonomy to Soviet protectorate, from a "people's republic" to an actual province of the Soviet Union. Beyond these former buffers of inner Asia lay the vast prize of China itself and the restive peoples to the south—India, Malaya, and the East Indies.

Thus the Iron Curtain closed down between the West and one Soviet satellite after another in Europe and Asia. Next might come Greece, where a communist revolt had been smoldering since the end of the war; then Turkey, and Iran; and still further to the south lay Africa, as tempting for the future as were China and the Indies to the east. Africa could be what it threatened to be if controlled by Nazi Germany, a springboard for a jump of power to South America. The Revolution, to use the words of its guides and fellow travelers, was "on the march" from the Heartland towards the Rimlands of the World Island. Beyond the Rimlands of the Old World, communist fifth columns, with leaders of revolution schooled in Moscow, mapped out the political terrain in every country everywhere. The United States, with its wide liberties and meager policing, afforded unparalleled facilities. . . .

Soviet intervention in the satellite states, the new Soviet alliances in Eastern Europe, and the increasing preponderance of Russian armed force, and gradual realization by the Western nations of the Soviet program for world revolution, frightened the democracies fringing on the Atlantic. Their heritage of freedom, so recently and so valiantly preserved, with Russia's aid, against the fascist conquest, seemed doomed to another even more formidable trial from their Ally of yesteryear.

Gar Alperovitz

UNCERTAINTY IN EASTERN EUROPE

Alperovitz, in the following review of Martin Herz's *Beginnings of the Cold War* (1966), challenges the traditional account of Soviet penetration of Eastern Europe. He emphasizes the complexity and contradictions of Soviet policy and the significance of chronology. Finally, Alperovitz, like Lippmann before him, argues that the United States aggravated Soviet fear of another invasion through weak neighbors.

ANY examination of the very earliest postwar period forces us to think about developments *before* 1947 when it was decided to contain the Soviet Union by "unanswerable force." Herz's study is important because it makes two serious judgments about this period: first, that in 1945 Soviet policy was by no means inexorably prescribed and expansionist; second, that mistakes made by American officials just after the war may well have prevented the kind of compromise and accommodation which is just beginning to emerge in Europe today.

These suggestions recall Walter Lippmann's *The Cold War,* published in 1947, which also argued—with greater candor and less detail—that the Russians might have been willing to accept a negotiated settlement in 1945 and 1946, but that US policy ignored opportunities to meet them halfway. Lippmann's now little-remembered book offered a powerful critique of Kennan's theory of Soviet expansion and American containment. If Herz's view is correct, accepted interpretations of American-Russian relations are called into question. And if Lippmann was right in saying that American policy helped to prevent an accommodation in 1945 and 1946, the Cold War itself must be regarded, at least in part, as the result of fundamental errors of American diplomacy. These are startling conclusions, but anyone willing to bring an open mind to Herz's book or to Lippmann's will find that they have exposed many weaknesses in the usual explanations of early events in the Cold War.

No one, of course, can be certain of "what might have been." But Herz refutes at least one accepted myth. Contrary to current historical reconstructions, there is abundant evidence that American leaders in 1945 were not much worried about the expansion of communism into *Western* Europe. That worry came later. In the days just after the war, most Communists in Italy, France, and elsewhere were cooperating with bourgeois governments. At Potsdam, in 1945, Truman regarded the Russians' desires for concessions beyond their area of occupation as largely bluff. The major issues in dispute were all in Eastern Europe, deep within the zone of Soviet military occupation. The real expansion of Soviet power, we are reminded, took place in Poland, Hungary, Bulgaria, Rumania, Czechoslovakia, and the eastern regions of Germany and Austria.

The US in 1945 wanted Russia to give up the control and influence the Red Army had gained in the battle against Hitler. American demands may have been motivated by an idealistic desire to foster democracy, but Herz's main point is that in countries like Rumania and Bulgaria they were about as realistic as would be Soviet demands for changes in, say, Mexico. Any such parallel has obvious limits, the most significant of which is not that democracy and communism cannot so easily be compared, but that Eastern Europe is of far greater

From Gar Alperovitz, "How Did the Cold War Begin?" pp. 6, 8, 9, 11. Reprinted from *The New York Review of Books,* VIII (March 23, 1967).

importance to Soviet security than is Mexico to American security: from the time of Napoleon—and twice in the lifetime of millions of present day Russians—bloody invasions have swept through the area of their "Middle West."

In the early Spring of 1945, negotiations concerning one border state—Poland—brought the main issue into the open. At Yalta and immediately thereafter, the US had mainly mediated between Stalin and Churchill on Poland; Roosevelt had warned Churchill that to make extreme demands would doom the negotiations. A month later, in the faltering last days of Roosevelt's life, the US itself adopted a new tough line, demanding that pro-Western and openly anti-Russian Polish politicians be given more influence in negotiations to set up a new government for Poland. As was predicted, the Russians balked at the idea of such an expansion of anti-Soviet influence in a country so important to their security, and the negotiations ground to a halt. Moreover, at this precise moment, Russian suspicions about the West deepened with Allen Dulles's concurrent but unrelated secret negotiations with Nazi generals in Switzerland. The result was a violent quarrel which shook the entire structure of American-Soviet relations. But this was only the beginning. The demands on the Polish question reflected the ideas of the men who were to surround the new President; led by Joseph Grew and James F. Byrnes, they soon convinced Truman to attempt to make stronger demands elsewhere in Eastern Europe.

For most of the year Roosevelt had been highly ambivalent toward such matters. By late 1944, however (in spite of wavering on the politically sensitive Polish issue in his dying days), Roosevelt concluded it would be a fundamental error to put too much pressure on Russia over other regions vital to her security. In September and October 1944, and in early January 1945, he gave form to his conclusion by entering into armistice agreements with Britain and Russia, which gave the Soviet military almost complete control of internal politics in each Eastern European ex-Nazi satellite. It was understood, for instance, that the Soviets would have authority to issue orders to the Rumanian government, and that, specifically, the Allied Control Commission would be "under the general direction of the Allied (Soviet) High Command acting on behalf of the Allied Powers." The Rumanian accords, and the similar but slightly less severe Bulgarian and Hungarian armistice agreements, served to formalize the famous Churchill-Stalin spheres-of-influence arrangement which, without FDR's agreement, had previously given the Russians "90 per cent" influence in Rumania, "80 per cent" influence in Bulgaria, and "75 per cent" influence in Hungary, in exchange for "90 per cent" British influence in Greece and a "50-50" split of influence in Yugoslavia. The armistice accords were also modeled after a previous understanding which had contained Soviet endorsement of dominant American-British influence in Italy. The Eastern European armistice agreements have been available to the public for years, but have been successfully buried, or avoided by most scholars. Herz has exhumed them, and he shows that they contain American endorsement of dominant Soviet influence in the ex-Nazi satellites.

At Yalta, in early February, 1945, Roosevelt pasted over these specific texts the vague and idealistic rhetoric of the famous Declaration on Liberated Europe. The President apparently wished to use the Declaration mainly to appease certain politically important ethnic groups in America; he devoted only a few minutes to the matter at the Yalta Conference, and the familiar rhetoric promising democracy was almost devoid of practical meaning. For example, who was to decide in given instances between the American and Soviet definitions of common but vague terms like "democratic"? Much more important, as Herz shows, in the broad language of the Declaration the Allies agreed merely to "consult" about matters within the liberated countries, not to "act," and they authorized consultations only when all parties agreed they were necessary. Thus the United States itself confirmed the

Russians' right to refuse to talk about the ex-Nazi satellites. The State Department knew this and, in fact, had tried to insert operative clauses into the Declaration. But Roosevelt, having just signed the armistice agreements, rejected this unrealistic proposal. Moreover, when the Soviets after Yalta crudely tossed out a Rumanian government they did not like, the President, though unhappy that he had not been consulted, reaffirmed his basic position by refusing to intervene.

Ironically, Herz's book lends credence to the old Republican charge that Roosevelt accepted a compromise at Yalta which bolstered Stalin's position in Eastern Europe. The charge, while correct in essentials, was silly in assuming that much else, short of war, could have been done while the Red Army occupied the area. The Republican politicians also ignored the fact that at Yalta Roosevelt could not expect a continued American military presence in Europe for very long after the war. This not only deprived him of leverage, it made an accommodation with Russia much more desirable for another reason: Red Army help became essential as a guarantee that Germany would not rise from defeat to start yet a third World War. Stalin also needed American help, as he too made clear, to hold down the Germans. Hence, underlying the American-Soviet plans for peace at Yalta was not "faith" but a common interest—the German threat—which had cemented the World War II alliance. From this 1945 perspective the crucial portion of the Yalta agreement was not the Declaration on Liberated Europe, nor even the provisions on Poland, but rather the understanding that the United States and Russia (with Britain and France as minor partners) would work together to control Germany. This meant, among other things, joint action to reduce Germany's physical power by extracting reparations from German industry.

Although Herz tends to play down the German issue, he does take up important economic matters that relate to it. He understands that Moscow was in a cruel dilemma which, had the US been shrewd enough, might have been resolved to the benefit of both American diplomacy and the economic health of Europe. The Russians were greatly in need of aid for their huge postwar reconstruction program. Importing industrial equipment from Eastern Europe was a possible solution, though a doubtful one, for taking this equipment would inevitably cause political problems. Reparations from Germany were another, but the key industrial sectors were in American hands. Finally, the United States itself was a potential source. Herz argues (as did Ambassadors Harriman and Winant at the time) that a US reconstruction loan for Russia would have been wise; it would have given US diplomacy strong leverage in a variety of negotiations. (Without other sources of aid for reconstruction the Russians were almost inevitably reduced to extracting industrial goods from either Germany or Eastern Europe.) American officials seriously considered such a loan, but, as Herz shows, they did not actively pursue it with the Russians—though one or two crude attempts were made to use a loan as a bludgeon in negotiations. With a future US troop commitment unlikely, and a large loan ruled out, the United States had no real bargaining power. Hence its attempts at intervention in Eastern Europe amounted to little more than bluster.

The State Department wanted to have it both ways: it wanted to hold the Russians to the vague promises of the Yalta Declaration; it also wanted to avoid the specific texts of the armistice agreements. But the Republicans, and even Secretary Byrnes in his later writings, understood the weakness of this position. The Republicans, for their part, also wanted to have it both ways. They wanted to argue both that Roosevelt gave the Russians all the authority they needed for their actions *and* that the Russians broke their agreements.

The Republican attack on Yalta came late in the Cold War, and was combined with a new demand that the US "roll back" Soviet influence. Few now realize how unoriginal the demand was, for a "roll back" effort—without its latter-day label—was, in fact, at the center of

Harry Truman's first postwar policy. The President, we now know, made this effort in a spurt of confidence derived from the new atomic bomb. But the policy failed in its continuing attempt to reduce Soviet control by expanding Western influence in Poland. It also failed in its bold follow-up effort to force the Russians to change the Bulgarian and Rumanian governments. Nevertheless, these opening moves of the postwar period helped to set the tone of the new Administration's attitude toward Russia. Truman, although publicly proclaiming his adherence to Roosevelt's policy of cooperation, seems to have understood that his approach differed fundamentally from his predecessor's. (In private, as Secretary of State Stettinius has written, he complained that the intervention in Poland rested on rather shaky diplomatic ground.) Indeed, by September 1945, the basic change in US policy was so clearly defined that, as Secretary of State Byrnes later wrote, the Russian complaint that Roosevelt's policy had been abandoned was "understandable."

What was the result? Like Herz, John Foster Dulles (who assisted Byrnes at the time) also believed that the Cold War began in 1945. Dulles emphasized in his book *War or Peace* (1950) that a new tough line of US policy was adopted at this time over dimly remembered issues deep within the Soviet-controlled Balkans. Herz prints almost the full text of the crucial 1945 Hopkins-Stalin talks, which reveal the equally important point that, in Russia, the change in American policy produced what Stalin termed "a certain alarm." A few thoughtful US officials recognized the significance of these developments. Secretary of War Henry L. Stimson, for example, tried to block the campaign to engage American prestige in Eastern Europe. In White House discussions he argued, first, that the demand for more Western influence in Poland was a mistake: "The Russians perhaps were being more realistic than we were in regard to their own security. . . ." He then tried to cut short efforts to intervene elsewhere, reminding Truman, as Stimson's diary shows, that "we have made up our minds on the broad policy that it was not wise to get into the Balkan mess even if the thing seemed to be disruptive of policies which the State Department thought were wise." Stimson pointed out that "we have taken that policy right from the beginning, Mr. Roosevelt having done it himself or having been a party to it himself."

When Stimson failed in his conservative effort to limit American objectives, the stage was set for one of the great tragedies of the Cold War. As Stimson understood, the Russians, though extremely touchy about the buffer area, were not impossible to deal with. Had their security requirements been met, there is evidence that their domination of Eastern Europe might have been much different from what it turned out to be. Churchill, too, thought the Russians were approachable. Obviously, conditions in Eastern Europe would not meet Western ideals; but Churchill judged, in late 1944 and early 1945, that Moscow was convinced it would be much easier to secure its objectives through moderate policies. In Greece at this time, as Churchill was to stress in *Triumph and Tragedy,* Stalin was "strictly and faithfully" holding to his agreement *not* to aid the Greek Communists. Even in much of the border area the Russians seemed willing to accept substantial capitalism and some form of democracy—with the crucial proviso that the Eastern European governments had to be "friendly" to Russia in defense and foreign policies. Finland serves as a rough model of a successful border state. Here, too, the armistice made the Soviets supreme, giving rights parallel to the Bulgarian and Rumanian accords plus the right to maintain Soviet military installations. However, the US made no independent effort to intervene; Finland maintained a foreign policy "friendly" to Russia; and the Russians were—as they still seem to be—prepared to accept a moderate government.

Although it is often forgotten, a modified application of the Finnish formula seemed to be shaping up elsewhere in 1945 and much of 1946. In Hungary, Soviet-sponsored free elections routed the Communist Party in 1945. In Bulgaria, a country with rather weak democratic traditions, the 1945 elections were complicated by competition for Great Power support among the various internal factions. Certainly the results were not perfect, but most Western observers (except the State Department) felt they should have been accepted. In Austria, the Communists were swamped in Soviet-run free elections in their zone in 1945, and, after a hesitant start, a free democratic government emerged for the entire country. In Czechoslovakia, from which the Red Army withdrew in December of 1945, democracy was so clearly acceptable to Soviet policy that the US had little to protest at the time.

Almost all of this was to change, of course. The freedoms in Hungary were to end in 1947. The initial pattern in Czechoslovakia was to be reversed in 1948. But writers who focus only on the brutal period of totalitarian control after 1947 and 1948 often ignore what happened earlier. The few who try to account for the known facts of the 1945–46 interlude usually do so in passing, either to suggest that the democratic governments "must have been" mere smokescreens, formed while Moscow waited for the US to leave the Continent; or that the Russians "must have been" secretly planning to take full control, but were methodically using the early period to prepare the groundwork for what came later. (Communists, too, like to ignore the 1945–46 period, for it suggests the possibility that Soviet Russia was more interested in an old-fashioned *modus vivendi* with the capitalists than in spreading World Communism. This was the essence of Tito's bitter complaint that Stalin tried to turn back the Yugoslav revolution.)

The Russians have displayed so much duplicity, brutality, and intransigence that it is easy to imagine the 1945–46 interlude as a mere smokescreen. But they also have a long history of protecting "socialism in one country" in a rather conservative, nationalistic way: the moderation of the 1945–46 interlude can be viewed as a logical extension of this tradition. That at least two quite different interpretations of their 1945–46 policy are conceivable is now rarely admitted, and the relative merits of each have not been seriously examined. Herz's study calls for a careful reappraisal of early post-war Soviet objectives. If the Russians were secretly harboring plans for an ultimate take over, they certainly were preparing a lot of trouble for themselves by sponsoring free politics, by pulling out the Red Army (it is not particularly shrewd to have to *re*-introduce foreign troops), by ripping up the Red Army's main rail connections across Poland—as they did in the fall of 1945. As well informed an observer as Averell Harriman believed, as he once testified to Congress, that Soviet policy in 1945 was ambivalent, that it could have become either more moderate within a framework of security and understanding with the West, or that it could have become hard-line and totalitarian, within the framework of insecurity and conflict. Harriman, though puzzled by the ultimate Russian decision in favor of the iron-fisted policy, clearly saw that Soviet expansion was neither inexorable nor inevitable.

At least one reason for Russia's shift to a tough line may be traced to mistakes made by US officials. As Stimson argued —and as history later showed—the demand for more influence in Soviet-controlled areas was almost certainly doomed from the start. This basic miscalculation stemmed, finally, from an attempt to overextend *American* diplomatic sway. Lippmann was, I believe correct in seeing that the other error was the failure of US policy makers to turn their energies to an early solution of the crucial German problem. Bolstered by the atomic bomb, which eliminated the threat that had been Roosevelt's central concern, American leaders dallied over Germany. Moreover, by refusing to hold to Roosevelt's agreement that a specific target for German reparations would be set (July, 1945), by permitting France to hamstring the German Control Commission (Fall, 1945), by halting German reparations shipments (Spring, 1946)—US policy suggested the very prospect Russia feared most: the abandonment of economic and political controls and the possibility that a new and powerful Germany would rise from the ashes of Nazism to become the bastion of Western capitalistic aggression in Europe. The United States had no such aggressive intent. Nonetheless, the US chose not to negotiate seriously on Germany until a full year-and-a-half after the war's end. Especially after Secretary Byrnes's tough speech in Stuttgart in the Fall of 1946, American policy was shortsighted enough to suggest a threat to Russia at the very time it was attempting to weaken Soviet control in the vital area which lay—protectively or threateningly—between German power and the Russian heartland. The Russians, who had no nuclear weapons, were far less casual about the question of security; their grip seemed to tighten in the buffer area month by month, as their worst fears about Germany seemed to come true.

The Russians were not easy to deal with, either in Germany or elsewhere. Nevertheless, if the hypothesis suggested by Lippmann's book is correct—and Herz's study indirectly supports it—there are reasons to believe that US policy itself may have to share responsibility for the imposition of totalitarian control in Eastern Europe, and possibly also for the subsequent expanding Communist agitation in Western Europe. The *addition* of increased insecurity to known Soviet paranoid tendencies may explain the rigidity which Soviet leaders displayed in their satellite policy after 1946. The first pattern seemed crudely similar to the Finnish or Austrian models. Would it have been reversed had the US seriously tried from the first to resolve the European security problem—as Lippmann urged? That Soviet actions may have been in part reactions to their judgments of American intentions may also help to explain why sustained Communist opposition developed in the West only *after* the clear breakdown of German control arrangements. It was not in 1945, but late in 1946 and in 1947 that the Italian and French Communists began to reverse their initial policy of cooperation with bourgeois governments. Was the changed focus of Communist politics part of the inexorable plan? Or was it primarily a rather shortsighted response to American policy itself?

Fred Warner Neal

SOVIET MILITARY AGGRESSION REAPPRAISED

In a short revisionist pamphlet on *U.S. Foreign Policy and the Soviet Union* (1961), Fred W. Neal of Claremont Graduate School, a former Consultant on Russian affairs in the Department of State (1946–1948), concluded that the United States overreacted to and misinterpreted Soviet ideology and rhetoric. Neal further developed this theme in a 1968 article which asserts that there was no imperative for war or conflict in Soviet ideology and that postwar Russia had no aggressive plans for Europe. Neal is also the author of *Titoism in Action: The Reforms in Yugoslavia after 1948* (1958).

THE general Washington view of Soviet Marxist theory has it that there is a Soviet ideological imperative to wage military war against capitalist states, to intervene militarily in underdeveloped areas and to work for world domination. The facts are that Marxist-Leninist theory sees capitalism being destroyed as a result of its own internal contradictions, country by country, taken advantage of by local revolutionaries. One of the contradictions concerns war. Up until Khrushchev, the theory proclaimed that wars were inevitable. Assuming as unquestionable the hostility of *capitalist states,* the theory did indeed foresee military conflict between the Soviet Union and its capitalist adversaries. But the war seen as inevitable by *Marxist-Leninist theory* was war between or among capitalist states or wars launched by capitalist states against socialist states.

The theory also foresees "wars of national liberation," and, moreover, it calls for support for them. In the military milieu of World War I, the Revolution, and the capitalist intervention in Russia, Lenin *did* see the future primarily in *terms* of military conflict, with the Revolution in Russia, once successful, giving military assistance to revolutionaries elsewhere. But in the basic ideology there is nowhere a call for military aggression by socialist states or for military intervention to aid foreign revolutionary movements. Indeed, Lenin set forth the tactical theory of objective conditions for revolution, which held that revolution could not be imported and could occur successfully only when the internal decay of a capitalist society was so advanced that the social fabric could be easily rent by domestic hands.

The Comintern, it is true, was created to aid and coordinate revolutionary activities, in short to aid Communists everywhere to do their best to bring about the objective conditions for revolution. But from the beginning the Comintern was tied exclusively to the Soviet Union, first as a result of trying to stem the capitalist invasion, and as a "general staff for world revolution"—which was what Lenin called it—it was not successful. Once Lenin saw that the earlier reports of the demise of capitalism were exaggerated, he called a halt to revolutionary activity, launched the NEP and concluded that capitalism, although certain to fall in the end, was in a period of some relatively long-run stability. This began the long period of the Soviet defensive that lasted more or less down to 1952.

Under Stalin, with his theory of the ebb and flow of the revolutionary tide, this took on such isolationist tones that Moscow and its minions actually spent more time trying to restrain Communist

From Fred Warner Neal, "The Cold War in Europe: 1945–1967," in N. D. Houghton, ed., *The Struggle Against History: U.S. Foreign Policy in an Age of Revolution* (New York, 1968), pp. 23–30.

revolutionary activity than to promote it. This was, of course, not because Stalin did not want to see Communism spread but because, adhering to his and Lenin's tactical theories, he was convinced that left-wing revolutionary activity could not then succeed. The task of the Communists was to secure a sound base, help the Soviet Union where they could and to wait. And if they would not do this—as with the Polish Communists before the war, for example—it was held better not to have a Communist Party at all rather than to have one that would risk everything by improper orientation and action.

Now this meant a sort of de facto coexistence, in the sense that the Soviet Union would try to avoid military conflict with the capitalist world if at all possible. It was to be a strictly temporary coexistence—war was still seen as inevitable and almost certain to involve the Soviet Union when it came. The USSR and its foreign minions would continue to denounce capitalism and the capitalists in harsh terms and make revolutionary propaganda where they could. But no matter how much hostility for capitalism was implicit in all this ideology, there was nothing calling for initiation of military action by Moscow. To make up for this lack, there has arisen a body of wholly false quotations attributed to Lenin, Stalin and others, in which they carefully explained that all Russians were waiting for was for the West to let down its guard. Many honest and otherwise perspicacious people have been taken in by this, but it in no way alters the facts about what the ideological pronouncements actually say and do not say.

Having determined to their satisfaction that Soviet ideology called for military aggression, the United States then proceeded to see evidence of it in what happened in Eastern Europe. There is no question that the Soviet Union long had its sights on extending its influence to Eastern Europe. In part, this was the natural attitude of a great power toward a core interest of geographic proximity. In part, it reflected Soviet reaction to the *cordon sanitaire* and Munich, under which hostile great powers extended their influence into this area. With the breakup of the pre-World War I empires, Eastern Europe represented something of a power vacuum. The traditional Russian influence there was excluded by the *cordon sanitaire,* and the Bolsheviks were too weak to do anything about it. It was doubtless the experience of the interwar period, in which Soviet influence was so unnaturally contained, that made it difficult for the United States and Britain to recognize that this was an abnormal situation in international politics and unlikely to continue long.

At this point, it is necessary to distinguish between the reality of the World War II agreements between the Soviet Union and the Anglo-American allies and the pseudohistory about them which is prevalent in the United States. This pseudohistory has it that Soviet diplomacy succeeded beyond all expectations by hoodwinking the Western powers; that the United States appeased the Soviets by "giving" them Eastern Europe; and that Moscow then violated the agreements by destroying democracy in that area.

It is important, in considering the reality, to see that as far as postwar goals are concerned, Moscow was singularly unsuccessful in its wartime diplomacy. The major political goals sought by Stalin at Teheran, Yalta, and Potsdam were: first, Western agreement to Soviet hegemony in Eastern Europe; second, United States assistance in rebuilding the USSR after the war; and third, a revision of the Montreux Convention giving Moscow some say in controlling the Dardanelles. Despite apparent agreement to these Soviet demands on the part of Roosevelt, Churchill, and even Truman, in the end the Soviets achieved none of them.

Specifically regarding Eastern Europe, two points are significant. First, the wartime agreements did little if any more than recognize the military realities. Just as the United States and Great Britain defeated the Nazis in the West and were in military possession of Western Europe, so the Soviet Union defeated the Germans in the East and were in military possession of Eastern Europe—the only difference being that Soviet power was well on the way to being ensconced in the East before the Nazis were subdued in the West. There was no alternative to recognizing this in the wartime agreements, and it was so recognized at the time. Moreover, there never had been a United States interest in Eastern Europe, which was clearly of the most vital concern to the USSR. The basically unwarranted idea that Yalta, for example, "gave" something to the Russians at the expense of the United States interests and ideals developed only later out of the anti-Communist vagaries of Washington's domestic politics.

Certainly, Moscow interpreted the wartime agreements as signifying Western acceptance of Soviet hegemony in Eastern Europe, and they probably were justified. It must be remembered that Yalta in effect underwrote the results of the Second Moscow Conference of 1944, where Churchill took the initiative in proposing to Stalin a division of spheres of influence which clearly acknowledged the dominant Soviet position in all of Eastern Europe except for Yugoslavia and Greece. And it was only after this position was reversed, by the challenge to Soviet policies in Bulgaria in the Anglo-American note of September, 1946, that one can distinguish beginnings of a clear Soviet "cold war attitude."

The wartime agreements were ambiguous about their references to political democracy. It is perhaps true that the naive Americans did not realize that the Soviets would utilize their dominant position in Eastern Europe to install the local Communists in power. It is hardly true, however, that the Soviets "destroyed" democracy in Eastern Europe. Democracy in its Western political sense had not flourished in this area—if one excludes Czechoslovakia—and less propitious conditions for it to be instituted, given the revolution-ridden chaos left by the Nazis, could hardly be imagined. You cannot destroy what doesn't exist, any more than you can give up something you don't have. In any event, the point is that first Soviet military domination and then local Communist domination came to Eastern Europe as a normal consequence of military occupation at the close of World War II.

A special word should be said about the case of Czechoslovakia. Those who purport to see what happened in Eastern Europe as evidence of Soviet Military aggression invariably cite Czechoslovakia as their most conclusive point. Ironically, it was in Czechoslovakia that the Soviet Union had the least to do with the coming of Communism. Not only were there no Soviet troops in Czechoslovakia at the time of the Communist coup d'état, but all Soviet military units withdrew from Czechoslovakia in 1945 after having allowed parliamentary democracy to be reinstituted there. The Communist take-over in Czechoslovakia may have had Soviet approval or even connivance, but it was done by the Czechoslovaks themselves and no one else. Yet four Secretaries of State have solemnly told the American people that the coup d'état [in 1948] in Czechoslovakia is one reason why we must be on our guard militarily.

The role of Soviet actions in Eastern Europe, although highly important, can be exaggerated in explaining United States fears of the USSR. Quite independently of this, even under Roosevelt, there were always powerful segments of Washington officialdom whose fear of and opposition to the Soviet Union were so great that it dominated their view of the world. However, President Roosevelt was monumentally sound in his recognition that in the postwar world there was either going to be some form of United States-Soviet cooperation or there was going to be dangerous instability. Roosevelt's emphasis on the importance of good relations with Moscow was always perturbing to many in his administration, and almost immediately after his death the views of this group became dominant. Its main spokesman was Secretary of Defense [James] Forrestal, in whose ultimate tragedy paranoia and deathly intense fear of the Soviet Union played a large part.

In George F. Kennan, the anti-Soviet group found an earnest but somewhat ambiguous philosopher, and in Harry

Truman they found a willing tool. Indeed, Truman, who brought to the Presidency a sort of average man, American Legion view of the world, mixed with Southern Baptist morality and New Deal liberalism, soon led the charge himself. As for Kennan, it is quite true that his reasoning was more sophisticated and was not predicated on the assumption that the Soviet Union was plotting military aggression. But, certainly, it was also quite confusing. Mr. Kennan has long since made it clear that he was not talking about military containment. As one rereads his "The Sources of Soviet Conduct" today, it appears to be a restrained statement.[1] But failing to identify just what aspects of Soviet conduct it was necessary to contain, and failing specifically to abjure military connotations, Kennan's persuasively written ideas seemed to advocates of the hard-line policy to be not only a justification of what they had done but also a justification of what they wanted to do. This was especially true of Kennan's thesis that the United States should adopt "a policy of firm containment designed to confront the Russians with unalterable counterforce at every point where they show signs of encroaching upon the interests of a peaceful and stable world."

Taken literally—as it was—this seemed to mean that Soviet influence had to be contained, by force, wholly within Soviet borders while United States influence was to spread throughout the world to make sure the Soviets were contained. If the Soviet Union, as a nation-state, had any vital interests at all outside its borders, this point was ignored in the containment doctrine, as was the fact that challenges to such vital Soviet interests—as the doctrine required—were certain to produce strong reactions and even counterchallenges. Unfortunately, Kennan's repeated subsequent disclaimers have never been able to overcome the impact of the interpretation placed on his words in 1947.

So earnestly did Americans believe in the containment doctrine, with its fear of Soviet aggression on the one hand and its refusal to accept the reality of the USSR on the other hand, that we were unable to conceive of any of our own actions as other than *defensive*. Yet it requires only the slightest trace of objectivity to realize that Moscow could only see as *aggressive threats* our war games along Soviet borders, missile emplacements on Soviet frontiers, air probes into the Soviet interior, and naval exercises in the Baltic and the Black Sea. Washington's unreality in this respect reached its height during the U-2 affair of 1960, when our position almost seemed to deny that the Soviet Union had a vital interest in its own territorial integrity. The wonder is that the chickens coming home to roost—in the form of Soviet missiles in Cuba—did not come sooner.

[1] Article in *Foreign Affairs,* XXV (July 1947), pp. 566–582. After service as Counselor to the American Embassy in Moscow, 1944–1946, Kennan returned to the United States to head the State Department's new Policy Planning Staff, formally established on May 2, 1947.

Klaus Epstein

THE DIVISION OF GERMANY

During World War II, the United States, Great Britain, and Russia decided to divide Germany into sections for the purpose of temporary military occupation. They agreed, too, to treat the country as a single economic unit, to break up large German corporations, and to demilitarize the nation. And a zone was granted to neighboring France. But the major powers could not decide Germany's eastern boundaries, and by 1947, as the Cold War produced more uncompromising policies, neither the United States nor Russia was willing to release control of its portion of Germany, and the division thus became permanent. In his review essay of Hans Peter Schwarz's *Vom Reich zur Bundesrepublik* (1966), Klaus Epstein discusses the reasons for the collapse of cooperation in Germany. He points out the unilateral policies of all occupants, the early disruptive posture of France, the uncertainty of Russian policy, and the growing American practice of drawing Western Germany into the Western European economy to contribute to the Marshall Plan. Security and economic recovery questions were closely interrelated in Germany. Before his death in 1967, Epstein was chairman of Brown University's Department of History and author of *The Genesis of German Conservatism* (1966).

THERE were, basically, five theoretically possible solutions to the German problem in 1945: a four-power agreement on a "Carthaginian peace"; a four-power agreement on a "neutralized" Germany standing outside existing power blocs; Soviet domination of all of Germany; Western domination of all of Germany, leading eventually to a free united Germany allied with the West; and a partition of Germany between a Western-oriented West Germany and an Eastern-dominated East Germany. Each of these solutions was promoted and hindered by several factors and attitudes among both Allies and Germans.

1. A "Carthaginian peace" was desired by strong currents of public opinion in all the victorious powers, an entirely understandable fact at a time when Nazi horrors were fresh in everyone's mind. Its ingredients would have been Allied annexation of broad German territories (e.g., annexation of the country up to the Oder-Neisse line by Russia and Poland, and of the Rhineland by France); internationalization of the Ruhr; a drastic economic policy of dismantling, reparations, and "industrial ceilings" in the spirit of the Morgenthau Plan; and permanent Allied controls over Germany to enforce this harsh policy upon a hungry, sullen, and rebellious "native" population. Such a policy was "objectively" impossible—at least in the long run—for two reasons: it could never win the support of the German people and hence could not be permanently acceptable to governments responsive to a "civilized" public opinion; and it presupposed permanent agreement between Russia and the United States not to mobilize German resources against one another. If it is accepted that the cold war between Russia and the U.S. was "inevitable" (even apart from conflict over Germany), then it is clear that a "Carthaginian peace" was based upon a utopian premise of continued Allied harmony.

2. A four-power agreement on a neutralized, united Germany, enjoying an

Excerpts from Klaus Epstein, "The German Problem, 1945–1950," ***World Politics*, XX (January, 1968), pp. 282–288, 297, 298–300. Reprinted by permission of *World Politics*.**

ever-increasing measure of self-government—in short, the solution applied to the Austrian problem in 1955—also meant that Germany would be subjected to punitive, discriminatory treatment, although the chances of winning German support obviously stood in inverse proportion to the degree of punishment and discrimination. Like the first, this solution was made virtually impossible by the mutual hostility of Russia and America in the cold war, as well as by the incompatibility of their aims, the basic factor behind the cold war. By 1947 these aims were made apparent in Germany by the Russians' "Sovietizing" their zone and making enormous reparations demands, while the Americans promoted democracy and free enterprise, subsidized their zone, and worked for the integration of Western Germany into the (Western) European Recovery Program.

3. The Soviet domination of all of Germany—and presumably all of Europe—was a genuine possibility if the U.S. were to relapse into isolationism, withdraw its troops from Europe, and fail to buttress the sagging Western European economy. These possibilities were taken very seriously indeed by many influential people until the Marshall Plan of 1947 and the negotiation of NATO in 1949. Thereafter Soviet domination could only be the result of victorious war.

4. The Western domination of all of Germany—and perhaps of much of Eastern Europe as well—could have been achieved only through a ruthless Western exploitation of military superiority in 1945 to impose unfavorable (though possibly "just") terms upon the Russians. Such a policy was advocated by Winston Churchill in June 1945, but it was never seriously considered by President Truman and would not have been supported by public opinion at the time.

5. The last theoretical solution was the partition of Germany at the zonal boundary of 1945, dividing a democratic West Germany from a Communist East Germany. The latter could be created and maintained only through Russian coercion; the former, though perhaps initiated originally by American pressure, could be maintained only with the voluntary concurrence of the majority of West Germans. Such concurrence could, in fact, be achieved because the American program of a West Germany integrated into Western Europe and the Atlantic Community offered West Germans broad advantages: psychological "rehabilitation" from the pariah status created by Nazism; a democratic libertarian constitutional structure; an economic revival promoted by Marshall Plan funds; security against Communist designs, as proved by the Berlin airlift and the permanent stationing of Allied troops; defeat of the French desire for dismemberment; and Allied refusal to recognize the Polish annexation of the Eastern territories. . . .

America's German policy was marked by continuous conflict between a "vindictive" Left, which strove for a "Carthaginian peace" in cooperation with Russia, and a "realistic" Right, which wanted to enlist West German resources in the cold war against communism. The Left believed itself to be carrying out the legacy of President Roosevelt; its program found an extreme expression in the Morgenthau Plan and a somewhat more moderate expression in the basic occupation directive, JCS 1067, of April 26, 1945. It wanted to cooperate with "our heroic Russian ally" in eliminating the triple evil of militarism, Junkerism, and big capital through a common policy administered through the Allied Control Council (the four-power authority, composed of the four Allied military commanders, set up at Berlin on July 30, 1945). Secretary of State James Byrnes and Deputy Military Commander (after 1947, Commander) Lucius Clay were initial supporters of this policy until they learned, by the late summer of 1946, that it meant economic ruin for the American Zone (necessitating food imports financed by the American taxpayer) and economic ruin for Western Europe (with the opportunity for Communist takeovers) because of the traditional interdependence of the German and Western European coal and steel economy. They were also appalled by the horrors perpetrated by the Russians in their zone, the Russian-encouraged expulsion of twelve million German refugees from Eastern Europe, and the astronomic Russian reparations demands, which far exceeded Germany's ability to pay (and would, if taken from the Western zones, be paid indirectly by the American government that subsidized those zones).

General Clay and other American military officers in contact with German realities began in fact a quiet sabotage of JCS 1067 by the summer of 1946; their sensible attitude was soon strengthened when the outbreak of the cold war between the U.S. and Russia made a viable West Germany seem desirable. Clay's "realism" was also reinforced by the declining influence of the "Carthaginian" school in Washington (following Henry Wallace's departure from the Cabinet), the development of the "containment policy" with George Kennan as its articulate spokesman, the replacement of Byrnes by Marshall as Secretary of State, and the Republican triumph in the congressional elections of 1946. Prominent Republicans like Herbert Hoover, and his main adviser on German policy, émigré economist Gustav Stolper, were ideologically sympathetic to German big business threatened by dismantling and above all placed "economic common sense" above vindictive passions. The result of the triumph of these new ideas of U.S. policy-making was a decision in the autumn of 1947 to promote the creation of a West German state closely linked with Western Europe—a policy which the Russians were bound to oppose and which the British and French supported only as the result of considerable American pressure.

The British constituted the smallest obstacle. Though Labourite Foreign Secretary Ernest Bevin was personally very anti-German . . . , he was essentially pragmatic in his outlook and maintained a constant feud with the Labourite left wing with its demand for a distinctly "socialist" foreign policy whose tenets included cooperation with Russia at Germany's expense. Bevin could count for support upon the bulk of the Labour party and upon the Tory opposition, especially Winston Churchill, whose advocacy of conciliation with Germany was no doubt promoted by his anticommunism. (In most ways British views paralleled those of the "realistic" American Right.) . . . Britain ceased to have an independent German policy by the autumn of 1946; at that time its inability to feed its zone (with its huge Ruhr industrial complex but inadequate agricultural hinterland) forced Britain to agree to an economic merger with the U.S. zone through the Bizonia agreement (September 4, 1946, effective January 1, 1947). The U.S. thenceforth paid the piper and called the tune in a common Anglo-American policy.

France's German policy in the first years after 1945, as formulated by General de Gaulle and implemented by Foreign Minister Georges Bidault, frankly aimed at terminating the "German danger" once and for all. It called for the permanent dismemberment of Germany, a veto upon the "central administrative bodies" contemplated by the Potsdam Conference, the internationalization of the Ruhr with a paramount voice for France, the dismantling of German industry and heavy reparations, and the long-term control of what remained of Germany by the armies of occupation. This policy could not, of course, win any indigenous German support; its implementation far exceeded France's strength in the face of American opposition; and it ignored France's dependence upon Marshall Plan aid (whose grant was implicitly made conditional upon France's cooperation in an economically "sensible" German policy). Luckily for the future of Franco-German relations, French policy shifted in 1948 (not least because of American pressure) from dismemberment in the tradition of Richelieu to conciliation in the spirit of a "new Europe" (a shift connected with Robert Schuman's replacing Bidault at the Foreign Office). The friction between civilian government and military occupation authorities (already noted in the case of Britain and the U.S.) became especially pronounced in the French case after 1948. The French zonal command under General Koenig remained stubbornly "Gaullist" in its outlook on German policy and did its (unsuccessful) best to sabotage the creation of a West German state in 1948–1949.

Russian policy toward Germany after 1945 is especially hard to analyze because revealing sources are unavailable. It is clear, however, that the Russians operated under well-nigh fatal handicaps in carrying out any policy requiring popular German support. They were burdened by the traditional Russophobia of most Germans, by memories of Goebbels' propaganda, by atrocities perpetrated by their troops in 1945, by their own understandable but impolitic desire for quick and heavy reparations, by the cession of the Oder-Neisse territories to Poland, and by their brutal expulsion of the twelve million Germans living in Eastern Europe. Additional handicaps were the hatred of communism felt by nearly all Germans. . . . The arbitrary and terroristic manner in which social reforms were imposed upon the East Zone caused general revulsion even among those Germans who believed that some of these reforms, e.g., the expropriation of the Junkers, were long overdue.

These handicaps (some inevitable, some created) suggest that the Russians never had any realistic chance in establishing any policy aiming at influence in Germany beyond their zonal boundary; this appears to have been the view of Colonel Tulpanov, the main "political officer" of the Soviet military government, and of the "radical" faction of the Moscow Politburo allegedly led by Zhdanov. Another group of Russians, however, including Ambassador Semjonov (the Foreign Office delegate at Berlin) and representing a "moderate" Moscow faction allegedly led by Beria, had some hope for the creation of centralized German institutions that they hoped either to dominate or, at least, to use to block the otherwise inevitable integration of West Germany into the anti-Soviet bloc promoted by American policy. The creation of "all-German institutions" was conspicuously advocated by Foreign Minister Molotov at the Four-Power Conference of Foreign Ministers held at Paris (July 1946) and at Moscow (April 1947); it was rejected by the Americans partly because it was accompanied by unacceptable reparation demands, partly because it flew in the face of American federalist ideas, and mostly (in 1947) because it would prevent the by then much desired integration of West Germany into the West. It should be added that the Russians proved slippery in matters of detail, perhaps because their proposals constituted more propaganda than policy. (Must the Russians not have reckoned with the probability that German central institutions would be dominated by anti-Communists?) It cannot be denied, however, that as propaganda their proposals were largely successful, not so much at the time (since objective needs drove most West Germans to support a West German state at the price of freezing partition) but for the future: they created the basis for the widely held view that the Americans were *at least* as responsible for Germany's partition as the Russians. The Russians probably felt they had nothing to lose by their proposals: if rejected, they were good propaganda; if accepted, they would block the Western integration of West Germany at least temporarily. Moreover, Russia could probably either influence or sabotage any centralized institutions established, and as a last resort it could always fall back upon its unchallenged control of its own East Zone.

* * *

The inevitable friction between West German and East German political leaders (even those who were not Russian stooges) was in fact but one aspect of the broader cold war that became the dominant reality of world politics in 1947. It made—so at least it appears today—the partition of Germany inevitable: Russia would not renounce control of its zone and abandon the Sovietization begun in 1945; America believed by 1947 that it needed German resources to promote the economic revival of Western Europe as part of the new policy of the containment of communism. Many West Germans, including Konrad Adenauer, were willing to go along with America's desire for a West German state. . . .

There can be no question, at any rate, that West Germany's support for a West German state was not *only* the result of the Germans' love of democracy, good Europeanism, and psychological desire to be accepted as partners of the free world. It was also promoted by solid economic considerations (the inducements of the Marshall Plan and the threat of its withdrawal) and American playing upon the Germans' fear of communism (for everyone knew that the abandonment of Berlin could easily set off a chain reaction ending in the communization of West Germany). The creation of the West German state proved justified in terms of promoting democracy, encouraging economic revival, permitting Germany to rejoin the Western world, and contributing to Western European unity and military security. All these gains were purchased, however, at the expense of freezing the country's partition and thereby perpetuating a source of constant international friction.

Who, it may be asked in conclusion, was ultimately responsible for Germany's partition? As suggested earlier, the obvious answer is Adolf Hitler, who launched an unnecessary war that ruined Germany and brought both American and Russian troops to the Elbe-Werra frontier dividing the Western zones from Russia's. Why was it, however, that an administrative demarcation line froze into a permanent state frontier? It appears that responsibility must be distributed, though scarcely in equal measure, between *both* the Russians and the Western Allies—though it is perhaps wrong to speak of "responsibility" (with its inevitable moral connotations) when describing a phenomenon made well-nigh "inevitable" by the general circumstances of the cold war and not deliberately "planned" by either side. The cold war between Russia and the U.S. after 1945 appears to have been inescapable in view of their conflicting ideologies, social systems, and power interests. The two nations confronted each other in the heart of Europe; each was eager (despite an initial preoccupation with purely vindictive policies) to impose its social system and ideology upon all of Germany if possible but, if the larger goal proved unattainable, upon its own zone as a minimum. There was, however, a major difference between Russian and American policy: the former had to rely upon direct coercion in view of Germany's endemic hostility to communism, whereas the latter could count upon a broad basis of voluntary support since democracy and capitalism were what most Germans wanted. The application of drastic economic pressures in 1948 to induce initial German cooperation does not, of course, invalidate this generalization.

This difference gave and gives the American program a major moral and political advantage in the eyes of all believers in self-determination. By denying East Germany self-determination, a principle that presumably ought to apply in Central Europe as well as in the lands of Asia and Africa, the Russians are primarily responsible for the creation and perpetuation of Germany's partition. To justify Russia's imperialist conduct one is forced to argue that self-determination—though usually a good principle—must be overridden in this case by other arguments and considerations such as Russia's alleged security needs, the chronic untrustworthiness (and political nonage) of the German people, the necessity of coercing the Germans (for their own and the world's good) into a desirable social revolution that they have been unable to achieve for themselves, the maintenance of a European equilibrium that would probably be threatened by the unification of Germany, and "the general opinion of mankind," which rightly or wrongly does not look upon German partition as a major grievance requiring urgent remedy.

It appears significant, when looking at the development of partition in the years 1945 to 1949, that the Western powers did not consider the avoidance of partition to be a major goal of their German policy. On the contrary, they frequently opposed Russian plans (whether sincere or not) for maintaining or restoring administrative unity and promoted policies certain to lead to partition. The French vetoed all plans in 1945–1946 for creating the "centralized administrative bodies" contemplated during the Potsdam Conference and included in its final communiqué. Secretary of State Marshall showed no interest in negotiating about Molotov's detailed plan for centralized administrative bodies (to be followed by a provisional government, nationwide elections, and the drafting of a constitution) at the Moscow Conference in April 1947. The pressure of the Allied military commanders prevented the West German premiers from placing the question of German unity on the agenda of the Munich *Ministerpräsidenten* conference of June 1947, though the Russian Zone premiers had made this a condition of their participation and, rightly or wrongly, left the conference when their wishes were not met. The creation of Bizonia (January 1, 1947) and the Frankfurt *Wirtschaftsrat* (June 25, 1947) were two steps on the road to ultimate partition, and the Anglo-American level-of-industries plan of August 29, 1947, though sensible and necessary, was undoubtedly a clear violation of the Allied Control Council decision of May 26, 1946 (a decision still influenced by the spirit of the Morgenthau Plan). The creation of the West German state, initiated at the London Six-Power Conference in March 1948 though completed only in September 1949, preceded in most of its phases the creation of the German Democratic Republic.

These regrettable facts, to which could be added the precipitate rejection of Russian reunification proposals in 1952–1953 without even any negotiation about their details, are not listed to "prove" primary Allied responsibility for Germany's partition. They indicate, however, that the Western Allies, then and presumably now, value other goals above Germany's reunification—a goal that is also felt to complicate other desirable objectives (for example, Western European unity and a détente with Russia).

Joseph Marion Jones

CURBING COMMUNIST EXPANSION: THE TRUMAN DOCTRINE

On March 12, 1947, President Truman went before Congress to appeal for a special foreign aid program for Greece and Turkey. Greece was stricken by a civil war between the Communist-led National Liberation Front and a conservative British-controlled Greek regime. Turkey was fearful of Soviet demands for joint control of the Dardanelles. Pronounced in an atmosphere of crisis, the Truman Doctrine pledged the United States to an ill-defined policy of containing Communism and the Soviet Union. Joseph Jones was a speechwriter in the Department of State in the early critical months of 1947, and helped prepare Truman's momentous address. His history of the development of the Truman Doctrine and the Marshall Plan, *The Fifteen Weeks* (1955), has been widely read and applauded. Jones writes that the Soviet Union was plotting to conquer the Near and Middle East, had fomented the Greek civil war, and that the Truman Doctrine was a vital revolution in American foreign policy which daunted Soviet hopes. Jones' work demonstrates that American officials closely intertwined economic and political questions in their diplomacy: that only through Greek recovery and eventual prosperity could a stable non-Communist Greek government, secure within an American sphere of influence, be organized.

After the devastation of World War II in Europe and Asia the power that had supported the imperial system was broken and the morality and the fact of rule by one people over another was everywhere challenged. Each day's cables, each day's newspapers and broadcasts, brought the story: From the Mediterranean eastward to the Sea of Japan nationalism was successfully asserting itself. In the very heart of the British Empire six independent states were emerging: India, Pakistan, Burma, Ceylon, Nepal, and Afghanistan. Revolutionary movements were challenging French and Dutch control in Indochina and Indonesia, with good prospects of success. The Philippines had achieved independence; Thailand had thrown off British influence. Victorious China had freed herself of Western controls. In the Middle East, colonies were moving toward self-government, mandated countries toward independence, all toward nationalistic self-assertion that weakened alliances. The Union Jack had been hauled down with great ceremony from the Cairo citadel, the green and white flag of Farouk I hoisted, and British troops concentrated at Suez, their future status under negotiation. Syria, Lebanon, Iraq, Jordan, Saudi Arabia, and Yemen had achieved (or were soon to achieve) full independence. Palestine, then ravaged by violence, was soon to make way for the new state of Israel. What was clearly happening was the sudden disappearance of the imperial system and the rise of independent, weak, nationalist states. This had happened in Europe hundreds of years earlier—and had led to centuries of bloody, nationalistic strife.

Moreover, in 1947, the prospects for strength and stability within each nationalistic unit were bleak. Effective self-government requires experience, discipline, and at least fair economic

From pp. 44–45, 46–47, 67–69, 72, 73–77, 17, 19–23, abridged from *The Fifteen Weeks: An Inside Account of the Genesis of the Marshall Plan.*

conditions. Democratic self-government requires in addition a high degree of literacy, a reasonable standard of living, and a substantial middle-class—assets that are in short supply throughout Asia. Only Japan possesses all these assets; several nations have none. Underlying these deficiencies, and the political instability they cause, are poverty, ignorance, undernourishment, and disease. Improvement in these conditions depends upon the efficient use and development of resources, including human resources. This requires outside capital and technical assistance, but capital will not invest where there is not political stability. There is thus a vicious circle in Asia, with political instability causing poor economic conditions and poor economic conditions causing political instability, which frightens away investment that might improve economic conditions.

Pressing down into this weakness, into this riot of nationalist disunity and self-assertion, was the expanding power of the Soviet Union. Ever since a Russian czar had married the daughter of the last Byzantine emperor four centuries earlier, the Russians had felt a sense of mission in Asia, as a result of which Imperial Russian control was extended from European Russia throughout north and central Asia. This expansionist urge, far from being reversed by the Bolshevik revolution, was merely reinforced by it. The chief practical difference was that the tactics of infiltration and propaganda were added to the standard forms of nineteenth-century expansionism. Monolithic in power and ideology, with a fanatical historical sense of mission, the USSR hung over fragmentized Asia in 1947, as it does today, like a dark and heavy sky over a patchwork countryside. In Manchuria, North China, and North Korea, Communist rain was coming down in sheets. Over the rest of China great spattering drops were falling. In northern Indochina a Communist-led nationalist revolution was raging. Communist agents trained in Moscow were busily organizing trouble throughout Southeast Asia. Each month brought new portents of the approaching storm. . . .

The barrier to the direct and immediate extension of Soviet power and influence into the Mediterranean, North Africa, and South Asia, was the land mass extending from the borders of Afghanistan westward to the Adriatic, comprising Iran, Turkey, and Greece. It was accordingly against these three countries that, beginning in 1945 and extending through 1948, the Soviet Union persistently deployed the powerful pressures of its diplomacy, its propaganda, and its apparatus for subversion; these were reinforced in Iran by direct armed intervention and in Greece by armed intervention of an indirect variety.

If the Soviet Union could gain control of Iran, not only would it command the oil riches of the Persian Gulf, but, more important, through that country—which has been described as the "Suez Canal of revolution"—it would be able to play a direct, open, and powerful role in the political evolution of the weak, newly independent countries of the Middle East and South and Southeast Asia.

Centrally located Turkey, anchored in Europe but extending far into Asia, astride the Dardanelles and commanding the Black Sea and the eastern Mediterranean—this was the real prize. For hundreds of years every holder of power in Europe had recognized the Turkish Straits as the key to still more power in Europe and Asia and had tried to secure control of it, meaning control of Turkey on both sides of the Straits. Catherine the Great had been obsessed by it, Napoleon had called it the key to world rule. Kaiser Wilhelm, Hitler, and Stalin had lusted after it. And needless to add, for a century and a half Great Britain and France had been keenly aware of it and were determined that it should not fall into hostile hands. In 1945, with British power crumbling and French power nonexistent, the Russians took a leaf from the history of the czars and began a drive to secure control of the Turkish Straits, which, if successful, would give them control of the eastern Mediterranean, dominion over the trade routes from Europe to the East, and the possibilities of infinite mischief in North Africa and the Middle East. The oil reserves of the Middle East and the uranium mines of Africa would be within grasp. And Soviet control of Greece would be a steppingstone to this end.

The backwash of these developments on Western Europe would be devastating —psychologically, politically, economically, and militarily. The entire continent of Europe would be fatally weakened in the face of an even more powerful Communist drive. . . .

There can be no question, on the basis of events as they unfolded from August 1946 onward, that there was a well-organized plot to bring part or all of Greece under Communist domination. The plot showed itself, in the not uncommon Communist manner, at Lake Success, New York, where the Ukrainian delegate to the United Nations Security Council, Dmitri Manuilsky, on August 25 brought unsubstantiated charges, which were dismissed shortly by the Council, that the Greeks were provoking border incidents with Albania, planning to wrest a portion of southern Albania by force, and persecuting minorities in Macedonia, Thrace, and Epirus—all these crimes aided and abetted, he charged, by British troops stationed in Greece. The plot was evident simultaneously at the Peace Conference in Paris, where Bulgarians pressed a claim for western Thrace, Yugoslavia demanded an independent Macedonia, and Molotov and his Balkan satellites loosed salvoes against the "monarcho-fascist" government of Greece, charging it with border provocations, territorial designs on Greece's neighbors, and internal terror and oppression. In the Soviet Union and the Communist-dominated Balkans the press and radio opened up a virulent campaign against Greece on these same points. And in Greece itself minor disturbances in the northern regions developed in August 1946 into organized, sustained, and well-supplied guerrilla activities, which prevented economic recovery and rapidly undermined what was left of the authority of the state. The guerrillas, numbering some 13,000, were armed, trained, and given border protection and guidance by the authorities in Yugoslavia, Bulgaria, and Albania. The poorly equipped and demoralized Greek Army was powerless to check their depredations.

This situation grew worse during the fall and winter. The Greek government repeatedly exposed it, the world press freely reported it, and the American Embassy in Athens kept it under close scrutiny. On December 19, 1946, following a request from the Greek government that cited chapter and verse of outside aid to Greek guerrillas, the Security Council of the United Nations appointed a Commission of Investigation and ordered it to Greece to report on the facts.

This was of course only a new phase, now with the covert help of foreign allies, of an armed effort to dominate Greece that had been carried on for several years by veteran Greek Communists. Had it not been for the understanding, farsightedness, and diplomacy of Prime Minister Winston Churchill and his intervention in Greek affairs in the face of widespread criticism, Greece's future would have been foreclosed well before the end of the war in Europe.

During the enemy occupation of Greece many guerrilla groups had been organized to harass the Germans, but bitter personal and political rivalries, which the Nazi occupiers encouraged, had led to a dissipation of much of their strength in fighting among themselves. The two groups which had finally absorbed or destroyed the weaker guerrilla organizations were the Communist-dominated EAM (National Liberation Front), with its army of about twenty thousand, known as ELAS (Peoples' National Army of Liberation), and its smaller rightist rival known as EDES, with about five thousand men, bitterly anti-Communist, under the leadership of General Zervas. For a period the two guerrilla groups had cooperated with each other, and with British agents, to carry out sabotage operations, but by the middle of 1943 they had fallen apart and, making no further significant contribution to the war effort, had resumed their fight for political power to be exercised at war's end. To Churchill it was obvious that these two contending groups of men, organized and with guns in their hands, would be in a position to move in when the Nazis retreated and that one or the other would determine the kind of government under which 7,500,000 Greeks would live for a long time to come.

The only other contender for Greek power was the Greek King in London, with the royalist politicians that composed his government in exile in Cairo and his Greek Brigade assembled in Egypt. To the King, as the head and symbol of a state that had fought as Britain's ally during the war, Churchill felt a very strong obligation, though he appears to have had a thinly veiled contempt for the "royalist politicians" who surrounded him. But Churchill's foremost loyalty was to Greece and its people. . . .

The horrors perpetrated by the Communists during the civil war of 1944–45 so revolted public opinion in faction-ridden Greece that a measure of cohesiveness was brought about, not in affirmation of a positive program but at least in opposition to Communism and its exponents in Greece. In the general election held on March 31, 1946, under the watchful eyes of fifteen hundred American, British, French, and South African official observers, who pronounced it on the whole a fair expression of opinion, the parties of the Right won a large majority, and on September 1, 1946, the King was recalled to Greece by a plebiscite. The EAM nevertheless remained exceedingly active and vocal, and whatever may have been its relations with Moscow before and during the civil war, as the wartime alliance of the powers disintegrated after the cessation of hostilities in Europe, it became the clearly recognized instrument of Soviet policy in Greece and the Balkans. . . .

Notwithstanding $700 million in direct foreign aid (from UNRRA, Great Britain, the United States, and organized charities), Greece in 1945 and 1946 managed merely to survive, and the country's ability to sustain itself economically was scarcely better in early 1947 than when German troops had evacuated the country in late 1944. Greece had always had a hard time making ends meet, the poverty of its natural resources being such that it had always needed more imports than could be paid for with exports. A large part of the exports had always gone to Central European markets, especially Germany, which after the war were closed. The Italian invasion, the German invasion, four years of cruel enemy occupation, and the scorched-earth policy of the retreating Germans had left Greece the most thoroughly destroyed, disorganized, and demoralized country in Europe.

In the first two years after liberation seven changes in government did little to improve things. Some progress was made in restoring emergency communications and in reviving agriculture, but industrial production and export trade had hardly done more than start a comeback. Foreign aid kept the country from starvation, but while most people were barely subsisting, profiteers, speculators, and black marketeers throve in ostentatious wealth and luxury, causing inevitable embitterment among the masses, and none of the seven Greek governments dealt effectively with the problem.

The end of the civil war in February 1945 and the nominal disarming and disbanding of the guerrillas brought a cessation of large-scale violence, but no peace and security. Widespread lawlessness and the uncertain intentions of Greece's neighbors to the north made necessary the maintenance of an army of 100,000 and police forces of half that number, far more than Greece had ever supported, with crushing, intolerable effects upon the budget. Notwithstanding, people lived in a perpetual state of fear. This, plus bitter social and political tensions that had grown out of civil strife, created a climate in which governments could hardly govern at all, much less engage in rational planning, develop an effective economic policy, or inaugurate and enforce the controls necessary to bring order out of economic and financial chaos. A psychology of helplessness and inertia prevailed, a feeling that individual efforts were futile, that Greece because of her sufferings was entitled, without determination and effort on the part of Greeks themselves, to be taken care of by Greece's rich allies.

This was the situation in the fall of 1946 when the heat was turned up under

Greece by her Communist neighbors. Well-supplied guerrilla bands spread terror and devastation. Refugees from the rural districts streamed into Athens and other cities. Communications were disrupted. A bad psychological, administrative, and economic situation rapidly turned worse. UNRRA was scheduled to end March 31, 1947, and the flow of life-sustaining supplies was already slowing down. Foreign exchange reserves were gone, and minimum import needs could not be financed. There was a prospect for a 1947 budget *deficit*, including provision for an expanded military establishment, of nearly $300 million, or three times the currency in circulation. By February 1947 prices were moving up steadily, threatening to skyrocket, and wage demands and social discontent were accumulating at a rapid rate.

The British had been the chief stabilizing and sustaining element in this chaotic situation. Not only had they helped finance the Greek Army, but 16,000 British troops, landed in Greece in October 1944 to aid in taking over control from the defeated Germans, had remained to help stabilize the country and organize and equip the Greek Army and police forces. British troops were not engaged in combat against the guerrillas in the north; nevertheless, concentrated in and around Athens, they were an important factor in maintaining order. But on February 3 the British government announced that for reasons of economy it was immediately withdrawing half its troops. The British Cabinet, confronted with financial disaster, had been debating for many weeks the matter of withdrawing all its forces, had decided upon such a course, to be effected in two stages, and although no date had been set for departure of the last contingent of 8000, it was expected to be soon. The Greeks felt abandoned and feared the worst.

Several times in 1946 the Greek government had asked the United States for increased financial aid, and Washington had done all it could under existing appropriations and authority, which were limited. Prime Minister Constantin Tsaldaris spoke to Secretary Byrnes early in October about Greece's need for financial assistance and military equipment. He raised the question with Byrnes again in December in New York, where he had come to request the United Nations to send a commission to Greece to investigate his charges of foreign aid to the Greek guerrillas. Secretary Byrnes and President Truman took the matter up with the Export-Import Bank, but as there was no reasonable assurance of repayment nothing further could be done under the law. In conversations between Tsaldaris and Undersecretaries of State Acheson and Clayton, it became apparent that the Greek economic and financial and administrative system was in complete chaos, that the Greeks had no documented case for loans but just wanted money and arms on a large scale, and that if granted they would probably be wasted. Accordingly, it was decided to send an American Economic Mission to Greece to make a thorough survey of the situation, and Paul A. Porter was selected to head the mission. He and his party arrived in Greece on January 18, 1947, approximately the same time as the commission appointed by the United Nations to investigate Greek frontier incidents. The United States representative on that commission was Mark Ethridge, editor and publisher of the *Louisville Courier-Journal* and the *Louisville Times*.

Porter, Ethridge, and the American Ambassador in Athens, Lincoln McVeagh, operated more or less as a team. By the latter part of February it was their combined judgment that unless Greece received immediate assurance of large-scale military and financial aid, the last vestiges of the authority of the Greek government would disappear within a matter of weeks in a skyrocketing inflation, strikes, riots, and public panic, leaving the field clear for the increasingly bold and successful Communist guerrillas to take over. One thing more was clear to them: aid in the old pattern, no matter how extensive, would not save the situation. Large-scale economic aid was necessary over a period of years, but it was equally important that this should be administered on the spot by an American mission large enough, expert enough, and exercising sufficiently direct participation in and sanctions over the Greek government to bring about a thorough reorganization of the Greek economy and administrative system. Otherwise the money would be lost, the supplies wasted, the errors of the past compounded.

There was never any doubt in Washington that aid to Greece would have to be accompanied by intervention in the country's internal affairs. When on March 3, 1947, the Prime Minister and the Foreign Minister of Greece addressed another urgent, formal appeal to the United States for financial and military aid, they also asked for "the aid of experienced American administrative, economic, and technical personnel to assure the utilization in an effective and up-to-date manner of the financial and other assistance given to Greece, to help to restore a healthy condition in the domestic economy and public administration and to train the young people of Greece to assume their responsibilities in a reconstructed economy." This was no accident. The message was drafted in the State Department and suggested to the Greek government.

To Americans in 1947 intervention was an ugly word. But in the long and turbulent history of Greece since the Golden Age mere foreign intervention had been among the nicer things that had happened to the Greek people. The more usual pattern had been, for more than two thousand years, foreign invasion, occupation, and indescribable oppression and exploitation. On the other hand, it had been the concerted, armed intervention of the British, French, and Russians in 1827–32 that had saved the Greek revolution started in 1821 against the centuries-old rule of the Ottoman Turks, and had resulted in the establishment of an independent monarchy under the protection of the three powers. Thereafter throughout most of the nineteenth century all three had intervened briefly but often, singly or jointly, in Greek affairs, but the net result of their rivalry and competitive intervention had been the maintenance, as a matter of common interest, of an independent Greece. The Nazi invasion and occupation of Greece in 1940–41 and the Soviet effort in 1946–47 to seize control were throwbacks to a much earlier pattern of conquest, rule, and oppression. Both sought the disappearance of an independent Greece, previously sustained by agreement for the common good.

* * *

The Speaker of the House, Joseph Martin, at 12:16 P.M. on March 12, 1947, declared the House in recess subject to the call of the Chair. The House and Senate were shortly to meet in joint session to hear a Special Message to be delivered in person by the President of the United States, Harry S. Truman. . . .

"Mr. President, Mr. Speaker, Members of the Congress of the United States, the gravity of the situation which confronts the world today necessitates my appearance before a joint session of the Congress. The foreign policy and the national security of this country are involved."

It had been just nineteen days earlier that the first in the chain of events leading to this appearance of the President before Congress had occurred, the official news that the British government could no longer aid in sustaining and strengthening Greece and Turkey. On the fourth day after Sichel's call (the four days covered a weekend) the State Department had ready a documented statement of position approved by Secretary Marshall. On the fifth day this position had been endorsed by the Secretary of War and the Secretary of the Navy and approved by the President. On the sixth day it had been laid by the President before congressional leaders of both parties, none opposing. On the seventh day a working party in the State Department had been appointed to draw up a detailed program of aid, draft a message to Congress for the President, and work up a program of public information. In the twelve following days all this had been done, the proposed program had been approved by the Cabinet and discussed again with congressional leaders, and the message had been polished and approved in the White House for final delivery. It had all gone like clockwork. No one in the government had opposed. No one had dragged his feet. Veterans in government service had never seen anything like the unanimity of view, and this on a matter recognized as a major turning point in American history. Nor had they ever before witnessed such efficiency in the government as that with which the job was done.

Now the President was displaying the end product to Congress, to the American people, to the world.

"One aspect of the present situation . . . concerns Greece and Turkey . . ."

President Truman described the tragic physical, financial, and economic condition of war-wrecked Greece, the threat to the very existence of the Greek state posed by the activities of the Communist-led terrorists in the north, the inadequacies of the Greek army, the urgent appeal of the Greek government to the United States. The British government, he said, could give no further financial or economic help after March 31. The question had been considered as to how the United Nations might assist in this crisis, but the situation was an urgent one requiring immediate action, and the United Nations and its related organizations were not in a position to extend help of the kind required.

"Greece must have assistance if it is to become a self-respecting democracy.

"The United States must supply this assistance.

"There is no other country to which democratic Greece can turn.

"No other nation is willing and able to provide necessary support for a democratic Greek government."

Mr. Truman emphasized that the Greek government had asked for our assistance in utilizing effectively the financial and other aid we might give to Greece and in improving its public administration. "It is of the utmost importance that we supervise the use of any funds made available to Greece," he said —and here he was interrupted by the first applause—"in such a manner that each dollar spent will count toward making Greece self-supporting, and will help to build an economy in which a healthy democracy can flourish."

The future of Turkey as an independent and economically sound state, the President continued, was clearly no less important to the freedom-loving peoples of the world than the future of Greece. Turkey, having been spared the disasters of war, was in much better condition than Greece, but nevertheless needed our support "in order to effect that modernization necessary for the maintenance of its national integrity. That integrity is essential to the preservation of order in the Middle East." If Turkey was to have the help it needed, the President concluded, the United States would have to supply it, for we were the only country able to do so. This was brief treatment indeed, but it is all the message contained about Turkey.

Up to this point President Truman had said things that had been more or less expected as a consequence of news leaks, discussions with congressmen over the previous two weeks, and background information officially given to the press. It was unique in our history that a President should ask Congress for an appropriation in time of peace to help foreign countries maintain their "integrity and independence"—financial aid to accomplish frankly political purposes—but it was a not illogical extension of Lend-Lease. But all the President had said thus far was but prologue. Now came the main drama.

"I am fully aware of the broad implications involved if the United States extends assistance to Greece and Turkey. . . .

"One of the primary objectives of the foreign policy of the United States is the creation of conditions in which we and other nations will be able to work out a way of life free from coercion. . . . To insure the peaceful development of nations, free from coercion, the United States has taken a leading part in establishing the United Nations. The United Nations is designed to make possible lasting freedom and independence for all its members. We shall not realize our objectives, however, unless we are willing to help free peoples to maintain their free institutions and their national integrity against aggressive movements that seek to impose upon them totalitarian regimes. This is no more than a frank recognition that totalitarian regimes imposed on free peoples, by direct or indirect aggression, undermine the foundations of international peace and hence the security of the United States. . . .

"At the present moment in world history nearly every nation must choose between alternative ways of life. The choice is too often not a free one. One way of life is based upon the will of the majority, and is distinguished by free institutions, representative government, free elections, guaranties of individual liberty, freedom of speech and religion, and freedom from political oppression. The second way of life is based upon the will of a minority forcibly imposed upon the majority. It relies upon terror and oppression, a controlled press and radio, fixed elections, and suppression of personal freedoms.

"I believe that it must be the policy of the United States to support free peoples who are resisting attempted subjugation by armed minorities or by outside pressures.

"I believe that we must assist free peoples to work out their destiny in their own way.

"I believe that our help should be primarily through economic and financial aid, which is essential to economic stability and orderly political processes."

Here, in its essence, was the Truman Doctrine. There was at this point no applause. It was as though the President's listeners were stunned, some perhaps dismayed, by the sweep, the boldness, of the President's utterance. The President went on.

"It is necessary only to glance at a map to realize that the survival and integrity of the Greek nation are of grave importance in a much wider situation. If Greece should fall under the control of an armed minority, the effect upon its neighbor, Turkey, would be immediate and serious. Confusion and disorder might well spread throughout the entire Middle East. Moreover, the disappearance of Greece as an independent state would have a profound effect upon those countries in Europe whose peoples are struggling against great difficulties to maintain their freedoms and their independence while they repair the damages of war. Collapse of free institutions and loss of independence would be disastrous not only for them but for the world. Discouragement and possibly failure would quickly be the lot of neighboring peoples striving to maintain their independence. Should we fail to aid Greece and Turkey in this fateful hour, the effect will be far reaching to the West as well as to the East. We must take immediate and resolute action."

President Truman asked Congress to appropriate $400 million for aid to Greece and Turkey and to authorize the detail of American civilian and military personnel to Greece and Turkey, at the request of those countries, to assist in the tasks of reconstruction and to supervise the use of United States aid. He also asked authorization to train selected Greek and Turkish personnel in the United States.

"This is a serious course upon which we embark. I would not recommend it except that the alternative is much more serious. . . . The seeds of totalitarian regimes are nurtured by misery and want. They spread and grow in the soil of poverty and strife. They reach their full growth when the hope of a people for a better life has died. We must keep that hope alive. The free peoples of the world look to us for support in maintaining their freedoms. If we falter in our leadership, we may endanger the peace of the world—and we shall surely endanger the welfare of our own nation. Great responsibilities have been placed upon us by the swift course of events. I am confident that the Congress will face these responsibilities squarely."

Richard J. Barnet

THE MISCONCEPTIONS OF THE TRUMAN DOCTRINE

Richard J. Barnet, in a recent study of America's response to revolutions in underdeveloped nations, disputes the traditional account of the Truman Doctrine as expressed by Jones. Barnet suggests that the United States worked under mistaken notions when it intervened in the Greek civil war. Pointing out that the Soviet Union was little involved in the Greek conflict, Barnet spells out the various alternative responses which he thinks might have been more realistic. Since 1963, Barnet has been co-director of an independent research center in Washington, D.C., the Institute for Policy Studies. He has worked for the Departments of Defense and State and the United States Arms Control and Disarmament Agency. He is also the author of *Who Wants Disarmament?* (1960), and *The Economy of Death* (1969).

IN THE name of the Truman Doctrine the United States supplied the military and economic power to enable the Greek monarchy to defeat an army of Communist-led insurgents in 1947–49 and won a victory which has become a model for U.S. relations toward civil wars and insurgencies. Almost twenty years later the President of the United States was defending his intervention in Vietnam by pointing to his predecessor's success in Greece. The American experience in Greece not only set the pattern for subsequent interventions in internal wars but also suggested the criteria for assessing the success or failure of counterinsurgency operations. Greece was the first major police task which the United States took on in the postwar world. One of the most important consequences of the American involvement in Greece in the 1940's was the development of new bureaucracies specializing in military assistance, police administration, and economic aid, committed to an analysis of revolution and a set of responses for dealing with it that would be applied to many different conflicts in the next twenty years.

In this chapter we shall look into the fateful series of decisions that culminated in the Truman Doctrine and its execution in Greece. To start this inquiry, we need to ask a basic question: Why did those in charge of the national security of the United States happen to define the problem in Greece in the way they did, and why did they use the power of the United States in the ways they did? To some the answer may be so obvious that the question itself is startling. Official history, as it always does, records these decisions as more or less inevitable responses to clear-cut challenges. There was no other practical or honorable choice.

To understand this turning point in American foreign policy, however, we must attempt to reconstruct the scene as it was seen through contemporary eyes. If we turn to Winston Churchill as chronicler, we find him, a few years after these events, expressing great surprise that the American intervention turned out the way it did. Alluding to Roosevelt's strong opposition to British military activities against the Greek Communists during the war, the former prime minister wrote, "I little thought . . . that the State Department, supported by overwhelming American public opinion, would in a little more than two years not

From pp. 97–101, 107–112, 121, 125–127, reprinted by permission of The World Publishing Company from *Intervention and Revolution: America's Confrontation with Insurgent Movements Around the World* by Richard J. Barnet. Copyright © 1968 by Richard J. Barnet.

only adopt and carry on the course we had opened, but would make vehement and costly exertions, even of a military character, to bring it to fruition."

The continuation of Britain's role in Greece was a highly accurate description of the American intervention, but it was hardly an inevitable one, especially in view of the bad press accorded the British Empire in the United States. Tradition suggested other definitions of the American Responsibility toward Greece. In late 1946 and early 1947 there were at least three other plausible ways for U.S. National Security Managers to look at the Greek crisis. Each would have dictated a form of intervention different from the Truman Doctrine. Each would have required a different definition of the American national interest. One was to continue to regard Greece primarily as a relief problem. At the end of September, 1946, the Food and Agriculture Organization reported that Greece urgently needed a minimum of one billion dollars from the United States and British governments. The United States had already provided most of the three hundred and forty-five million dollars spent on Greek relief in 1945 and 1946, and the Truman administration was planning to spend sixty million dollars more, but the Republican-controlled Eightieth Congress, elected on the economy slogan "Had Enough?" appeared unwilling to support a major project of international charity. Greek officials argued that raids by insurgents, which resumed in September, 1946, were a major factor in preventing economic recovery. But a U.S. mission under Paul Porter, which arrived in January, 1947, found that the most pressing crises were due to the collapse of the Greek currency, the resultant panic over the disappearance of gold reserves, and a strike by the entire Greek civil service.

The problem of Greece might, alternatively, have been regarded as a traditional crisis of Balkan politics. The Peace Conference held in the summer and fall of 1946 dramatized the depth and bitterness of the conflict between Greece and her Balkan neighbors, particularly Bulgaria and Yugoslavia, over disputed territories. The prime minister devoted most of his opening speech to parliament in 1946 to Greece's territorial claims. When the United States refused to back Greece's demands for northern Epirus and for certain adjustments of the frontier with Bulgaria, Greek politicians from left to right called the settlement "a most cruel injustice" and an occasion for "deepest mourning." Bulgaria and Yugoslavia made no secret of their desire to annex parts of Macedonia and Thrace. In conversations with Americans, Greek officials stressed the danger that the Soviet Union might encourage the newly communist Balkan regimes to satisfy their territorial ambitions and thereby at the same time extend the area of Soviet influence. Thus the problem might have been seen principally as one calling for international mediation. In effect, the United States, Britain, and the Soviet Union might have continued their informal agreements during the war, establishing zones of respective "responsibility" in the Balkans and jointly guaranteeing the frontiers. However, the Great Powers would have had to agree on what their respective roles in the Balkans were to be, and it was the lack of agreement on this very issue that fanned the growing East-West suspicion into the Cold War.

The third way to look at Greece in 1946–47 was as a problem of internal political collapse. The ultrarightist government of Constantine Tsaldares; established after the British army had helped put down the communist-led ELAS rebellion in 1945, attempted to root out opposition by force. The government ousted the leadership of the Greek Federation of Labor and replaced it with government appointees. In October, 1946, the Greek government dismissed seventeen university professors and twenty-six senior civil servants on purely political grounds, although most of them were not communists. "The internal situation is much worse than it has ever been. Law and order are nonexistent," a former Liberal premier told a group of visiting British M.P.'s. Like the Diem government in Vietnam ten years later, the Tsaldares regime conducted what the U.S. correspondents for the *Herald Tribune* and Associated Press termed "a desperate effort to halt a growing rebellion and wipe out not only Communists but all democratic, liberal, and republican elements." The government armed right-wing supporters, and often with the collaboration of the police, encouraged them to terrorize political opponents. "This tactic," a former Progressive (moderate) party minister wrote in October, 1946, "drives the people to the hills, since no Greek is willing to be beaten without reason, only because he is an opponent of the party in power." The government was rapidly polarizing the country by limiting the expression of political choices either to wholehearted support of Tsaldares' reactionary policy or to wholehearted opposition by joining communist-led guerrilla bands in the hills. A British parliamentary delegation, made up of Labour, Conservative, and Liberal members, visiting Greece in late summer 1946, condemned the government terrorism and urged sweeping reforms, including the restoration of constitutional liberties, an amnesty, the reestablishment of an independent labor movement, the end of political deportations, and the formation of an "all-Party Government . . . to include all sections with the possible exception of the Extreme Left." The establishment of a regime which "resembled a dictatorship," the report observed discreetly, "would have fatal consequences." As these observers saw it, the government should attempt to accommodate the mounting political opposition in Greece, not repress it.

The United States made a few modest efforts in late 1946 to persuade the Greek government to move in the direction of reform. On October 18, Ambassador Lincoln MacVeagh showed King George II a letter from the President suggesting that the United States was prepared to grant "substantial aid and supplies" but that "the Greek Government should help persuade American public opinion that the rulers of Greece constituted no oligarchy of reactionaries, bent on exploiting U.S. aid in order to tyrannize their political opponents." The government should be broadened so that Americans might come to see that all Greeks, except the communists, were united.

However, in the minds of the U.S. National Security Managers, the Greek crisis soon took on a very different significance. Greece was still a relief problem, still a point of tension in age-old Balkan rivalries, and more than ever, a revolution with deep domestic political roots. But more than any of these, Greece was now seen as a pawn in a global struggle. Keeping Greece noncommunist had become the central concern of the United States.

When President Truman announced the decision to help the Greek monarchy win the civil war, he stressed that the commitment was prompted by the "terrorist activities of several thousand armed men, led by communists." The United States was to use its power to put down violence. But, clearly, violence itself was not the issue, for throughout 1946, according to correspondents of the London *Times* and other U.S. and British papers, the Greek government itself had been carrying out mass arrests, tortures, beatings, and other retaliation against those who had been on the wrong side of the earlier civil war that ended in January, 1945. The foreign minister had resigned in early 1946, charging "terrorism by state organs." In Greece, as elsewhere, the violence of constituted authorities, however oppressive their rule, was judged by one criterion and the violence of insurgents by another. President Truman alluded to the corruption and brutality of the Greek government by conceding that it was "not perfect." But while the fascist character of the government genuinely bothered some members of the U.S. government, most National Security Managers shared the judgment of former Secretary of State James Byrnes: "We did not have to decide that the Turkish Government and the Greek Monarchy were outstanding examples of free and democratic governments."

It was enough that the guerrillas were communists and as such constituted, according to Joseph Jones, the State Department official who drafted the original Truman Doctrine message, an "instrument" of Soviet "expansionism." What was happening in Greece was important to officials in Washington only as it affected U.S. interests, as the State Department saw them. This is, of course, the standard by which governments customarily judge internal developments in other countries. The interesting question is why the Truman administration saw the mounting insurgency in Greece as a threat to the American national interest.

* * *

When the resistance began in 1941–42, the communist-led guerrillas had no contacts at all with Moscow. The prewar links between the Greek Communist party and Moscow, "tenuous and unreliable" as they were, had been completely cut off by the Axis occupation. In July, 1943, eight Soviet officers arrived at the ELAS headquarters to assess the prospects of the guerrillas. The Soviet military mission reported that ELAS was "just a rabble of armed men, not worth supporting." Requests for Soviet aid went unanswered; Bulgarian guerrillas operating just over the border with Soviet support also ignored the struggle in Greece. As the Italians and then the German occupation forces withdrew in 1944, the rival guerrilla forces began to attack each other. The British supported EDES; ELAS captured most of its arms from the retreating Axis armies. General Scobie, the British commander, sought to reconcile the various guerrilla bands and to persuade them to operate in separate areas. Meanwhile he installed a government in Athens under George Papandreou, a monarchist politician.

The Soviet-satellite Bulgarian army occupied parts of Macedonia and Thrace. The Soviets, consistent with their agreement with Churchill to leave Greece primarily to British influence, ordered the Bulgarian troops to evacuate Greek soil. By the end of 1944 ELAS controlled most of the countryside of Greece and occupied all cities, towns, and villages except for Athens, Salonika, Piraeus, and a few other centers where British troops were stationed. EAM, the political arm of the communist-guerrilla movement, began to administer large areas of the country, making use of secret police and their power over the distribution of UNRRA supplies. Openly agitating against the Papandreou government and the government secret police, they charged, accurately, as it turned out, that the government was killing and imprisoning leftist partisans while protecting former Nazi collaborators. The civil war began when ELAS, still in political control of far more of Greece than the Athens government, refused to surrender its arms unless EDES also agreed to disarm. The revolt which flamed over the whole peninsula required a British force of seventy-five thousand to crush it.

In February, 1945, the British arranged a cease-fire at Varkiza. The guerrillas agreed to surrender their arms, provided an immediate plebiscite on the return of the king was held, to be followed by free elections. ELAS did surrender far more weapons than anyone in the British army thought they had had, but they hid most of their small arms and automatic weapons in the mountains. The government, which had yet to condemn a single Nazi collaborator, carried out wholesale arrests and executions of former ELAS fighters. EAM charged that at least five hundred had been murdered and twenty thousand arrested in the first five months after the cease-fire. The government countered with a discovery of the bodies of eighty-eight hundred hostages allegedly murdered by the ELAS during the fighting. In the civil war both sides had taken hostages and practiced terrorism. Now, with ELAS disarmed, the government and the bands of royalist guerrillas who supported it were responsible for most of the terror and political murder.

The Greek government was not only repressive but also hopelessly corrupt. Tsaldares spent about fifty percent of the budget on the army and the police, six percent on reconstruction. Capital was fleeing the country. The rich knew how to escape taxation, and inflation was rampant. At the end of the war the drachma was valued at one hundred and forty-nine to the dollar. A year later it was five thousand to the dollar. Much UNRRA aid was diverted to the black market. In 1947 an American investigating team found huge supplies rotting in warehouses at a time when seventy-five percent of Greek children were suffering from malnutrition. The British proceeded to reconstruct the army, which they put in the hands of monarchist officers, including, as Ernest Bevan admitted in the House of Commons, two hundred and twenty-eight former officers of the Nazi security battalions in Greece. They also strengthened the police, leaving it under the direction of the police chief, who for three years had served the Nazis.

In 1945 and 1946 the British installed, successively, a general and an admiral as prime minister of Greece. Both filled provincial administrative posts with monarchist sympathizers before the British replaced them with an aged Liberal politician, Themistokles Sophoulis. On March 31, 1946, an election was held, which resulted in a clear-cut victory for the monarchists. Although termed a fair election by numerous Allied observers, this verdict, as Howard K. Smith, the CBS correspondent who visited Greece shortly after the elections, concluded, is open to doubt:

> With all power and armed force in the hands of the right and with the countryside under the terror of ubiquitous and merciless rightist bands, the Greek peasant was in no mood to be heroic; . . . I visited a village outside Athens and was told by peasants through a neutral Greek interpreter that they had been threatened with having their village burned down if they did not yield a majority monarchist vote in the elections. In this village the newspaper of the Liberal Party—the party of the Premier of Greece [Sophoulis]—was forbidden to be read on pain of beatings.

Meanwhile the EAM was in the throes of an internal debate between those who favored attempting a slow political route to power and those who wanted to resume the fight. As the government repression mounted, the militants in the EAM grew stronger. Noncommunist politicians from the six parties that made up the original Liberation Front resigned. Many ex-ELAS leaders, "spurred on by what would happen to them if they were arrested, took to the hills and began collecting former comrades around them." According to Major Edgar O'Ballance's recent account of the civil war, this trend was "spontaneous rather than centrally organized or inspired," although the Greek Communist party tried to keep control over these fast-moving events.

At the end of 1945 ELAS was reorganized as the "Greek Democratic army" with the help of members of the Bulgarian and Yugoslav general staffs. In the beginning Stalin apparently approved of the cooperation, although Soviet promises of assistance were never fulfilled. The relationship between the other Balkan communist regimes and the Greek communists was ambivalent from the first. Relations with Albania were the best, probably because the Greek Communist party had renounced the claim still pressed by the Athens government to annex the Albanian province of northern Epirus. In 1946 a communist government was established in Tirana which permitted the Greek Democratic army to build camps on its soil near the border to be used as rear bases for incursions into Greece. A Radio Free Greece was set up on Albanian soil. Actual military aid, however, was small.

Tito, in Yugoslavia, was more uncertain about aiding the Greek rebels. His political plans at the time called for a Balkan federation under his own control, and particularly a communist Slav Macedonia, which would in all events be detached from Greece. In 1946 he did offer food, use of army camps, and a few transport vehicles, but little else. The question of Yugoslav aid provoked dissension within the Greek Communist party between nationalists, who were suspicious of Tito's territorial aims, and those party leaders who put ideological solidarity above all else.

In late 1946 Bulgaria also came under the full control of a communist government. Dimitroff, the party chief, was also a nationalist with an interest in annexing Thrace as well as the city of Salonika.

By October, 1946, the Greek Democratic army, which had reached the level of six thousand men, was carrying on hit-and-run raids throughout northern Greece. The government, unable to deal with them either by using the thirty-thousand-man police force or by arming loyal villagers, secured British permission to use the national army, now at a strength of one hundred thousand men. The domestic political life of the country was moving toward a new crisis when Tsaldares, against all the pressures of the British to broaden his extreme-right-wing government, eliminated all the opposition parties from the cabinet and closed down two communist newspapers.

The Balkan neighbors now agreed to step up their aid to the communist rebels, but at a price. General Markos, the commander of the Greek Democratic Army, made agreements with Albania, Yugoslavia, and Bulgaria for the detachment from Greece of its Slavic areas and for other territorial adjustments most unfavorable to Greece. By March, 1947, when the Truman Doctrine was announced, the rebel force stood at about seventeen thousand men. Making increasing use of Yugoslav territory for regrouping and medical care, the rebels carried out raids of mounting intensity, using terrorist techniques in the countryside, including the taking and executing of hostages. General Zervas, the former head of the EDES, who was appointed minister of public order in early 1947, carried out an extensive program of political murder of his own.

By the time President Truman asked Congress for military aid for Greece, the communists had developed a political and intelligence network that included about fifty thousand active workers who were engaged in collecting information and supplies and carrying out sabotage and other acts of terrorism. An additional two hundred and fifty thousand sympathizers gave the rebels assistance from time to time.

A Yugoslav general was now attached to the headquarters of the Democratic army at Bulkes, Yugoslavia. The Soviet Union, which had recognized the Greek government almost immediately, withdrew its ambassador in April, 1947. Stalin gave no aid to the rebels, however. The Soviets limited their involvement to a handful of military liaison officers whose function was to observe the arrangements worked out between the Yugoslavs and the Greek guerrillas. A Balkan joint staff was formed under Yugoslav domination. Tito agreed to give more weapons and supplies in return for the right to veto any changes in the high command of the Greek Democratic Army. The Greeks were unhappy about the arrangement and distrustful of the Yugoslavs, but they had nowhere else to turn. The International Brigade of communist volunteers, of which some of the rebels had dreamed, and some had, indeed, been promised, never materialized. By 1948 about seventy-five percent of the rebels' small arms were coming from the Balkan neighbors, mostly Yugoslavia; none came from the Soviet Union directly, nor, so far as one can determine, did Stalin transmit weapons to the Greeks through the Balkan satellites. . . .

Crucial to this analysis besides the dubious use of the term "democratic" was the assumption of "Soviet direction." As we have seen, the Soviets in fact were giving neither aid nor direction. A few months later they would vainly seek to persuade Yugoslavia to cut off the substantial aid which they were giving. "What do you think," Stalin exclaimed to the Yugoslav vice-premier in early 1948, "that Great Britain and the United States—the United States, the most powerful state in the world—will permit you to break their line of communication in the Mediterranean? Nonsense. And we have no navy. The uprising in Greece must be stopped, and as quickly as possible." Indeed, the Soviet attitude toward Greece conformed perfectly to the Stalinist pattern. Since the Greek guerrillas had taken action independent of the Red army and Stalin's direction, the Kremlin viewed them as a nuisance and a possible threat to the diplomatic relations of the Soviet Union. Stalin saw them as potential clients of the Yugoslavs, whose claims to a role of independent political leadership in the Balkans he was already attempting to crush.

During the feverish days of preparation for the Truman Doctrine speech, no one in the national-security bureaucracy appears to have ventured a political analysis of the Greek rebels, their relations with Russia, Yugoslavia, or the other Balkan neighbors. The fifth-column analogy from World War II dominated official thinking. The possibility that men had taken to the hills for reasons of their own and not as agents of a foreign power was never seriously considered. "The president has determined to take a stand to 'aid' Greece, as a counter-Russia move," David Lilienthal wrote in his diary for March 9. Writing a grocery-store executive in Michigan, Senator Vandenberg made it clear that he had the same understanding of the purposes behind the new policy. It was a holding action to prevent the sweep of Soviet power in a "chain reaction" from the Dardanelles to the China Sea. "I think the adventure is worth trying as an alternative to another 'Munich' and perhaps to another war. . . ."

When the Truman Doctrine was launched, some members of the State Department believed that a massive infusion of American power and money could establish a stable, moderate, reasonably democratic government and that the military operations should be regarded as instruments to set up the preconditions for bringing about political and social change. But by 1943 it had become clear that the military and political goals were incompatible. In supplying weapons and characterizing the struggle primarily as a Hitler-like fifth-column operation rather than as a conflict among Greeks over the sharing of political and economic power, by stressing the external rather than the internal aspects of the problem, the United States strengthened those forces in Greece with the least interest in reform.

When the conflicts became apparent between democratization and reform, on the one hand, and military security, on the other, those in Washington genuinely interested in reform lowered their sights. Ports and railroads were repaired; the Corinth Canal was repaired. The distribution of food prevented thousands from starving. A remarkable antimalaria campaign started under UNRRA was brought to a successful conclusion. A thousand miles of good highways were built. No progress, however, was made on the basic economic and political problems that were tearing apart the country. "Even as we undertook to bolster the economy of Greece to help her combat Communist agitation," Harry Truman records ruefully in his memoirs, "we were faced with the desire of the Greek Government to use our aid to further partisan political rather than national aims." By the end of 1947 the United States had transferred substantial funds earmarked for economic reconstruction to the military effort, and most of the "reconstruction" programs that remained were road and port programs for the direct support of the counterinsurgency campaign. In the year following the arrival of the U.S. economic mission, the cost of living jumped fifty-three percent. In March, 1948, the Greek government announced that thirty-two percent of the population was on relief.

With the help of substantial American military equipment—seventy-four thousand tons arrived in the last five months of 1947—including artillery, dive-bombers, and stocks of napalm, the strength of the Greek National army was brought up to one hundred and thirty-two thousand and the National Guard to about fifty thousand. They faced a guerrilla force, which, despite heavy casualties, remained at about twenty-three thousand men. The guerrillas had no armor, no aircraft, and little artillery. While the first U.S. aid was pouring into Greece, Tito stepped up his aid, including much needed artillery, but for it he extracted a price. Substantial parts of Greece were to be detached and joined to a Yugoslav federation. The other satellite countries encouraged the rebel leader General Markos to announce a Free Democratic government, but when he did on Christmas Eve, 1947, not one communist country, including the Soviet Union, ever recognized it.

Despite the overwhelming superiority

of the government forces, the guerrillas were achieving considerable successes with a series of raids throughout 1947 and the first six months of 1948. In 1948 they lost almost thirty-two thousand men under increasing air bombardment, but, remarkably, they managed to replenish their force and to maintain it at about the same level as before.

The expulsion of Tito from the Cominform in June, 1948, did not result in the immediate end of Yugoslav aid or in the closing of the border between Greece and Yugoslavia. But it did promote a split in the Greek Communist party between those, like General Markos, who thought Tito's guns were more valuable than Stalin's dubious good wishes, and the old political functionary, Zakhariadis, who believed that allegiance to Stalin could somehow be translated into something more helpful than an occasional surveillance by Soviet officers. The Stalinist faction won, and the defeat of the guerrilla movement began.

In July, 1949, Tito announced that he would close the border, but for the last six months he had already drastically curtailed his assistance. More important, Zakhariadis, growing desperate at the defections of the communist neighbors and the mounting guerrilla casualties, took charge of the military operations himself. He gambled that he could blunt the impact of American aid by switching from insurgent raids to full-scale conventional warfare. The results were disastrous for the communists. The rebels, in large battles for the first time, suffered major setbacks and on May 3, 1949, they broadcast an offer for a cease-fire. While they had offered twenty such proposals since 1946, this one contained substantially softer terms. However, it too was ignored by Greece and the United States.

In the final six months of the war General Van Fleet initiated a campaign for "the systematic removal of whole sections of the population" in an effort to separate the guerrillas from the supporting population. In his recent analysis of the war Major Edgar O'Ballance attaches great importance to this tactic.

> This was more far-reaching than is generally realized. It removed the people; it demarcated a "front line," it prevented "back infiltration" and it caused a blanket of silence to descend. . . . The harsh policy of displacing thousands of people was a difficult decision for a democratic government to take, even in wartime, and the Greek Government hesitated for a long time. However, once this policy was put into effect it paid handsome dividends. . . .

On October 16, 1949, with rebel resistance almost at an end, the guerrilla radio announced that the "Greek Democratic army" had decided to "cease-fire" in order "to prevent the complete annihilation of Greece." The civil war was over.

Robert H. Ferrell

THE MAGNANIMITY OF THE MARSHALL PLAN AND THE OBSTRUCTIONISM OF RUSSIA

A little more than three months after the President's enunciation of the Truman Doctrine, Secretary of State George C. Marshall, speaking to a Harvard University commencement (June 5, 1947), invited European nations to undertake a joint economic reconstruction plan with American assistance. As in the Truman Doctrine, economic uplift was linked to political stability, anti-Communism, and security against Soviet expansion. The plan was more than Marshall's; it had been in the making for months as leading Americans learned of the severity of Europe's postwar prostration. Churchill described Europe in early 1947 as "a rubble heap, a charnel house, a breeding-ground of pestilence and hate." Short of food, living still amidst the war's destruction, and lacking dollars to buy from the most productive and prosperous country in the world—the United States, desperate Europeans applauded Marshall's offer of help. Congress approved Marshall Plan aid in early 1948. But the European Recovery Program became Western European, because the Soviet Union and its neighbors remained outside and attacked the plan. In his account of the Marshall Plan from 1947 to its conclusion in 1952, Robert Ferrell of Indiana University writes that the Marshall Plan probably prevented a new world war. Ferrell is also the author of *American Diplomacy in the Great Depression* (1957).

THE speech read much better than it sounded. The Secretary called on Europe to pull itself together, with only assistance—not direction—from the United States. He had determined that there would not be another lend-lease in which Europeans would bring their shopping lists to the United States and the American Government trim demands down to some reasonable amount, never sure that countries with the most overblown requirements came out best after the reduction. Marshall's demand was European leadership. "It would be neither fitting nor efficacious for this government to undertake to draw up unilaterally a program designed to place Europe on its feet economically. This is the business of Europeans. The initiative, I think, must come from Europe. The role of this country should consist of friendly aid in the drafting of a European program and of later support of such a program so far as it may be practical for us to do so. The program should be a joint one, agreed to by a number, if not all, European nations."

How would the Europeans react? The British Government showed immense enthusiasm at the prospect of American aid under a plan, even if the Americans seemed uncertain of details. When after Marshall's speech the Permanent Undersecretary of State for Foreign Affairs, Sir William Strang, came to Ernie Bevin with the suggestion that the Washington Embassy ask for explanation of the speech, Bevin almost literally jumped into action. "Bill," said he, "we know what he *said*. If you ask questions, you'll get answers you don't want. Our problem is what *we do*, not what *he meant*." Bevin arranged a meeting in Paris of the European foreign ministers—Britain,

From Robert H. Ferrell, *George C. Marshall* (New York, 1966), pp. 111–114, 117–123, 132–134. Volume XV of *The American Secretaries of State and Their Diplomacy*, edited by Robert H. Ferrell and Samuel Flagg Bemis. Reprinted by permission of Cooper Square Publishers, Inc.

France, and Russia. He announced his intention to the Americans, saying he was going to Paris for preliminary talks with Premier Paul Ramadier and Foreign Minister Bidault, and would be glad to carry any message. The British Ambassador in Washington, Lord Inverchapel, bringing these tidings to Secretary Marshall, expressed hope that Will Clayton would come to London soon and not delay because of Bevin's proposed foreign ministers session in Paris. Meanwhile Bevin told a member of the American Embassy in London that the United States was in the same position in 1947 where Britain had been at the end of the Napoleonic Wars. In 1815, he said, Britain held about thirty per cent of the world's wealth. The United States after the Second World War held about fifty per cent. Britain for eighteen years after Waterloo, Bevin ruminated, had practically given away her exports, but the result had been stability and a century of peace.

The French were apprehensive of Bevin's fast footwork, and showed both their usual postwar sensitivity to France's European prestige and a certain fear for the opinions of French communists. Bidault told the American Ambassador in Paris, Jefferson Caffery, that he was not too happy about Bevin coming over, as it looked as if Bevin were trying to steal the show after the new American *démarche*. Caffery thought privately that Bidault wanted to steal the show but Bevin had beat him by a day or two. Ramadier remarked that France and the other West European countries were heading for economic and financial disaster and would get there during the latter part of 1948 unless someone headed off Europe's troubles. The communists had been demonstrating high glee at the prospect of chaos, and their tactics of obstruction greatly bothered him.

As soon as Bevin arrived the question arose of Soviet cooperation. Both Bevin and Bidault told Caffery, separately, that they hoped the Soviets would refuse to cooperate, and in any event they would go ahead full steam. A momentary embarrassment occurred when Bevin and Bidault were deep in their cooperative planning stage, preparing for the Soviets: the French minister of information inadvertently gave out an announcement that they were planning, before they had opportunity to communicate with the Russians, and the ministry then had to deny that the two foreign ministers were planning.

Shortly after this initial Anglo-French diplomacy in Paris, Will Clayton and Ambassador Lewis Douglas held some sessions with members of the British Cabinet in London. . . .

The third London meeting, June 26, turned attention to expected Russian difficulties at the forthcoming Anglo-French-Russian conversations in Paris. Clayton said he thought there would have to be radical change in the Russian position on European recovery and other matters before the American people would approve financial assistance to Russia. Clayton thought the Russians might not need short-term assistance with the "three f's"—food, fuel, and fiber—for they had these, but might require long-term credits. Dalton said the Russians, not members of the International Bank, could not borrow, but could join the Bank if they wished. An aide interjected that this course seemed unlikely because as a member of the Bank the USSR would have to reveal its gold holdings. Dalton closed the session by reverting to the note that the timetable for the US loan to the UK was so erroneous, that Britain could take on convertibility only with great trouble.

The meeting of the three foreign ministers now opened in Paris, on June 27. The United States, not present, had exact recounting of the conversations. Molotov at the outset proposed to ask the US for further information, and then ran into the Franco-British opinion that the three nations should draft a plan. Bidault offered a compromise, asking clarification on the extent of US willingness to help with a proposal. Jefferson Caffery obtained the notion from what he heard of the meetings that the French, in event of Soviet tactics of delay or obstruction, would let Bevin get out in front and carry the ball. Fortunately Anglo-French unity held. It proved fairly easy for Bidault and Bevin to stay together in their proposals as the meeting turned into a considerable trial for Foreign Minister Molotov: Bidault told Caffery that Molotov's "hungry satellites are smacking their lips in expectation of getting some of your money. He is obviously embarrassed."

The Russians may have tried, but if so without success, to stir trouble for the French Government by encouraging the communists. Bevin told Caffery that the 140 technical advisers and assistants, so-called, whom Molotov brought along for the conference had little if anything to do with the discussion. He believed these Russians were all agents, brought along in view of the Communist National Congress then in session at Strasbourg, all in hope of getting communists back into cabinet positions in the government.

The Paris conference quickly came to an end. Bevin took the French proposal and reduced it to a single page, taking out the extra words, and sent this page to Bidault and Molotov on the morning of July 1. That afternoon the Russian Foreign Minister reiterated arguments of previous days—no infringement on sovereignty of European states, each should establish its needs and submit total dollar costs to the United States. Bidault strongly supported Bevin. One of Molotov's aides brought in a partly decoded telegram from Moscow repeating the old arguments. Bevin said to Molotov that the Russians wanted a blank check from the Americans, and what would happen if he, Bevin, went to Moscow and asked for a blank check from the Russians? The meeting of July 1 adjourned on this note. The final meeting, held next day, brought a clean break. Bevin presided. Molotov repeated his arguments, and finished by saying that any joint Anglo-French action without Russia might have very grave consequences. Bidault said the French would go with the British. Bevin said that he, like Bidault, proposed to carry on.

The following day, July 3, the British and French governments invited all European states to meet in Paris and draw up a proposal for the American Government.

Despite the break at Paris the Russians still were welcome to attend. Secretary Marshall had never excluded Russia from his offer. There had been Department discussion of Russian participation, with advisers taking positions pro and con, but Marshall decided to give the Soviets a chance. In reply to the Secretary's questions Kennan had advised, "Play it straight." The Soviet Union and its satellites were great producers of food and raw materials that Western Europe needed and it was sensible to encourage East-West trade. The Secretary could confront the Russians with their own Marxist maxim, "From each according to his ability, to each according to his need." There would have to be sharing of information on economic and financial conditions about which the Russians traditionally had been secretive. If they changed their spots and came in, so much the better. Marshall privately described his offer as including "everything up to the Urals" and he meant it. He said "if Europe was to be divided he was not going to be the person to divide it, therefore U.S.S.R. should be let in on the plan."

This great opportunity Stalinist diplomacy threw away. If they had participated in the plan the Russians could have made congressional approval of Marshall Plan outlays difficult if not impossible; Congress was in a suspicious mood, unlikely to approve billions of dollars for Russia and the satellites. Or if by some minor miracle the plan with Russian participation passed Congress, the Soviets could have ruined economic planning for Europe by sabotaging it—delaying, evading, all the devices of which they were masters. Staying out of the plan, they ensured its success.

Unfortunately for the apparent unity of the Eastern block they did not stay out of the Marshall Plan quickly enough—a confusion of signals between Moscow and the satellites led to an open Russian veto of participation by the Czechoslovak and Polish governments. Those two regimes gave tentative indication of desire to join the plan. They took pains to say that, although they wished to send delegates to the organizing meeting in Paris which was to open on July 12, final acceptance depended on the scope of the plan. Then came the belated advice from Moscow. The Polish Government backed water immediately. Foreign Minister Modzelewski had some trouble informing Ambassador Griffis that his country was not sending a representative to Paris, talked continuously and refused to look Griffis in the face. Modzelewski had told Griffis a few days before that the Poles would go to Paris. But the Czechoslovak Government got into the worst trouble. President Eduard Benes told an American diplomat on July 9 that he did not anticipate a Soviet veto on Czechoslovak membership in the plan, but that in event of a veto a showdown would occur in the Prague government, forcing a choice between East and West. That very afternoon a telephone message arrived in the Czechoslovak capital from the delegation, including Prime Minister Klement Gottwald, which had gone to Moscow for consultation. The message, of course, told of a Soviet veto. The Russians had said the Americans were trying to buy up Europe, that Czechoslovak membership in the Marshall Plan would be an act of hostility against the USSR. Stalin advised the Prague regime to withdraw its acceptance and justify this action by pointing to the fact that nonparticipation of the other Slav nations and the other East European states had created a new situation. The Czechoslovaks had had two interviews, first Gottwald alone with Stalin, then a reception of the entire delegation by Stalin and Molotov. The second session was fairly relaxed, although the Russians made their points clearly and categorically. The first meeting *à deux,* Gottwald and Stalin, was the business meeting, and not so pleasant: Gottwald had returned to his hotel almost scared, and said he had never seen Stalin so angry.

Lacking Russian and satellite attendance, representatives of the sixteen nations met in Paris on July 12: Austria, Belgium, Denmark, France, Greece, Iceland, Ireland, Italy, Luxembourg, the Netherlands Norway, Portugal, Sweden, Switzerland, Turkey, and the United Kingdom. Under chairmanship of Sir Oliver Franks the Europeans set up an interim Committee of European Economic Cooperation (CEEC), drew up a report, and presented it to the United States on September 22.

The Russians meanwhile organized a meeting at Warsaw where the satellites received from Moscow their own bogus economic plan, known as the Molotov Plan. The Russians announced a revived Comintern, the Communist Information Bureau ("Cominform"), on July 6, 1947. . . .

On March 15, 1948, the interim Committee of European Economic Cooperation (CEEC) representing sixteen countries and the zones of Western Germany gathered in Paris to form the Organization for European Economic Cooperation (OEEC). To OEEC the ECA (and its successor at the end of 1951, the Mutual Security Administration) between April 3, 1948 and June 30, 1952 gave $13,348,800,000. Three nations took over half this sum: The United Kingdom obtained $3,189,800,000; France $2,713,600,000; Italy (including Trieste) $1,508,800,000. West Germany received $1,390,600,000. The Netherlands received $982,100,000 under the Marshall Plan. Other states tapered off with lesser sums, down to Iceland with $29,300,000.

The program ended on June 30, 1952, as Marshall insisted it should. In a private meeting at the State Department in 1949 after he had left the secretaryship he said that "it ought to be terminated in 1952. Part of the reason why they imply it cannot be terminated then comes from the opponents of the present appropriations, and part comes from the foreign fellows who naturally would like to see it prolonged beyond 1952, but you have got to stop somewhere." By its end the plan had turned from an economic to a military arrangement. Prior to June, 1950, there had been stipulation that no Marshall Plan aid should go into military supplies. This did not prohibit European nations from shifting budget appropriations, and American administrators had hoped the plan would ease pressure to cut military appropriations. Early in 1951 with the Korean War at a crucial stage the United States informed the Europeans that aid under the plan would have to go for defense. By 1952 eighty per cent of aid was in weapons, the other twenty per cent in defense support.

Contrary to some feeling expressed at the plan's inauguration, it did not disrupt the American economy. Far from bankrupting the country, it stimulated production and probably braked a fall in demand for American food and industrial products, for the initially large postwar domestic demand had slowed down. The money involved in the plan, $13,348,800,000, was a stupendous sum. But inquiry into the peculiar statistics of American consumption showed a domestic liquor bill of more than thirteen billions, an athletic bill of far more than thirteen billions, a tobacco bill of more. The economy had plenty of slack. It is true that the Marshall Plan added large budget deficits to the national debt—moving beyond $250,000,000,000 by 1952. The Korean War added far more. Americans could congratulate themselves that because of the Marshall Plan they did not have to spend even more in an enormous war in Europe.

Thomas G. Paterson

THE MARSHALL PLAN RECONSIDERED

In the following re-evaluation of the development of the Marshall Plan, Paterson stresses the frank self-interest of the program, its domestic support, and the manner in which it was proposed. He writes that the Marshall Plan was presented in such a way as to preclude Soviet or Eastern European participation. In arguing that the anti-Sovietism of the plan made more permanent the division of the world into spheres, he also suggests that a viable alternative was ignored.

AFTER European officials responded to the call in Secretary Marshall's commencement address at Harvard University on June 5, 1947, for European initiative in a large-scale foreign aid plan, the Truman administration began to cultivate public endorsement of a European Recovery Program (ERP). Its task was not an easy one, for as late as November 1947, 40 percent of the American people had never heard of the Marshall Plan. With the help of the State Department, the Committee for the Marshall Plan to Aid European Recovery was organized to combat that ignorance. Comprised largely of prominent business executives, such as Robert Patterson, former secretary of war and Wall Street corporation lawyer, Philip Reed of General Electric, Allen Dulles of Sullivan and Cromwell, Thomas Lamont of J. P. Morgan, and H. D. Collier of Standard Oil of California, this committee joined with leading farm and labor groups to publicize the ERP in full-page newspaper advertisements, circulate petitions, organize speaker forums, and initiate letter campaigns directed at Congress. The very stature of the members, the close cooperation with the State Department, and the access to audiences assured the committee a considerable influence.

Standing with the almost solid front of business leadership in endorsing the Marshall Plan were the American Federation of Labor, the Congress of Industrial Organizations, Americans for Democratic Action, Veterans of Foreign Wars, and the American Farm Bureau Federation. A significant ally of the administration was Republican Senator Arthur Vandenberg of Michigan. Vandenberg helped head off opposition to the plan by suggesting the appointment of the bipartisan Harriman Committee (President's Committee on Foreign Aid), which shared much material and many ideas with the Department of Interior (Krug Committee), and the Council of Economic Advisers. These three committees issued similar reports in the fall of 1947 indicating that the United States could undertake a large foreign aid program without seriously straining the economy, but with some controls, and arguing that indeed such a program was vital to the goals of American foreign and domestic policy. Vandenberg also assured his colleagues that the ERP would be a "business venture," and, as James Forrestal put it, with "business management." It was assumed by many congressmen before the passage of the ERP that the administrator of the program would be a prominent industrialist (Paul Hoffman, president of Studebaker, was named by Truman).[1]

[1] Opposition to the Marshall Plan came from those who thought the United States could not afford the program (Hearst press), that it would be inflationary (Illinois Manufacturers Association), that the ERP was socialistic

From pp. 97–101 in "The Quest for Peace and Prosperity: International Trade, Communism, and the Marshall Plan" by Thomas G. Paterson. Reprinted by permission of Quadrangle Books, Inc., from *Politics and Policies of the Truman Administration* edited by Barton J. Bernstein,

Events in Europe also spurred passage of the Marshall Plan. The dollar shortage in Europe was becoming more acute. The fear that the Communist party would win the Italian elections in April 1948 persuaded some to vote acceptance before then, to influence the outcome. Soviet pressures on Finland, and the communist *coup d'état* in Czechoslovakia in February also aroused congressional concern. And by early 1948 it was clear that West Germany would be included in the ERP, as the United States drastically trimmed back its decartelization and dismantling operations there. The Truman administration used these events to help create a crisis atmosphere. The President appeared before Congress in mid-March to plead alarmingly for temporary selective service, universal military training, and the Marshall Plan, and leaks from American military officials suggested administration fears of a serious and sudden conflict with the Soviet Union.

The administration's propaganda job was helped by the Soviet Union's rejection of the Marshall Plan, thus assuring Americans that the plan would be an anti-communist effort. In fact, the plan was presented in such a way that the Soviet Union and the Eastern European countries could not participate. Russian Foreign Minister V. M. Molotov had gone to the Paris meeting of European nations interested in Marshall's proposal in June 1947 with a staff of eighty-nine, but the conferees encountered disputes immediately. The Russians were suspicious of a private French-British meeting before the conference began, and the British were frankly cool to Molotov's delegation in Paris. Fearful that the United States would manipulate the Marshall Plan for diplomatic purposes, Molotov rejected the British-French call for a Big Three steering committee to draw up country surveys. He responded that the sovereignty of each potential recipient had to be maintained, and that a Big Three committee, with American overlordship, might meddle in internal affairs. The Soviet Union could not accept the "decisive hold" of the United States over the recovery program, especially since the Marshall Plan followed so closely behind the Truman Doctrine and many anti-Soviet speeches by government officials like Dean Acheson, and after the United States had refused to grant a loan to the Russians in 1945–1946 unless they accepted American trade principles and opened up Eastern Europe to American trade. Soviet control over Eastern Europe was not firm or decided in early 1947 (the Czechoslovak *coup*, for example, was in part a response to the Marshall Plan), and the massive influx of American-directed dollars would challenge Russian influence.[2]

The Soviet Union was also wary of the French-British proposal, prepared before the Paris gathering, that the European economies be integrated. Russia interpreted this to mean that the *status quo ante bellum* would be perpetuated; that is, that Western Europe would be the industrial center, with Eastern Europe the supplier of raw materials, especially grains and coal. The Russians feared the subordination of the agricultural East to the industrial West. The Eastern European countries had developed plans, probably with Russia's prodding, for industrialization. They were undeveloped countries, and their economic difficulties had been augmented by the war's destruction. Vera Micheles Dean wrote in 1948 that "experts on Eastern Europe believe that only through industrialization accompanied by modernization of agriculture can the countries of this region solve their rural overpopulation problems, and ultimately raise their living standards." And a student of Eastern European history adds: "It is also understandable that the new regimes would wish, from a general feeling of patriot-

(Henry Hazlitt and the National Economic Council), that Europe was beyond saving (Virgil Jordan of the National Industrial Conference Board), that it was a scheme of business trusts (American Labor party), that the United States should work through the United Nations (National Farmers Union), and that it divided Europe (Henry Wallace).

[2] Will Clayton, who attended the Paris conference, later discussed an episode which reveals the tenor of the meeting: "He [Molotov] tried to get Bevin [British Foreign Minister] to tell him what the U.S. and Britain had talked about. But Bevin would not tell him unless he was sure Molotov would come along."

ism, to diminish their countries' economic dependence on foreign countries." George Kennan later stated that in fact the United States expected from Russian participation the flow of raw materials to help the revival of the Western European economy.

The Soviet Union, then, considered the Marshall Plan another example of American pressure to isolate and challenge Communist nations, and *Pravda* asked: "Why . . . deliberately obscure the phraseology of Mr. Marshall's presentation of the Truman doctrine to the world?" The Soviet Union's response was to tighten its grip on Eastern Europe. Between July 12 and July 29, 1947, Russia secured a number of trade agreements with her neighbors and eventually attempted to mold them into a cumbersome "Molotov Plan." The International Communist Information Bureau (Cominform) was organized in September 1947 as the Russian propaganda agency. In February 1948 Czechoslovakia was dragged into the communist camp, after Jan Masaryk had tried desperately to steer a middle course between East and West and had failed to attract American foreign aid. The Marshall Plan, as it was presented, served to solidify developing international blocs and to realize Secretary of State James Byrnes's simplistic division of the world in 1946 into "friends" and "enemies."

The Soviet Union might have asked, if the Marshall Plan was not a weapon of American foreign policy, why the United States did not work through the United Nations or the existing and viable Economic Commission for Europe (ECE), rather than through a nationalistic, American-directed organization. Perhaps there *was* an alternative for the United States. The United Nations' Economic Commission for Europe was a working body which counted the Soviet Union as a member. Kennan had suggested a program utilizing the ECE, and Walt W. Rostow, assistant to the ECE Executive Secretary, wrote in 1949 that many world leaders saw the ECE as a means of reducing Soviet-American tensions. He pointed out that Russia did not disrupt the ECE, even after the Marshall speech. But the United States chose to form an organization it could control directly, and rejected the offer of the United Nations' Trygve Lie for a program through the ECE.

Perhaps the question of the invitation to Russia in the first place is not terribly relevant. It would have been the utmost of illogic and contradiction for Congress to approve funds for the Soviet Union so shortly after the passage of the anti-Soviet Truman Doctrine, the curtailment of United Nations Relief and Rehabilitation Administration supplies to Russia, and at a time when vociferous complaints were being made against trade with the Soviets. From fragmentary evidence it appears that American leaders did not expect the Soviet Union to accept. Clayton and Kennan told Marshall to "Play it straight," and Clayton made it emphatic that although Russia would be invited, the United States would "run this show." It may have been Henry Wallace who prompted the State Department not to exclude Russia from the offer of aid. Both State Department staffman Joseph Jones and Ambassador to Great Britain Lewis Douglas have mentioned as relevant Wallace's early 1947 speech in which he advocated a massive European reconstruction plan with a large part of the assistance going to Russia. Yet there was really no gamble in offering Russia access to a recovery program. As indicated, the Soviet Union could not have accepted membership in an administration dominated and directed by Americans and motivated by a desire to curb Soviet influence in the world. Thus many Europeans and Americans interviewed in the "Marshall Plan Project" considered the American invitation a gesture and diplomatic finesse, placing the burden of rejection on the Soviet Union.

Norman A. Graebner

THE EXTENSION OF THE COLD WAR TO ASIA

The Cold War originated in Europe, and was later thrust upon underdeveloped nations in Latin America, Africa, and Asia. Norman A. Graebner of the University of Virginia indicates below that the assumptions of the European conflict were transferred to Asia with the establishment of the People's Republic of China in 1949. Americans interpreted Mao Tse-tung's government as an appendage of Soviet foreign policy. Similarly, the civil war in Indo-China (Vietnam) was viewed from the United States as part of an international Communist plan, rather than as a national movement. Indeed, the containment doctrine had become global. Graebner's works include *Ideas and Diplomacy* (1964), *Cold War Diplomacy, 1945–1960* (1962), and *The New Isolationism* (1956).

UNITED States involvements in East Asia during the immediate postwar years, extensive as they were, had not brought the United States into any direct conflict with Soviet purpose. The Truman Doctrine of March, 1947, had announced a sweeping United States commitment to intervene everywhere in the world where governments might be threatened by communism regardless of the security interests involved or the prospects of success for any American effort. In practice, however, the Truman Doctrine had been limited to Greece and Turkey, and Secretary of State George C. Marshall had pointedly refused in 1948 to extend it to China. The emerging cold war, whatever its demands on American emotions and resources, remained a European phenomenon.

Perhaps the comparative complacency with which Americans viewed the Far East was natural enough. For two long generations Japan had been the major, if not the exclusive, threat to a balanced and stable Orient. But the Japan of the late 1940's was an occupied nation, its military power broken. The continuing collapse of European colonialism in South and Southeast Asia threatened that region's historic stability.

But, nevertheless, to Americans generally even the Communist-led revolution in Indochina represented the ideal of self-determination far better than did French colonial policy. No aggressor had appeared anywhere on the scene to challenge the independence of the new Asian states, whatever their internal weakness.

China was the critical problem of the Far East. But even as Chiang Kai-shek slowly went down before Mao Tse-tung and his Chinese Communists in 1948 and 1949, the United States government did not recognize in this transferal of power in China any threat of aggression or danger to the United States. Indeed, until 1949 the United States did not reject the possibility of establishing normal and satisfactory relations with the new regime. To the extent that numerous Americans and potential critics of United States policy anticipated the Communist victory in China with deep regret, they regarded the new leadership as dangerous to Chinese traditions and to China's historic relations with the United States. They feared above all that Mao might slam shut the Open Door and thus deprive American scholars, missionaries, travelers, officials and merchants of their former access to a country which was for them a region of immense charm. But even for the friends of China and of Chiang the closing of the Open Door and the subsequent mistreatment

From Norman A. Graebner, "Global Containment: The Truman Years," *Current History,* 57 (August, 1969), pp. 77–83, 115–116. Reprinted by permission of Current History, Inc. and the author.

of American officials in China were not necessarily indications of Mao's aggressive intent toward China's neighbors. Communist influence and behavior in China might be tragic but did not automatically comprise a threat to United States security interests.

Still, there existed in 1949 a marked ambivalence in American attitudes toward the impending retreat of Chiang Kai-shek to the island of Formosa. Some Americans recalled Lenin's blueprint for Russian expansion: "First we will take Eastern Europe, then the masses of Asia. Then we will surround America, the last citadel of capitalism." The Western world could not ignore the fact that soon 900,000,000 people would be living under Communist-led governments. Indeed, with the collapse of Nationalist China late in 1949, the United States entered a period of deep intellectual crisis. What mattered during these critical months of decision was the role which American officials, editors and political leaders—the creators of public opinion—chose to assign to the U.S.S.R. in the triumph of Communist power in China. The State Department's White Paper on China, published in August, 1949, publicly viewed the impending Communist victory in China as a legitimate expression of popular approval and thus no real challenge to Asian stability. But what had once appeared indigenous was beginning to loom as possibly the initial triumph of Soviet aggression as it moved into the Asian sphere.

After mid-1949, United States officials were no longer ruling out the possibility that China was being induced "to accept a disguised form of foreign rule"—as George F. Kennan expressed it in a radio program. Even in the China White Paper the new Secretary of State, Dean Acheson, had called attention to the danger of Soviet imperialism in the Far East and reaffirmed United States opposition

> to the subjugation of China by any foreign power, to any regime acting in the interest of a foreign power, and to the dismemberment of China by any foreign power, whether by open or clandestine means. . . .

That the Chinese had indeed become puppets of the Soviet Politburo appeared to pass beyond any shadow of doubt when, in February, 1950, the world read the terms of the new Sino-Soviet Treaty of Friendship, Alliance and Mutual Assistance. By its terms the Soviets promised China considerable financial and technical aid. Acheson admitted that the Chinese people might welcome such promises but, he added,

> they will not fail, in time, to see where they fall short of China's real needs and desires. And they will wonder about the points upon which the agreements remain silent.

Acheson warned the Chinese that, whatever China's internal development, they would bring grave trouble on themselves and the rest of Asia "if they are led by their new rulers into aggressive or subversive adventures beyond their borders."

The concept of a single conspiracy, global in its pretensions and centering in Moscow, had not won universal acceptance. Indeed, many American scholars at mid-century rejected the notion completely. Journalist Walter Lippmann, speaking before the Chicago Council on Foreign Relations on February 22, 1950, reminded his audience:

> While it is true that we have lost our power and for the time being most of our influence in China, it by no means follows that Russia has won control of China or has achieved an enduring alliance with China.

Most writers on Far Eastern subjects agreed with Acheson's warning of January that the United States should not introduce the use of military force into Asia. But the final Communist victory in China, added to the interpretation of the Sino-Soviet Pact which official Washington ascribed to it, propelled the administration logically toward the extension of the containment principle to include the Far East. By March, 1950, the Chinese revolution alone seemed sufficient to demonstrate Soviet expansionist tendencies toward Asia.

* * *

Much of the fear of further Soviet aggression eventually centered on Indochina where the French, as late as 1949, continued the struggle for their Asian empire against the determined opposition of Vietnamese nationalist Ho Chi Minh. At one time the United States had supported Ho and as late as 1949 it had revealed no official interest in his defeat. Within the context of global containment, however, the fact that Ho was a Marxist and Moscow-trained made him sufficiently suspect as an agent of Soviet imperialism to bring the full weight of United States policy against him. What embarrassed United States containment policy in Indochina at mid-century was the French reluctance to grant the region its independence.

The French promised independence for Indochina in the Elysée Agreements of March, 1949. In June, the State Department welcomed the creation of the new state of Vietnam and expressed the hope that the March agreements would "form the basis for the progressive realization of the legitimate aspirations of the Vietnamese people." The United States accepted the new Vietnamese leader, Bao Dai, with enthusiasm as the nationalist answer to Ho Chi Minh. Meanwhile the French, conscious of the growing United States fear of Soviet expansion into Asia, insisted that they were fighting for Western security in the Far East and therefore deserved United States military aid. Only the refusal of the French National Assembly to ratify the Elysée Agreements stalled the French request for United States military support in Asia in late 1949.

The events of January and February, 1950, finally rendered Ho Chi Minh a mortal enemy of the United States. On January 14, to meet the challenge of Bao Dai and French policy, Ho declared the establishment of the Democratic Republic of Vietnam, under his control, as the only lawful government representative of the Vietnamese people. At the same time Ho announced that his country would

> consolidate her friendly relations with the Soviet Union, China and other People's Democracies, actively to support the national liberation movements of colonial and semi-colonial countries. . . .

Before the end of the month both China and the U.S.S.R. had recognized the Democratic Republic. In a press release, Acheson declared that this

> should remove any illusion as to the "nationalist" character of Ho Chi Minh's aims and reveals Ho in his true colors as the mortal enemy of native independence in Indochina.

Eventually, the French Assembly ratified the agreements which established the new state of Vietnam, the Kingdom of Laos and the Kingdom of Cambodia as independent states within the French Union. On February 6, 1950, Ambassador Jessup declared in Singapore that the United States would view any armed Communist aggression against the new states of Indochina as a matter of grave concern. On the following day, the United States and Great Britain extended *de jure* recognition to the three Associated States of Laos, Vietnam and Cambodia, and sent a note of congratulations to Bao Dai, the chief of the new Vietnam state. The notion that Bao Dai had better claims to Vietnamese leadership than Ho and that he would ultimately triumph became official doctrine in Washington. Loy Henderson expressed it well when he said

> The United States is convinced that the Bao Dai Government of Viet Nam reflects more accurately than any rival claimants to power in Viet Nam the nationalist aspirations of the people of that country. It hopes by its policies with regard to Viet Nam, to contribute to the peaceful progress of Vietnamese people toward the realization of the fruits of self-government. . . . My government is convinced that any movement headed by a Moscow-recognized Communist such as Ho Chi Minh must be in the direction of subservience to a foreign state, not in that of independence and self-government.

Still the United States faced a dilemma in Indochina which belied its stated faith in either Bao Dai or the French. To give military aid to the French would lend additional credence to the charge that United States policy in Asia was primarily military and strategic with little or no genuine concern for the political advancement of the Vietnamese people. To channel aid to the government in Saigon, with Bao Dai spending his time at Dalat far removed from the activities of his government, gave no promise of effective utilization at all. Finally on May 8, 1950, Acheson, with French Foreign Minister Robert Schuman, negotiated an arrangement whereby France and the governments of Indochina together would carry the responsibility for Indochinese security and development. United States aid would simply contribute to that objective.

Again the motives of containment were clear.

> The United States Government [wrote Acheson] convinced that neither national independence nor democratic evolution exist in any area dominated by Soviet imperialism, considers the situation to be such as to warrant its according economic aid and military equipment to the Associated States of Indochina and to France in order to assist them in restoring stability and permitting these states to pursue their peaceful and democratic development.

In his request to Congress for military assistance funds in June, President Truman acknowledged the nation's determination "to preserve the freedom and integrity of Indochina from the Communist forces of Ho Chi Minh." In December, 1950, the United States signed a Mutual Defense Assistance Agreement with France, Vietnam, Cambodia and Laos for indirect United States military aid to the three states of Indochina.

* * *

With the outbreak of the Korean War, Washington officials pushed United States rearmament in Europe and Asia with a greater sense of urgency under the assumption that the non-Soviet world had entered a period of great peril and had only a short time to prepare before the enemy reached the peak of its power. In the President's budget message of 1951, military aid became an established policy of the United States. The first Mutual Security Act, adopted that year, implied that thereafter economic aid would be used primarily to expand the military base of the recipient countries.

During 1952, military assistance to Asia grew in importance relative to Europe. The bulk of the military aid channeled into Asia went to four countries regarded as especially vulnerable to Soviet-Chinese aggression: the Republic of China on Formosa, the Republic of Korea, the Republic of Vietnam and Japan. In Korea, the United States supported one of the largest non-Communist armies in the world at a cost of almost $1 billion per year. In Indochina, the United States eventually underwrote 80 per cent of the financial cost of the French effort.

That the globalization of containment would produce diminishing returns was evident even as the policy unfolded. Containment in Europe had promised success because the threat was purely military—the danger of a Red Army marching westward. The region guaranteed by NATO, moreover, comprised the seat of an ancient civilization with a tradition of political, economic and military efficiency. In Asia and the Middle East, the danger was less that of marching armies than of guerrilla warfare and subversion. This reduced containment to a matter of political, not military, effectiveness. For no government that failed to establish a broad governing base would long remain in power whatever moral and physical support it received from the United States.

Even as a venture in power, containment in Asia was prejudiced from the start. Unlike the nations of Europe, the Asian nations lacked the skilled manpower and industrial bases to develop self-sustaining military strength. Whereas the military structures of such countries would never be strong enough to resist aggression, they would always exceed in cost what the Asian economies could support. Thus they threatened the United States with an endless financial drain without contributing much useful defense.

It was essentially the absence of political stability that rendered the borderlands along the Asian periphery of Russia and China an unfortunate area in which to establish the barriers against Communist expansion. Such an effort at containment, warned Walter Lippmann in *The Cold War* (1947), would compel the United States to stake its policies

> upon satellites, puppets, clients, agents about whom we know very little. Frequently they will act . . . on their own judgments, presenting us with accomplished facts that we did not intend, and with crises for which we are unready. The "unassailable barriers" will present us with an unending series of insoluble dilemmas. We shall have either to disown our puppets, which would be tantamount to appeasement and defeat and the loss of face, or must support them at an incalculable cost on an unintended, unforeseen and perhaps undesirable issue.

From such dilemmas there would be no escape, for through the critical years of 1949 to 1951 United States officials had created an image of Asia which would not die, an image calculated to introduce the element of fear on a massive scale into the American conceptualization of the challenges which the United States faced. Global containment, responding to the challenge of an insatiable Soviet-based Communist monolith, elevated every Communist-led maneuver to first-level importance even where United States security interests were unclear and strategic conditions unfavorable. The policy would ultimately exact its toll in costly military involvements and a deeply divided nation.

III. WHOSE RESPONSIBILITY? THE SCHOLARS DEBATE

Arthur M. Schlesinger, Jr.

LENINIST IDEOLOGY AND STALINIST PARANOIA

One of the most prolific writers on American history, author of studies of the Jacksonian period, the New Deal years, and the Kennedy Administration (*A Thousand Days* in 1965), Arthur Schlesinger taught for many years at Harvard University before becoming Special Assistant to President John F. Kennedy. In the following essay, he concedes that Russia had major postwar recovery problems and security fears, and that American policy was sometimes rigid and misunderstood Soviet intentions. But he defends the traditional story of the Cold War's origins by placing responsibility for the conflict squarely in Moscow. There was nothing the United States could have done to change the course of events, he concludes, because Russia was driven by an uncompromising and controlling ideology and by Stalin's excessive paranoia.

THE Cold War in its original form was a presumably mortal antagonism, arising in the wake of the Second World War, between two rigidly hostile blocs, one led by the Soviet Union, the other by the United States. For nearly two somber and dangerous decades this antagonism dominated the fears of mankind; it may even, on occasion, have come close to blowing up the planet. In recent years, however, the once implacable struggle has lost its familiar clarity of outline. With the passing of old issues and the emergence of new conflicts and contestants, there is a natural tendency, especially on the part of the generation which grew up during the Cold War, to take a fresh look at the causes of the great contention between Russia and America.

Some exercises in reappraisal have merely elaborated the orthodoxies promulgated in Washington or Moscow during the boom years of the Cold War. But others, especially in the United States (there are no signs, alas, of this in the Soviet Union), represent what American historians call "revisionism"—that is, a readiness to challenge official explanations. No one should be surprised by this phenomenon. Every war in American history has been followed in due course by skeptical reassessments of supposedly sacred assumptions. So the War of 1812, fought at the time for the freedom of the seas, was in later years ascribed to the expansionist ambitions of Congressional war hawks; so the Mexican War became a slaveholders' conspiracy. So the Civil War has been pronounced a "needless war," and Lincoln has even been accused of manœuvring the rebel attack on Fort Sumter. So too the Spanish-American War and the First and Second World Wars have, each in its turn, undergone revisionist critiques. It is not to be supposed that the Cold War would remain exempt.

In the case of the Cold War, special factors reinforce the predictable histori-

From Arthur M. Schlesinger, Jr., "Origins of the Cold War," *Foreign Affairs*, 46 (October, 1967), pp. 22–25, 26–27, 28–30, 31–32, 34–35, 42–47, 48–50, 52.

ographical rhythm. The outburst of polycentrism in the communist empire has made people wonder whether communism was ever so monolithic as official theories of the Cold War supposed. A generation with no vivid memories of Stalinism may see the Russia of the forties in the image of the relatively mild, seedy and irresolute Russia of the sixties. And for this same generation the American course of widening the war in Viet Nam—which even non-revisionists can easily regard as folly—has unquestionably stirred doubts about the wisdom of American foreign policy in the sixties which younger historians may have begun to read back into the forties.

It is useful to remember that, on the whole, past exercises in revisionism have failed to stick. Few historians today believe that the war hawks caused the War of 1812 or the slaveholders the Mexican War, or that the Civil War was needless, or that the House of Morgan brought America into the First World War or that Franklin Roosevelt schemed to produce the attack on Pearl Harbor. But this does not mean that one should deplore the rise of Cold War revisionism. For revisionism is an essential part of the process by which history, through the posing of new problems and the investigation of new possibilities, enlarges its perspectives and enriches its insights.

More than this, in the present context, revisionism expresses a deep, legitimate and tragic apprehension. As the Cold War has begun to lose its purity of definition, as the moral absolutes of the fifties become the moralistic clichés of the sixties, some have begun to ask whether the appalling risks which humanity ran during the Cold War were, after all, necessary and inevitable; whether more restrained and rational policies might not have guided the energies of man from the perils of conflict into the potentialities of collaboration. The fact that such questions are in their nature unanswerable does not mean that it is not right and useful to raise them. Nor does it mean that our sons and daughters are not entitled to an accounting from the generation of Russians and Americans who produced the Cold War.

The orthodox American view, as originally set forth by the American government and as reaffirmed until recently by most American scholars, has been that the Cold War was the brave and essential response of free men to communist aggression. Some have gone back well before the Second World War to lay open the sources of Russian expansionism. Geopoliticians traced the Cold War to imperial Russian strategic ambitions which in the nineteenth century led to the Crimean War, to Russian penetration of the Balkans and the Middle East and to Russian pressure on Britain's "lifeline" to India. Ideologists traced it to the Communist Manifesto of 1848 ("the violent overthrow of the bourgeoisie lays the foundation for the sway of the proletariat"). Thoughtful observers (a phrase meant to exclude those who speak in Dullese about the unlimited evil of godless, atheistic, militant communism) concluded that classical Russian imperialism and Pan-Slavism, compounded after 1917 by Leninist messianism, confronted the West at the end of the Second World War with an inexorable drive for domination.

The revisionist thesis is very different. In its extreme form, it is that, after the death of Franklin Roosevelt and the end of the Second World War, the United States deliberately abandoned the wartime policy of collaboration and, exhilarated by the possession of the atomic bomb, undertook a course of aggression of its own designed to expel all Russian influence from Eastern Europe and to establish democratic-capitalist states on the very border of the Soviet Union. As the revisionists see it, this radically new American policy—or rather this resumption by Truman of the pre-Roosevelt policy of insensate anti-communism—left Moscow no alternative but to take measures in defense of its own borders. The result was the Cold War. . . .

Peacemaking after the Second World War was not so much a tapestry as it was a hopelessly raveled and knotted mess of yarn. Yet, for purposes of clarity, it is essential to follow certain threads. One theme indispensable to an understanding of the Cold War is the contrast between two clashing views of world order: the "universalist" view, by which all nations shared a common interest in all the affairs of the world, and the "sphere-of-influence" view, by which each great power would be assured by the other great powers of an acknowledged predominance in its own area of special interest. The universalist view assumed that national security would be guaranteed by an international organization. The sphere-of-interest view assumed that national security would be guaranteed by the balance of power. While in practice these views have by no means been incompatible (indeed, our shaky peace has been based on a combination of the two), in the abstract they involved sharp contradictions.

The tradition of American thought in these matters was universalist—*i.e.* Wilsonian. Roosevelt had been a member of Wilson's subcabinet; in 1920, as candidate for Vice President, he had campaigned for the League of Nations. It is true that, within Roosevelt's infinitely complex mind, Wilsonianism warred with the perception of vital strategic interests he had imbibed from Mahan. Moreover, his temperamental inclination to settle things with fellow princes around the conference table led him to regard the Big Three—or Four—as trustees for the rest of the world. On occasion, as this narrative will show, he was beguiled into flirtation with the sphere-of-influence heresy. But in principle he believed in joint action and remained a Wilsonian. His hope for Yalta, as he told the Congress on his return, was that it would "spell the end of the system of unilateral action, the exclusive alliances, the spheres of influence, the balances of power, and all the other expedients that have been tried for centuries—and have always failed."

Whenever Roosevelt backslid, he had at his side that Wilsonian fundamentalist, Secretary of State Cordell Hull, to recall him to the pure faith. After his visit to Moscow in 1943, Hull characteristically said that, with the Declaration of Four Nations on General Security (in which America, Russia, Britain and China pledged "united action . . . for the organization and maintenance of peace and security"), "there will no longer be need for spheres of influence, for alliances, for balance of power, or any other of the special arrangements through which, in the unhappy past, the nations strove to safeguard their security or to promote their interests."

Remembering the corruption of the Wilsonian vision by the secret treaties of the First World War, Hull was determined to prevent any sphere-of-influence nonsense after the Second World War. He therefore fought all proposals to settle border questions while the war was still on and, excluded as he largely was from wartime diplomacy, poured his not inconsiderable moral energy and frustration into the promulgation of virtuous and spacious general principles. . . .

It is true that critics, and even friends, of the United States sometimes noted a discrepancy between the American passion for universalism when it applied to territory far from American shores and the preëminence the United States accorded its own interests nearer home. Churchill, seeking Washington's blessing for a sphere-of-influence initiative in Eastern Europe, could not forbear reminding the Americans, "We follow the lead of the United States in South America"; nor did any universalist of record propose the abolition of the Monroe Doctrine. But a convenient myopia prevented such inconsistencies from qualifying the ardency of the universalist faith.

There seem only to have been three officials in the United States Government who dissented. One was the Secretary of War, Henry L. Stimson, a classical balance-of-power man, who in 1944 opposed the creation of a vacuum in Central Europe by the pastoralization of Germany and in 1945 urged "the settlement of all territorial acquisitions in the shape of defense posts which each of these four powers may deem to be necessary for their own safety" in advance of any effort to establish a peacetime United Nations. Stimson considered the claim of Russia to a preferred position in Eastern Europe as not unreasonable: as he told President Truman, "he thought the Russians perhaps were being more realistic than we were in regard to their own security." Such a position for Russia seemed to him comparable to the preferred American position in Latin America; he even spoke of "our respective orbits." Stimson was therefore skeptical of what he regarded as the prevailing tendency "to hang on to exaggerated views of the Monroe Doctrine and at the same time butt into every question that comes up in Central Europe." Acceptance of spheres of influence seemed to him the way to avoid "a head-on collision."

A second official opponent of universalism was George Kennan, an eloquent advocate from the American Embassy in Moscow of "a prompt and clear recognition of the division of Europe into spheres of influence and of a policy based on the fact of such division." Kennan argued that nothing we could do would possibly alter the course of events in Eastern Europe; that we were deceiving ourselves by supposing that these countries had any future but Russian domination; that we should therefore relinquish Eastern Europe to the Soviet Union and avoid anything which would make things easier for the Russians by giving them economic assistance or by sharing moral responsibility for their actions.

A third voice within the government against universalism was (at least after the war) Henry A. Wallace. As Secretary of Commerce, he stated the sphere-of-influence case with trenchancy in the famous Madison Square Garden speech of September 1946 which led to his dismissal by President Truman:

> On our part, we should recognize that we have no more business in the *political* affairs of Eastern Europe than Russia has in the *political* affairs of Latin America, Western Europe, and the United States. . . . Whether we like it or not, the Russians will try to socialize their sphere of influence just as we try to democratize our sphere of influence. . . . The Russians have no more business stirring up native Communists to political activity in Western Europe, Latin America, and the United States than we have in interfering with the politics of Eastern Europe and Russia.

Stimson, Kennan and Wallace seem to have been alone in the government, however, in taking these views. They were very much minority voices. Meanwhile universalism, rooted in the American legal and moral tradition, overwhelmingly backed by contemporary opinion, received successive enshrinements in the Atlantic Charter of 1941, in the Declaration of the United Nations in 1942 and in the Moscow Declaration of 1943.

The Kremlin, on the other hand, thought *only* of spheres of interest; above all, the Russians were determined to protect their frontiers, and especially their border to the west, crossed so often and so bloodily in the dark course of their history. These western frontiers lacked natural means of defense—no great oceans, rugged mountains, steaming swamps or impenetrable jungles. The history of Russia had been the history of invasion, the last of which was by now horribly killing up to twenty million of its people. The protocol of Russia therefore meant the enlargement of the area of Russian influence. Kennan himself wrote (in May 1944), "Behind Russia's stubborn expansion lies only the age-old sense of insecurity of a sedentary people reared on an exposed plain in the neighborhood of fierce nomadic peoples," and he called this "urge" a "permanent feature of Russian psychology." . . .

The unconditional surrender of Italy in July 1943 created the first major test of the Western devotion to universalism. America and Britain, having won the Italian war, handled the capitulation, keeping Moscow informed at a distance. Stalin complained

> The United States and Great Britain made agreements but the Soviet Union received information about the results . . . just as a passive third observer I have to tell you that it is impossible to tolerate the situation any longer. I propose that the [tripartite military-political commission] be established and that Sicily be assigned . . . as its place of residence.

Roosevelt, who had no intention of sharing the control of Italy with the Russians, suavely replied with the suggestion that Stalin send an officer "to

General Eisenhower's headquarters in connection with the commission." Unimpressed, Stalin continued to press for a tripartite body; but his Western allies were adamant in keeping the Soviet Union off the Control Commission for Italy, and the Russians in the end had to be satisfied with a seat, along with minor Allied states, on a meaningless Inter-Allied Advisory Council. Their acquiescence in this was doubtless not unconnected with a desire to establish precedents for Eastern Europe.

Teheran in December 1943 marked the high point of three-power collaboration. Still, when Churchill asked about Russian territorial interests, Stalin replied a little ominously, "There is no need to speak at the present time about any Soviet desires, but when the time comes we will speak." In the next weeks, there were increasing indications of a Soviet determination to deal unilaterally with Eastern Europe—so much so that in early February 1944 Hull cabled Harriman in Moscow:

> Matters are rapidly approaching the point where the Soviet Government will have to choose between the development and extension of the foundation of international cooperation as the guiding principle of the postwar world as against the continuance of a unilateral and arbitrary method of dealing with its special problems even though these problems are admittedly of more direct interest to the Soviet Union than to other great powers.

As against this approach, however, Churchill, more tolerant of sphere-of-influence deviations, soon proposed that, with the impending liberation of the Balkans, Russia should run things in Rumania and Britain in Greece. Hull strongly opposed this suggestion but made the mistake of leaving Washington for a few days; and Roosevelt, momentarily free from his Wilsonian conscience, yielded to Churchill's plea for a three-months' trial. Hull resumed the fight on his return, and Churchill postponed the matter. . . .

Meanwhile Eastern Europe presented the Alliance with still another crisis that same September. Bulgaria, which was not at war with Russia, decided to surrender to the Western Allies while it still could; and the English and Americans at Cairo began to discuss armistice terms with Bulgarian envoys. Moscow, challenged by what it plainly saw as a Western intrusion into its own zone of vital interest, promptly declared war on Bulgaria, took over the surrender negotiations and, invoking the Italian precedent, denied its Western Allies any role in the Bulgarian Control Commission. In a long and thoughtful cable, Ambassador Harriman meditated on the problems of communication with the Soviet Union. "Words," he reflected, "have a different connotation to the Soviets than they have to us. When they speak of insisting on 'friendly governments' in their neighboring countries, they have in mind something quite different from what we would mean." The Russians, he surmised, really believed that Washington accepted "their position that although they would keep us informed they had the right to settle their problems with their western neighbors unilaterally." But the Soviet position was still in flux: "the Soviet Government is not one mind." The problem, as Harriman had earlier told Harry Hopkins, was "to strengthen the hands of those around Stalin who want to play the game along our lines." The way to do this, he now told Hull, was to

> be understanding of their sensitivity, meet them much more than half way, encourage them and support them wherever we can, and yet oppose them promptly with the greatest firmness where we see them going wrong. . . . The only way we can eventually come to an understanding with the Soviet Union on the question of non-interference in the internal affairs of other countries is for us to take a definite interest in the solution of the problems of each individual country as they arise.

As against Harriman's sophisticated universalist strategy, however, Churchill, increasingly fearful of the consequences of unrestrained competition in Eastern Europe, decided in early October to carry his sphere-of-influence proposal directly to Moscow. Roosevelt was at first content to have Churchill speak for him too and even prepared a cable to that effect. But Hopkins, a more rigorous universalist, took it upon himself to stop the cable and warn Roosevelt of its possible implications. Eventually Roosevelt sent a message to Harriman in Moscow emphasizing that he expected to "retain complete freedom of action after this conference is over." It was now that Churchill quickly proposed—and Stalin as quickly accepted—the celebrated division of southeastern Europe: ending (after further haggling between Eden and Molotov) with 90 percent Soviet predominance in Rumania, 80 percent in Bulgaria and Hungary, fifty-fifty in Jugoslavia, 90 percent British predominance in Greece.

Churchill in discussing this with Harriman used the phrase "spheres of influence." But he insisted that these were only "immediate wartime arrangements" and received a highly general blessing from Roosevelt. Yet, whatever Churchill intended, there is reason to believe that Stalin construed the percentages as an agreement, not a declaration; as practical arithmetic, not algebra. For Stalin, it should be understood, the sphere-of-influence idea did not mean that he would abandon all efforts to spread communism in some other nation's sphere; it did mean that, if he tried this and the other side cracked down, he could not feel he had serious cause for complaint.

* * *

Yalta remains something of an historical perplexity—less, from the perspective of 1967, because of a mythical American deference to the sphere-of-influence thesis than because of the documentable Russian deference to the universalist thesis. Why should Stalin in 1945 have accepted the Declaration on Liberated Europe and an agreement on Poland pledging that "the three governments will jointly" act to assure "free elections of governments responsive to the will of the people"? There are several probable answers: that the war was not over and the Russians still wanted the Americans to intensify their military effort in the West; that one clause in the Declaration premised action on "the opinion of the three governments" and thus implied a Soviet veto, though the Polish agreement was more definite; most of all that the universalist algebra of the Declaration was plainly in Stalin's mind to be construed in terms of the practical arithmetic of his sphere-of-influence agreement with Churchill the previous October. Stalin's assurance to Churchill at Yalta that a proposed Russian amendment to the Declaration would not apply to Greece makes it clear that Roosevelt's pieties did not, in Stalin's mind, nullify Churchill's percentages. He could well have been strengthened in this supposition by the fact that *after* Yalta, Churchill himself repeatedly reasserted the terms of the October agreement as if he regarded it, despite Yalta, as controlling.

Harriman still had the feeling before Yalta that the Kremlin had "two approaches to their postwar policies" and that Stalin himself was "of two minds." One approach emphasized the internal reconstruction and development of Russia; the other its external expansion. But in the meantime the fact which dominated all political decisions—that is, the war against Germany—was moving into its final phase. In the weeks after Yalta, the military situation changed with great rapidity. As the Nazi threat declined, so too did the need for coöperation. The Soviet Union, feeling itself menaced by the American idea of self-determination and the borderlands diplomacy to which it was leading, skeptical whether the United Nations would protect its frontiers as reliably as its own domination in Eastern Europe, began to fulfill its security requirements unilaterally.

In March Stalin expressed his evaluation of the United Nations by rejecting Roosevelt's plea that Molotov come to the San Francisco conference, if only for the opening sessions. In the next weeks the Russians emphatically and crudely worked their will in Eastern Europe, above all in the test country of Poland. They were ignoring the Declaration on Liberated Europe, ignoring the Atlantic Charter, self-determination, human freedom and everything else the Americans considered essential for a stable peace. "We must clearly recognize," Harriman wired Washington a few days before Roosevelt's death, "that the Soviet program is the establishment of totalitarianism, ending personal liberty and democracy as we know and respect it."

At the same time, the Russians also began to mobilize communist resources in the United States itself to block American universalism. In April 1945 Jacques Duclos, who had been the Comintern official responsible for the Western communist parties, launched in *Cahiers du Communisme* an uncompromising attack on the policy of the American Communist Party. Duclos sharply condemned the revisionism of Earl Browder, the American Communist leader, as "expressed in the concept of a long-term class peace in the United States, of the possibility of the suppression of the class struggle in the postwar period and of establishment of harmony between labor and capital." Browder was specifically rebuked for favoring the "self-determination" of Europe "west of the Soviet Union" on a bourgeois-democratic basis. The excommunication of Browderism was plainly the Politburo's considered reaction to the impending defeat of Germany; it was a signal to the communist parties of the West that they should recover their identity; it was Moscow's alert to communists everywhere that they should prepare for new policies in the postwar world.

The Duclos piece obviously could not have been planned and written much later than the Yalta conference—that is, well before a number of events which revisionists now cite in order to demonstrate American responsibility for the Cold War: before Allen Dulles, for example, began to negotiate the surrender of the German armies in Italy (the episode which provoked Stalin to charge Roosevelt with seeking a separate peace and provoked Roosevelt to denounce the "vile misrepresentations" of Stalin's informants); well before Roosevelt died; many months before the testing of the atomic bomb; even more months before Truman ordered that the bomb be dropped on Japan. William Z. Foster, who soon replaced Browder as the leader of the American Communist Party and embodied the new Moscow line, later boasted of having said in January 1944, "A post-war Roosevelt administration would continue to be, as it is now, an imperialist government." With ancient suspicions revived by the American insistence on universalism, this was no doubt the conclusion which the Russians were reaching at the same time. The Soviet canonization of Roosevelt (like their present-day canonization of Kennedy) took place after the American President's death.

The atmosphere of mutual suspicion was beginning to rise. In January 1945 Molotov formally proposed that the United States grant Russia a $6 billion credit for postwar reconstruction. With characteristic tact he explained that he was doing this as a favor to save America from a postwar depression. The proposal seems to have been diffidently made and diffidently received. Roosevelt requested that the matter "not be pressed further" on the American side until he had a chance to talk with Stalin; but the Russians did not follow it up either at Yalta in February (save for a single glancing reference) or during the Stalin-Hopkins talks in May or at Potsdam. Finally the proposal was renewed in the very different political atmosphere of August. This time Washington inexplicably mislaid the request during the transfer of the records of the Foreign Economic Administration to the State Department. It did not turn up again until March 1946. Of course this was impossible for the Russians to believe; it is hard enough even for those acquainted with the capacity of the American government for incompetence to believe; and it only strengthened Soviet suspicions of American purposes.

The American credit was one conceivable form of Western contribution to Russian reconstruction. Another was lend-lease, and the possibility of reconstruction aid under the lend-lease protocol had already been discussed in 1944. But in May 1945 Russia, like Britain, suffered from Truman's abrupt termination of lend-lease shipments—"unfortunate and even brutal," Stalin told Hopkins, adding that, if it was "designed as pressure on the Russians in order to soften them up, then it was a fundamental mistake." A third form was German reparations. Here Stalin in demanding $10 billion in reparations for the Soviet Union made his strongest fight at Yalta. Roosevelt, while agreeing essentially with Churchill's opposition, tried to postpone the matter by accepting the Soviet figure as a "basis for discussion" —a formula which led to future misunderstanding. In short, the Russian hope for major Western assistance in postwar reconstruction foundered on three events which the Kremlin could well have interpreted respectively as deliberate sabotage (the loan request), blackmail (lend-lease cancellation) and pro-Germanism (reparations).

Actually the American attempt to settle the fourth lend-lease protocol was generous and the Russians for their own reasons declined to come to an agreement. It is not clear, though, that satisfying Moscow on any of these financial scores would have made much essential difference. It might have persuaded some doves in the Kremlin that the U.S. government was genuinely friendly; it might have persuaded some hawks that the American anxiety for Soviet friendship was such that Moscow could do as it wished without inviting challenge from the United States. It would, in short, merely have reinforced both sides of the Kremlin debate; it would hardly have reversed deeper tendencies toward the deterioration of political relationships. Economic deals were surely subordinate to the quality of mutual political confidence; and here, in the months after Yalta, the decay was steady.

The Cold War had now begun. It was the product not of a decision but of a dilemma. Each side felt compelled to adopt policies which the other could not but regard as a threat to the principles of the peace. Each then felt compelled to undertake defensive measures. Thus the Russians saw no choice but to consolidate their security in Eastern Europe. The Americans, regarding Eastern Europe as the first step toward Western Europe, responded by asserting their interest in the zone the Russians deemed vital to their security. The Russians concluded that the West was resuming its old course of capitalist encirclement; that it was purposefully laying the foundation for anti-Soviet régimes in the area defined by the blood of centuries as crucial to Russian survival. Each side believed with passion that future international stability depended on the success of its own conception of world order. Each side, in pursuing its own clearly indicated and deeply cherished principles, was only confirming the fear of the other that it was bent on aggression.

Very soon the process began to acquire a cumulative momentum. The impending collapse of Germany thus provoked new troubles: the Russians, for example, sincerely feared that the West was planning a separate surrender of the German armies in Italy in a way which would release troops for Hitler's eastern front, as they subsequently feared that the Nazis might succeed in surrendering Berlin to the West. This was the context in which the atomic bomb now appeared. Though the revisionist argument that Truman dropped the bomb less to defeat Japan than to intimidate Russia is not convincing, this thought unquestionably appealed to some in Washington as at least an advantageous side-effect of Hiroshima.

So the machinery of suspicion and counter-suspicion, action and counter-action, was set in motion. But, given relations among traditional national states, there was still no reason, even with all the postwar jostling, why this should not have remained a manageable situation. What made it unmanageable, what caused the rapid escalation of the Cold War and in another two years completed the division of Europe, was a set of considerations which this account has thus far excluded.

Up to this point, the discussion has considered the schism within the wartime coalition as if it were entirely the result of disagreements among national states. Assuming this framework, there was unquestionably a failure of communication between America and Russia, a misperception of signals and, as time went on, a mounting tendency to ascribe ominous motives to the other side. It seems hard, for example, to deny that American postwar policy created genuine difficulties for the Russians and even assumed a threatening aspect for them. All this the revisionists have rightly and usefully emphasized.

But the great omission of the revisionists—and also the fundamental explanation of the speed with which the Cold War escalated—lies precisely in the fact that the Soviet Union was *not* a traditional national state. This is where the "mirror image," invoked by some psychologists, falls down. For the Soviet Union was a phenomenon very different from America or Britain: it was a totalitarian state, endowed with an all-explanatory, all-consuming ideology, committed to the infallibility of government and party, still in a somewhat messianic mood, equating dissent with treason, and ruled by a dictator who, for all his quite extraordinary abilities, had his paranoid moments.

Marxism-Leninism gave the Russian leaders a view of the world according to which all societies were inexorably destined to proceed along appointed roads by appointed stages until they achieved the classless nirvana. Moreover, given the resistance of the capitalists to this development, the existence of any non-communist state was *by definition* a threat to the Soviet Union. "As long as capitalism and socialism exist," Lenin wrote, "we cannot live in peace: in the end, one or the other will triumph—a funeral dirge will be sung either over the Soviet Republic or over world capitalism."

Stalin and his associates, whatever Roosevelt or Truman did or failed to do, were bound to regard the United States as the enemy, not because of this deed or that, but because of the primordial fact that America was the leading capitalist power and thus, by Leninist syllogism, unappeasably hostile, driven by the logic of its system to oppose, encircle and destroy Soviet Russia. Nothing the United States could have done in 1944–45 would have abolished this mistrust, required and sanctified as it was by Marxist gospel—nothing short of the conversion of the United States into a Stalinist despotism; and even this would not have sufficed, as the experience of Jugoslavia and China soon showed, unless it were accompanied by total subservience to Moscow. So long as the United States remained a capitalist democracy, no American policy, given Moscow's theology, could hope to win basic Soviet confidence, and every American action was poisoned from the source. So long as the Soviet Union remained a messianic state, ideology compelled a steady expansion of communist power. . . .

A temporary recession of ideology was already taking place during the Second World War when Stalin, to rally his people against the invader, had to replace the appeal of Marxism by that of nationalism. ("We are under no illusions that they are fighting for us," Stalin once said to Harriman. "They are fighting for Mother Russia.") But this was still taking place within the strictest limitations. The Soviet Union remained as much a police state as ever; the régime was as infallible as ever; foreigners and their ideas were as suspect as ever. "Never, except possibly during my later experience as ambassador in Moscow," Kennan has written, "did the insistence of the Soviet authorities on isolation of the diplomatic corps weigh more heavily on me . . . than in these first weeks following my return to Russia in the final months of the war. . . . [We were] treated as though we were the bearers of some species of the plague"—which, of course, from the Soviet viewpoint, they were: the plague of skepticism.

Paradoxically, of the forces capable of bringing about a modification of ideology, the most practical and effective was the Soviet dictatorship itself. If Stalin was an ideologist, he was also a pragmatist. If he saw everything through the lenses of Marxism-Leninism, he also, as the infallible expositor of the faith, could reinterpret Marxism-Leninism to justify anything he wanted to do at any given moment. No doubt Roosevelt's ignorance of Marxism-Leninism was inexcusable and led to grievous miscalculations. But Roosevelt's efforts to work on and through Stalin were not so hopelessly naïve as it used to be fashionable to think. With the extraordinary instinct of a great political leader, Roosevelt intuitively understood that Stalin was the *only* lever available to the West against the Leninist ideology and the Soviet system. If Stalin could be reached, then alone was there a chance of getting the Russians to act contrary to the prescriptions of their faith. The best evidence is that Roosevelt retained a certain capacity to influence Stalin to the end; the nominal Soviet acquiescence in American universalism as late as Yalta was perhaps an indication of that. It is in this way that the death of Roosevelt was crucial—not in the vulgar sense that his policy was then reversed by his successor, which did not happen, but in the sense that no other American could hope to have the restraining impact on Stalin which Roosevelt might for a while have had.

Stalin alone could have made any difference. Yet Stalin, in spite of the impression of sobriety and realism he made on Westerners who saw him during the Second World War, was plainly a man of deep and morbid obsessions and compulsions. When he was still a young man, Lenin had criticized his rude and arbitrary ways. A reasonably authoritative observer (N. S. Khrushchev) later commented, "These negative characteristics of his developed steadily and during the last years acquired an absolutely insufferable character." His paranoia, probably set off by the suicide of his wife in 1932, led to the terrible purges of the mid-thirties and the wanton murder of thousands of his Bolshevik comrades. "Everywhere and in everything," Khrushchev says of this period, "he saw 'enemies,' 'double-dealers' and 'spies.'" The crisis of war evidently steadied him in some way, though Khrushchev speaks of his "nervousness and hysteria . . . even after the war began." The madness, so rigidly controlled for a time, burst out with new and shocking intensity in the postwar years. "After the war," Khrushchev testifies,

> the situation became even more complicated. Stalin became even more capricious, irritable and brutal; in particular, his suspicion grew. His persecution mania reached unbelievable dimensions. . . . He decided everything, without any consideration for anyone or anything.
>
> Stalin's wilfulness showed itself . . . also in the international relations of the Soviet Union. . . . He had completely lost a sense of reality; he demonstrated his suspicion and haughtiness not only in relation to individuals in the USSR, but in relation to whole parties and nations.

A revisionist fallacy has been to treat Stalin as just another Realpolitik statesman, as Second World War revisionists see Hitler as just another Stresemann or Bismarck. But the record makes it clear that in the end nothing could satisfy Stalin's paranoia. His own associates failed. Why does anyone suppose that any conceivable American policy would have succeeded?

An analysis of the origins of the Cold War which leaves out these factors—the intransigence of Leninist ideology, the sinister dynamics of a totalitarian society and the madness of Stalin—is obviously incomplete. It was these factors which made it hard for the West to accept the thesis that Russia was moved only by a desire to protect its security and would be satisfied by the control of Eastern Europe; it was these factors which charged the debate between universalism and spheres of influence with apocalyptic potentiality.

Leninism and totalitarianism created a structure of thought and behavior which made postwar collaboration between Russia and America—in any normal sense of civilized intercourse between national states—inherently impossible. The Soviet dictatorship of 1945 simply could not have survived such a collaboration. Indeed, nearly a quarter-century later, the Soviet régime, though it has meanwhile moved a good distance, could still hardly survive it without risking the release inside Russia of energies profoundly opposed to communist despotism. As for Stalin, he may have represented the only force in 1945 capable of overcoming Stalinism, but the very traits which enabled him to win absolute power expressed terrifying instabilities of mind and temperament and hardly offered a solid foundation for a peaceful world. . . .

The point of no return came on July 2, 1947, when Molotov, after bringing 89 technical specialists with him to Paris and evincing initial interest in the project for European reconstruction, received the hot flash from the Kremlin, denounced the whole idea and walked out of the conference. For the next fifteen years the Cold War raged unabated, passing out of historical ambiguity into the realm of good versus evil and breeding on both sides simplifications, stereotypes and self-serving absolutes, often couched in interchangeable phrases. Under the pressure even America, for a deplorable decade, forsook its pragmatic and pluralist traditions, posed as God's appointed messenger to ignorant and sinful man and followed the Soviet example in looking to a world remade in its own image.

In retrospect, if it is impossible to see the Cold War as a case of American aggression and Russian response, it is also hard to see it as a pure case of Russian aggression and American response. "In what is truly tragic," wrote Hegel, "there must be valid moral powers on both the sides which come into collision. . . . Both suffer loss and yet both are mutually justified." In this sense, the Cold War had its tragic elements. The question remains whether it was an instance of Greek tragedy—as Auden has called it, "the tragedy of necessity," where the feeling aroused in the spectator is "What a pity it had to be this way"—or of Christian tragedy, "the tragedy of possibility," where the feeling aroused is "What a pity it was this way when it might have been otherwise."

Once something has happened, the historian is tempted to assume that it had to happen; but this may often be a highly unphilosophical assumption. The Cold War could have been avoided only if the Soviet Union had not been possessed by convictions both of the infallibility of the communist word and of the inevitability of a communist world. These convictions transformed an impasse between national states into a religious war, a tragedy of possibility into one of necessity. One might wish that America had preserved the poise and proportion of the first years of the Cold War and had not in time succumbed to its own forms of self-righteousness. But the most rational of American policies could hardly have averted the Cold War. Only today, as Russia begins to recede from its messianic mission and to accept, in practice if not yet in principle, the permanence of the world of diversity, only now can the hope flicker that this long, dreary, costly contest may at last be taking on forms less dramatic, less obsessive and less dangerous to the future of mankind.

William A. Williams

AMERICAN INNOCENCE QUESTIONED

In his rebuttal to Schlesinger and in his defense of revisionism, William A. Williams of Oregon State University denies that America was helpless in the early Cold War and that Stalin was uniquely paranoid. Williams finds Schlesinger short on evidence and remiss in not discussing the impact of the atomic bomb on diplomacy. For many years an historian at the University of Wisconsin, Williams was one of the first scholars to question the traditional Department of State explanation for the coming of the Cold War. In his *American-Russian Relations, 1761–1947* (1952) and *The Tragedy of American Diplomacy* (1959), he demonstrated his technique of imaginatively and provocatively reinterpreting the history of American foreign relations. Professor Williams' *The Roots of the Modern American Empire* (1969) is a major reinterpretation of American expansion in the late nineteenth century.

THERE is a great book to be written some day explaining how Schlesinger and a good many other historians of his generation came by the power to render such flat-out psychiatric judgments without professional training and without direct access to their subjects. My own candidates for that undertaking are Robert Coles, Abraham H. Maslow or Rollo May, men who somehow acquired a sense of the limits of their approach even as they mastered its discipline.

Meanwhile, the first point to be made about Schlesinger's attempt to fix the origins of the cold war in Stalin's paranoia is that *no major American policy maker between 1943 and 1948 defined and dealt with the Soviet Union in those terms.* Schlesinger offers not the slightest shred of evidence that such was the case. The reason is simple: there is no such evidence.

Even if Schlesinger's characterization of Stalin as a paranoid were granted, the argument would still be unable to account either for the nature or the adoption of American policy. There is only one circumstance in which his proposition would become directly relevant: If a different American policy had been carefully formulated and then seriously tried over a significant period of time, only to fail because of Russian intransigence, then Schlesinger's argument that Stalin's paranoia caused the Cold War would bear on the case.

It is particularly important to grasp that point because Schlesinger does not introduce paranoia until after he has demonstrated that Stalin was acting on a rational and conservative basis. Long before he mentions paranoia, Schlesinger notes the ambivalence of Soviet leaders toward an accommodation with the United States, and makes it clear that American leaders were operating on that estimate of the situation—not on the proposition that the Russians were paranoid. While entering the caveat that "no one, of course, can know what was really in the minds of the Russian leaders," he nevertheless concludes that "it is not unreasonable to suppose that Stalin would have been satisfied at the end of the war to secure . . . 'a protective glacis along Russia's western border.' . . . His initial objective was very probably not world conquest but Russian security." And he makes it clear that Stalin kept his word about giving the British the initiative in Greece.

Schlesinger does not resort to explain-

From William A. Williams, "The Cold War Revisionists," *The Nation,* 205 (November 13, 1967), pp. 492–495. Reprinted by permission.

ing Soviet action in terms of paranoia until he has to deal with American efforts to exert direct influence on affairs in Eastern Europe. Then he casually asserts that it was a factor: "given the paranoia produced alike by Russian history and Leninist ideology, [American action] no doubt seemed not only an act of hypocrisy but a threat to security."

That offhand introduction of paranoia as a primary operational factor in historical explanation staggers the mind. It is simply not convincing to hold that a man (in this instance, Stalin) who believes he has negotiated a clear security perimeter is paranoid because he reacts negatively when one of the parties to the understanding (in this case the United States) unilaterally asserts and acts on a self-proclaimed right to intervene within that perimeter. When examined closely in connection with foreign affairs, the most that can be made of Schlesinger's argument is that Stalin may have had strong paranoid tendencies, and that the American thrust into Eastern Europe (and elsewhere throughout the world) could very well have pushed him gradually into, and perhaps through, the psychic zone separating neurosis from psychosis.

The most significant aspect of Schlesinger's argument that emerges at this point is his admission that America's assertion of its right to intervene anywhere in the world, and its action in doing so in Eastern Europe, had a primary effect on Soviet behavior. For in saying that, however he qualifies it later, Schlesinger has granted the validity of one of the major points made by the critics of the official line on the cold war. Many criticisms could be made of his description of the nature and dynamism of American global interventionism, which he labels "universalism," but the most important weakness in his analysis is the failure to discuss the explicit and implicit anti-communism that was a strong element in the American outlook from the moment the Bolsheviks seized power in 1917. That omission gravely undercuts the attempt he makes later to substantiate a vital part of his argument.

For, having admitted the reality and the consequences of American interventionism, Schlesinger faces the difficult problem of demonstrating the truth of three propositions if he is to establish Soviet responsibility for the cold war. First, he must show that a different American policy could not have produced other results. Second, he must sustain the thesis that the Soviet response to American universalism was indeed paranoid. Third, he must prove that the American counter-response was relevant and appropriate.

Schlesinger's argument that an alternate American policy would not have made any difference has two themes. He says that a serious effort to negotiate around the Soviet bid for a $6 billion loan would "merely have reinforced both sides of the Kremlin debate" because "economic deals were merely subordinate to the quality of mutual political confidence." That judgment completely overlooks the impact which a serious American economic proposal would have made on the "quality of political confidence."

In the end, however, Schlesinger falls back on Soviet paranoia as the reason that a different approach would have made no difference. Here, however, he introduces a new factor in his explanation. In the early part of the argument, he holds that the Soviets "thought *only* of spheres of influence; above all, the Russians were determined to protect their frontiers, and especially their border to the west, crossed so often and so bloodily in the dark course of their history." But later Schlesinger suggests that the paranoia was partially caused, and significantly reinforced, by the Marxist ideology of capitalist antagonism and opposition.

However, Soviet leaders did not detect capitalist hostility merely because they were viewing the world through a Marxist prism. Such enmity had existed, and had been acted upon, since November, 1917, and anti-communism was an integral part of the universalism that guided American leaders at the end of World War II. As Schlesinger demonstrates, willy-nilly if not intentionally, American leaders were prepared to work with Russian leaders if they would accept key features of the American creed. It is possible, given that truth, to construct a syllogism proving that Stalin was paranoid because he did not accept the terms. But that kind of proof has nothing to do with serious historical inquiry, analysis and interpretation.

The real issue at this juncture, however, is not how Schlesinger attempts to establish Stalin's paranoia. The central question is whether or not Soviet actions are accurately described as paranoid. The evidence does not support that interpretation. Consider the nature of Soviet behavior in three crucial areas.

First, the Russians reacted to American intervention in Eastern Europe by consolidating their existing position in that region. Many Soviet actions implementing that decision were overpowering, cruel and ruthless, but the methods do not bear on the nature of the policy itself. The Soviet choice served to verify an important point that Schlesinger acknowledges: Stalin told Harriman in October, 1945, that the Soviets were "going isolationist" in pursuit of their national interests. Russian policy at that time in Eastern Europe was neither paranoid nor messianic Marxism.

Second, the Soviets pulled back in other areas to avoid escalating a direct national or governmental confrontation with the United States. They did so in the clash over rival claims for oil rights in Iran; and that policy was even more strikingly apparent in Stalin's attempt to postpone Mao's triumph in China. In the first instance, prudence belies paranoia. In the second, any messianic urges were suppressed in the national interest.

Third, the Soviets acquiesced in the activities of non-Russian Communist movements. While the term *acquiesced* is not perfect for describing the complex process that was involved, it is nevertheless used advisedly as the best single term to describe the *effect* of Soviet action. Stalin and his colleagues no doubt sought results other than those that occurred in many places—China and Yugoslavia come particularly to mind—and clearly tried to realize their preferences. Nevertheless, they did acquiesce in results that fell far short of their desires.

Schlesinger makes a great deal, as do all official interpreters of the cold war, of the April, 1945, article by Jacques Duclos of the French Communist Party. Let us assume that Duclos wrote the article on orders from Moscow, even though the process that produced the action was probably far more complex than indicated by that simple statement. The crucial point about Duclos' article is that it can be read in two ways. It can be interpreted as a messianic cry for non-Soviet Communist parties to strike for power as part of a general push to expand Russian boundaries or the Soviet sphere of influence. But it can as persuasively be read as primarily a call for non-Soviet Communists to reassert their own identity and become militant and disruptive as part of the Russian strategy of consolidation in the face of American universalism.

Official explanations of the cold war generally imply that American leaders heard the Duclos piece as a bugle call for Communist aid in behalf of Soviet expansion. In truth, no significant number of American leaders feared a Russian military offensive at any time during the evolution of the cold war. When the Duclos article appeared, and for a long period thereafter, they were far more concerned with devising ways to use the great preponderance of American power to further the universalism and interventionism of the United States in Eastern Europe and elsewhere.

But the most astonishing use of the Duclos article by any defender of the official line on the cold war is made by Schlesinger when he employs it to avoid any serious discussion of the impact of the dropping of two atomic bombs in August, 1945. In truth, astonishing is a very mild word for Schlesinger's performance on this point. He says merely that the Duclos article came many months before the bombs were dropped, and then proceeds to ignore the *effect* of the bomb on Soviet leaders. All he adds is a flat assertion that the critics are "not convincing" in their argument that "the bomb was dropped less to defeat Japan than to intimidate Russia" (which is a strained interpretation of what they have said). That is not even to the point, for one could agree that the bomb was dropped only to finish the Japanese and still insist that it had a powerful effect on Soviet thought and action in connection with its future relations with the United States.

The argument could be made, of course, that only a Russia gone paranoid would have been upset by the American act. The issue of psychotic behavior might better be raised about the Americans. It could also be maintained that the United States had no responsibility for the effects of the bomb on Soviet leaders because the motive in using it was not anti-Soviet. That is about like saying that a man who constantly interferes in the affairs of his neighbors, and who suddenly starts using a 40-millimeter cannon to kill cats in his back yard, bears no responsibility for the neighbor's skepticism about his good intentions. Schlesinger is fully warranted in making a careful examination of the period before the bomb, but he has no justification for so nearly ignoring the role of the bomb in the origins of the cold war.

Finally, there is the question of the relevance and appropriateness of the American response to the Soviet policy of consolidation in Eastern Europe, and the related call for non-Russian Communists to reassert their identity and policies. The answer, put simply and directly, is that the increasingly militarized holy war mounted by American leaders was grossly irrelevant to the situation and highly conducive to producing problems that were more dangerous than those the policy was supposed to resolve.

Melvin Croan

STALIN'S RATIONALITY AND DOMESTIC IMPERATIVES

In a 1967 London meeting of the Institute of Contemporary History held in association with the University of Reading, Melvin Croan, of the Political Science Department, University of Wisconsin, disputed Schlesinger's emphasis on Stalin's paranoia. Although tending to agree with Schlesinger that the Soviet Union was largely responsible for the Cold War, Croan commented that Stalin was quite rational in measuring his nation's postwar weakness, his own precarious domestic position, and the need for the renewed ideological mobilization of the Russian people.

LET me only suggest that whatever Stalin's aberrations, his abnormal psychology, the Cold War, or something like it, from his point of view made perfectly rational good sense. That is to say the Cold War was . . . "system functional" for the Soviet regime. And I must say that my own view of the Soviet Union in world affairs in those initial post-war years is certainly not the one embodied in the official American view of Soviet policy under Stalin, namely that the Soviet Union was hell-bent on expansion, armed to the teeth, ready to begin the march to the Atlantic. Rather I think I tend to subscribe in this case, not to Karl Deutsch's but to Isaac Deutscher's view of the Soviet Union as really a relatively weak pole in the bipolar system: a system, a country, a regime which showed a fearsome face to the outside world but one which was, in the decisive view of its leaders, seriously weakened as a result of the war and potentially vulnerable in the postwar international political system.

In my reading of them, those kinds of policies and series of actions which so escalated the Cold War from the Soviet side, did not mark any innovation in the general tenor of Stalinist foreign policy. I accept Deutscher's view of Russia as a relatively weak (in its own perception), threatened power (in its leadership's perception—the only perception that counted—namely, Stalin's perception). . . . Furthermore, as I see it, Stalin himself had been pretty much disabused of revolution, or revolutionism, as a result of the disastrous failure in China in 1927. His objectives after that time right up until his death really were primarily, obviously, survival for the Soviet regime, which meant survival for Stalin's own regime. Second, and related, Stalin sought security for the Soviet Stalinist regime. Third, in his quest for security he inclined towards isolationism—not just isolation, but isolationism—as not only a goal but also as a framework, a psychology. The first manifestation of this we find in a kind of Soviet version of splendid—indeed heroic—isolationism during the period of collectivization and industrialization. It was an isolationism that could not be operated only because of aggressive German and Japanese policies. This was an isolationism which, however, could not in its earlier form, say from 1928 to 1934, be recaptured in the post-1945 bipolar world, in which, by virtue of the migration of power to the United States on the one side and the Soviet Union on the other, opting out of international politics was itself no longer a real option.

I think we must begin by looking at the way in which the postwar Soviet Union must have appeared to its ruler, to Stalin himself. He could not have failed

From "Origins of the Post-War Crisis—A Discussion," ***Journal of Contemporary History,*** **3 (April, 1968), pp. 233–237. Reprinted by permission of George Weidenfeld & Nicolson Ltd., London.**

to be aware of Russia's weakness and vulnerability. First of all there was the tremendous loss in population, variously estimated between fifteen and twenty million casualties. Then there was the precipitous decline of industrial production, so that, despite the relocation of industry to Siberia, to the Urals, at the end of the war industrial production was only 50 percent of what it had been in 1939. Moreover, as Stalin must have seen it, one-third of the Soviet post-war population was deemed to have been exposed to what were then called "harmful ideological influences," that is to say, the population of those Soviet territories that had been under German occupation, the population of areas that had been absorbed into the post-war Soviet state and had never been indoctrinated in Marxist-Leninist ideology, the *Ost-Arbeiter,* slave labourers, who had returned from Germany, and, last but not least, those troops who had seen a standard of living in the liberated and occupied areas of Europe to the west of Soviet Russia which was considerably higher than what they had grown up with and considerably at variance with what they had been given to expect.

Then we must also consider that, to meet the necessities of survival during the war, the entire apparatus of Soviet government had been considerably transformed in a number of ways. All the networks of party control had been modified in the interests of getting specific jobs done. Moreover, the party itself had suffered tremendous losses, in the rank and file and among the cadres. Here is one level at which quantification in history makes some sense. You find that on the eve of the war, in June 1941, there were 4.2 million party members; at the end of the war there were 5.8 million; but some 60 per cent of the 5.8 million were new wartime recruits. In fact, in the first months of the war—and this bears testimony to the active role of the party in the war effort—the losses in party lives between June 1941 and December 1941 were well over one million. One can also see that though by the end of the war the physical instruments of control were intact, the underlying ideological framework had been badly shaken; in a sense deliberately shaken, in the interests of rallying popular support and of cementing the wartime alliance with the West, precisely because the wartime alliance itself was necessary, or deemed to be necessary, for the survival of the Soviet state. During the war there occurred a profound down-playing of Marxism-Leninism, a dilution of ideology along many lines through the introduction of all sorts of patriotic themes, through the re-definition of bourgeois democracy as almost a special form of Soviet democracy (or vice versa), bourgeois democracy in this case meaning the American and British government and social systems. This kind of thing in turn led intellectuals to hope for a relaxation of the dictatorship after the war and also to think perhaps of the possibility of more fruitful, more purposive, and more continuing cooperation with the West; to envisage, in other words a downplay of ideological conflict, indeed the establishment of that something which to this very day is taboo in the Soviet Union, namely, ideological co-existence between the Soviet regime and western democratic regimes.

This is the sense in which it seems to me that ideology was enormously important for the origins of the Cold War. Because if one begins with a sense of a badly-shaken Soviet political system, and if one accepts, as I do, Stalin's consciousness of the need for and utility of absolute dictatorial political power, and if one also adds that Stalin, 66 years old at the end of the war, was bound to consider the struggle for the succession, it seems to me that one gets a series of domestic imperatives which led to the need for an objective enemy. All this was reinforced by Stalin's desire to re-establish the kind of political controls which he deemed necessary for the massive task of reconstruction. In turn, all these objectives, it seems to me, could have been accomplished only through a regeneration of ideology, through—more specifically—the objectification of an external enemy. If one thinks of the alternatives, if one thinks of the conceivable price, from Stalin's point of view, that the Soviet system would have had to pay, or would have run the risk of having to pay, for a continuation of the co-operation, intermittent though it may have been, which occurred during the war between the Soviet Union and the West, then I think one reaches the conclusion that such an alternative course was quite simply intolerable to Stalin. . . .

. . . But it also seems to me that the very ideological threat to the Soviet system implicit in American universalism—alas, not nearly strong enough to make it at that time a real threat—nonetheless did reinvigorate Stalin's drive for Soviet ideological purity, for it highlighted the need for ideological legitimacy for the Stalinist dictatorship at home and for the reimposition—and I would stress the word "reimposition"—of the Stalinist style of rule *inside* the Soviet Union—all in order to mobilize the Soviet population for the mammoth tasks of reconstruction, a reconstruction of those internal bases of international power which, once successfully completed, made the Soviet Union a truly dynamic global power, but really only in the era of "competitive coexistence" ushered in by Khrushchev some time after Stalin's death.

These observations leave open the question of whether the Cold War at its most intense and rigid was really inevitable or not. The answer to that question depends on one's philosophy of history, I suppose. All I want to suggest is that a continuation of those tentative lines of co-operation between Russia and the West which had developed during the war was, for a variety of quite understandable domestic Soviet considerations, quite unacceptable to Stalin. Given his point of view, which I regard *not* as the assessment of a madman but rather as the perception of a rather shrewd power-attuned leader, conscious of his own objectives and all too aware of those domestic Soviet realities that seemed to call their attainment into question—something like the Cold War as it actually occurred would have been the likely outcome irrespective of western policies. Perhaps Stalin himself would have preferred non-involvement in world affairs altogether. But isolationism was no longer a genuine alternative for a Soviet Union which, despite all its manifold post-war weaknesses, still was one of the two major power centres in a bipolar international system. This being the case, further scholarly progress towards excavating the roots of the Cold War, can, it seems to me, come by concentrating more closely than has heretofore been the case upon the domestic foundations of Soviet foreign policy. Once again, in this case as in so many others, a critical reexamination of the sins of commission and omission of the diplomacy of one side or the other may be necessary, but it can never be sufficient. In the case of the Cold War, it is high time to assert the primacy not of *Aussenpolitik* but rather of *Innenpolitik*.

Adam B. Ulam

REVISIONISM AND THE FUTILITY OF THE QUESTION

In 1968 Adam Ulam published his lengthy and thoughtful *Expansion and Coexistence: The History of Soviet Foreign Policy, 1917–67*. He depicted a weak and cautious postwar Russia with no blueprint for expansion, and a realistic Stalin who would not risk a military clash with the stronger United States. Ulam also argued that the atomic bomb did not cause "either panic or undue apprehension" in the Kremlin, and hence that American monopoly of the nuclear weapon until 1949 was not central to the developing Cold War. In the following review of revisionism and the Alperovitz thesis, Ulam vigorously chides revisionists for distorting history. Although Ulam suggested in his book that postwar disunity was inevitable and that the conflict stemmed largely from the demands of Soviet totalitarianism, he here urges scholars to reach beyond the question of responsibility to study alternative policies and attitudes which might have at least reduced international tension. Indeed, much recent scholarship has investigated alternatives, as the essays by Neal, Barnet, and Paterson indicate. Ulam has been on the faculty of Harvard University since 1946, and is also the author of *Titoism and the Cominform* (1952).

THERE is no better way of summarizing the main preoccupation of American writing and thinking on international affairs since World War II than by recalling the titles of two celebrated Russian novels of the 19th century: *Who Is Guilty*? and *What Is To Be Done*? To be sure, the books' authors, Herzen and Chernyshevsky, both belonged to the radical camp, while in the United States the preoccupations epitomized by the two titles have been shared by writers of different ideological coloration and political aims. But the fact remains that, confronted by the puzzling and depressing phenomenon of the Cold War, historians, men of affairs, and finally, to a smaller or larger extent, all of us have sought to assess the responsibility for and the means of getting out of the dangerous predicament in which the republic and the world have found themselves for the past quarter century.

But the universality of this concern and the understandable emotions it arouses does not excuse the historian from his special responsibility, which is, to use the current jargon, "telling it like it is"—or rather, was. Before he becomes a philosopher of history or a judge, he must tell us what actually happened. His primary duty is not to be attuned to the currently fashionable trends in public thinking or to be a counselor to statesmen. It is to ascertain what, in terms of our knowledge, is a fact, what could be a reasonable hypothesis, and what must remain a conjecture. If he does not meet that test, he is a moralist or a publicist but not an historian.

Now, all this might appear a platitude, and a pedantic one at that. But it must be said before we proceed to consider the by now considerable literature concerning the origins of the Cold War. Much of this literature reflects what has come to be known as the revisionist point of view. This view challenges the main thesis underlying American policies since World War II: that the responsibility for

From Adam Ulam, "On Modern History: Re-reading the Cold War," *Interplay Magazine*, 2 (March, 1968), pp. 51–53. Reprinted by permission of *Interplay Magazine*, © March, 1968.

the drastic deterioration in US-Soviet relations since 1945 must be attributed wholly or mainly to the actions and designs of the rulers of the Soviet Union. On the contrary, some, almost all of the blame, say the revisionists, depending on the given author, can be traced to actions and intentions of American policy-makers.

Let us for the moment leave apart the wider question of whether the whole inquiry is meaningful or profitable. But do the arguments adduced by the revisionists make sense in their own terms? Mr. Schlesinger, who once impatiently brushed off the whole school, has since come to believe that historical revisionism in general "is an essential part of the process by which history . . . enlarges its perspectives and enriches its insights." Hence one should not deplore the rise of Cold War revisionism. Well, let us see. Dr. Alperovitz's *Atomic Diplomacy, Hiroshima and Potsdam* (New York, 1965) is the most concentrated dose of the revisionist argument. Its thesis is simple: the first atomic bomb was dropped not because of any military necessity but in order to *impress the Russians.* Subsequently, US policymakers used their monopoly of the atom bomb as a bargaining weapon in order to wrest from the Russians their sphere of influence in Eastern Europe. Since that sphere had been conceded by Roosevelt, Truman's policy represented a significant reversal of American foreign policy. Confronted with this breach by the United States of the solemn pledges he had secured, Stalin naturally withdrew into a policy of isolation, suspicion and hostility toward the West. Hence the Cold War.

Now some reviewers have criticized Alperovitz's book by questioning his assertion that Truman reversed Roosevelt's policy vis-à-vis Russia, by expostulating that it is impossible to talk about the Cold War without taking into account Stalin's personality, etc. Justified as these complaints are, they miss the central point. The book stands or falls with the thesis that there was in fact "atomic diplomacy," *i.e.*, that in bargaining with the USSR over Eastern Europe or any other area, the United States used its possession of the bomb as a threat or a bargaining counter. Hence one would expect Alperovitz to adduce at least a single instance of an American negotiator saying in effect to a Russian during the period in question (1945–46), "You ought to remember we have the bomb," or "If you go easy on the Poles we might share our nuclear know-how with you." Or he might offer a *public* statement by an American official that "the Russians ought to keep in mind before they go too far in Rumania that we have this weapon." Dr. Alperovitz does not cite any such instances because there weren't any. . . .

Dr. Alperovitz quotes what various US officials committed to their diaries or what they said to each other concerning the US diplomatic position being strengthened by its possession of the atomic bomb. But what does that prove? If one Soviet official said to another in 1945, "We have larger land forces in Europe than the West has," is this a *prima facie* case for maintaining that the Soviets were blackmailing the British and Americans?

But if no case at all can be made for the existence of "atomic diplomacy" in 1945 or for many years afterwards, can one rescue something from the revisionist argument by adopting Dr. Alperovitz's secondary complaint, *i.e.*, that no *positive* policy was being pursued to dissipate Soviet fears and suspicions? Why did the US quibble over the character of governments the USSR was establishing in its sphere of interests in Eastern Europe? Why, especially, did not the US offer to share its nuclear technology with the USSR, as indeed was suggested at one time by Secretary Stimson? Here the argument must hinge on circumstantial evidence concerning the Russians' (*i.e.*, Stalin's) probable reaction to the US possession of the bomb, and to the United States' quibbling over the extent of Russian influence in Eastern Europe. And as such, it fares no better than the one about the US having practiced atomic diplomacy in 1945. . . .

Would an American offer of sharing the alleged atomic secrets have made the

Russians less suspicious, more tractable, more humane in their policies in Eastern Europe and elsewhere? This is implicit in all the revisionists' writings, since it is not a part of their argument that Soviet policies in Eastern Europe were *entirely* blameless, or that the governments there represented *exactly* the popular will. Soviet repressions and exactions are held as an understandable over-reaction to American atomic blackmail. But as we have seen, Dr. Alperovitz has just argued that had Stalin not been afraid of the atom bomb he would have asked for more rather than less. . . .

Could Stalin's fears have been appeased by a firm agreement on spheres of influence throughout the world between the two superpowers? As I tried to point out in my recent book, if carefully qualified, this argument possesses some validity. But in its extreme form it has its own unreality. With the war over, it was simply impossible for public opinion in the West to remain indifferent to tales of repression, violence and destruction which were pouring in from the East. Had democratic countries been able to practice such cold-blooded realism in foreign policy, it can be argued that there would have been no reason for World War II. What was Hitler doing in Poland and the Japanese in China but carving out their spheres of influence? In the vastly different world of 1968 the Soviet effort to discipline Czechoslovakia —and that by means infinitely more humane than those employed by Stalin in Eastern Europe between 1945–48—still sent a shock through the world.

Could "tougher" policies have worked? Surely—had America been ruled by a dictator or an oligarchy, there was little that this country could not have gotten by threats and pressure. "American omnipotence" was for the period 1945–1950 not a myth but very close to being a reality. The main factor here was not the wretched bomb, but the fantastic record of American industry and production during the war; and secondly, the vast American manpower—in comparison with every other belligerent barely tapped. As against it, Russia's economy was in ruins and Stalin faced his own people with their expectations, which were to be cruelly disappointed, that their sacrifices had won them the right for a better and freer life than they had had before the war. But the real America of 1945 could no more embark upon a pushful foreign policy than Stalin could have instituted a two-party democracy. In fact, for anybody with even a superficial knowledge of the period, it is evident that the main concern of the American policy-makers was not to deny Russia the fruits of victory nor to destroy the Russian Revolution, as the revisionists tell us in their tirades, but to prevent the American people from lapsing back into isolationism when confronted with the sinful and complex postwar world.

Within the limits circumscribed by the character of both societies, there was still a great deal that skillful, well-informed and alert diplomacy could have accomplished. On the Polish issue, a key one in inter-allied diplomacy between 1943–45, the Western leaders and their diplomatic advisers were abysmally ignorant. They simply could not keep up with Stalin, who was excellently informed and who could take the most outrageous liberties with facts without any of his interlocutors catching on. Thus a careful study of the Teheran Conference will bear out the conclusion that on Poland the Soviets were offered more than they had expected. Soviet diplomacy was alert and tenacious. It perceived and exploited the West's fears and foibles. At Teheran Stalin played masterfully on Churchill's embarrassment over the delay on the second front, and his obvious apprehension that the invasion of the Continent might bring casualties on the scale of those of World War I. At Yalta the Russians diagnosed carefully the exaggerated importance attached by the Americans to the framework of the United Nations. The Russians would raise objections concerning membership, procedures, etc., and then drop them in a manner that would earn American gratitude and the feeling that it would be too embarrassing now to quibble over Poland or the German reparations.

Soviet diplomacy was not superhuman nor were the Russians rigid in their thinking, with a blueprint worked out for every contingency. On the German issue, it is obvious, the Soviets in 1945 were not clear in their own mind what they wanted, what kind of Germany would eventually serve their interests best. But American diplomacy was operating by fits and starts. People were already asking questions unanswerable because of their vastness and impracticality. Was Soviet Russia out to conquer the world or was Stalin going to abide faithfully by the charter and spirit of the United Nations? That there were a great number of possibilities and opportunities between those majestic and fatuous alternatives was but dimly perceived.

An American philosophy of international relations was thus launched on that course of grandiose rhetoric that in due time was to produce the would-be magic solutions and incantations: "massive retaliation," preparation for "brushfire wars" and eventually the "we were guilty" chant of the revisionists. While looking for a sign in heaven indicating who was right or for a magic formula to solve *all* problems, we have overlooked those occasions where tenacious, well-informed diplomacy could have made a difference, and where hard bargaining rather than posturing might have brought partial solutions and lowered the international tension. It is in illuminating those occasions—such as the German question in 1947 and 1952, or the opportunities presented for American diplomacy by the already irrefutable evidence of the Sino-Soviet conflict in the late '50s—that the historian can be of help to the men of affairs and to public opinion, rather than by pondering the unanswerable and futile question: who started it all?

Thus one cannot endorse a tolerant view of "cold war revisionism" which sees in it but a necessary part of a dialogue that will lead to a deeper historical truth. As history this revisionism is fallacious. As polemic it is an attempt to exploit the currently fashionable mood of guilt, which is as harmful as a guide to reflection and action as is national arrogance and moral self-righteousness.

Walter LaFeber

THE IMPACT OF REVISIONISM

In assessing and explaining the work of the revisionists, LaFeber takes issue with Adam Ulam's interpretation. LaFeber does not find a distortion of history in revisionist writing, but rather new evidence and insight lacking in the traditional studies, or what he calls "Liberal" histories. He also points out the importance of experience and environment in the scholarship of all historians, and suggests that scholars will indeed move beyond revisionism as issues change in the 1970's.

CARL Becker once observed that a professor is a man who thinks otherwise. One might add that a professor is often a person who professes and that a history professor is one who professes history, at least most of the time.

These are essential traits of a group which is becoming known for advocating a new revision of post-1945 American diplomatic history. The new revisionists think otherwise because they have not accepted the American government's explanation of how and why the Cold War developed.

They have, moreover, revised and challenged the work of those most influential historians, who might best be identified as the Liberals, who have essentially followed the government's explanations in writing their own histories of the Cold War. Often identified also as "New Left," these revisionists have such widely-varying relationships to that term that they are perhaps better studied through their view of history rather than their call to politics.

The historians who might be considered such revisionists include Gar Alperovitz, Richard J. Barnet, Barton Bernstein, Denna Frank Fleming, Lloyd C. Gardner, David Horowitz, Gabriel Kolko, Thomas J. McCormick, Marcus Raskin, William Appleman Williams, and, although he is not a professional historian, Carl Oglesby. Highly influential because of his brilliant analysis of the 1917–1920 period, Arno Mayer should also be included on this list. Others have mined similar historical veins, but these names are sufficient for present purposes.

There are also some who are perhaps better known, who have influenced the men listed above, and who have become recognized particularly for their dissent from the government's Cold War strategies. These include Frederick L. Schuman, Walter Lippmann, Hans Morgenthau, Fred Warner Neal, O. Edmund Clubb, James P. Warburg, and to an interesting if limited extent, the more recent George F. Kennan. . . .

After World War II, revisionists have believed that the fundamental error was a gross miscalculation of Communism and Russian Communist intentions. They argue that in the 1944–1946 years, Stalin had considerably more flexibility and posed a less aggressive threat to the West than the Liberals have been willing to admit.

The revisionists of course will have nothing to do with those who argue that Communism as an ideological monolith continues to be the enemy, that Chinese or North Vietnamese Communism has picked up where Stalinism and North Korean Communism left off. But between these two groups (the revisionists on the one hand and the current Vietnam Cold Warriors on the other), there is a middle group with which the revisionists disagree also.

These historians in the middle [the Liberals] have argued that Communism as an ideology cannot be dismissed as a

From Walter LaFeber, "War: Cold," ***Cornell Alumni News,*** **71 (October, 1968), pp. 24–26, 28–29. Reprinted by permission.**

threat to American interests, and this group has often focused particularly upon the threat posed by the far left within American society. Flourishing in the late 1940s with Reinhold Niebuhr as its intellectual godfather and Arthur Schlesinger Jr.'s *The Vital Center* as its call to action, the emphasis upon the role of Communist ideology, particularly as that ideology acted as a primary cause of the split between East and West in 1945, recently reappeared in Mr. Schlesinger's influential article on the causes of the Cold War in the October 1967 issue of *Foreign Affairs*.

Rebuttals to Schlesinger's argument came from Alperovitz, Williams, and Gardner, and each of them placed considerably less importance on Marxist-Leninist ideology. Revisionists tend instead to see traditional Russian national interest as determinative in Soviet foreign policy. To accomplish this, they must argue more historically than the Liberals, for they have to go back beyond 1945 and even beyond 1917 to make their point stick. . . .

Recently the focus of this debate has been on the events of 1945, in part because of Alperovitz's detailed analysis of America's "atomic diplomacy" during the middle part of that year, and partly because Arthur Schlesinger Jr. has made the events of Yalta through Potsdam the pivot of his argument in the *Foreign Affairs article*. On perhaps the critical question of this discussion, Louis Halle recently argued the Liberal position in his book, *The Cold War as History:* "The initiative in the Cold War had, from the beginning, been with Moscow."

Halle observed that American policymakers did not realize as early as they should have that Western and Central Europe formed a near-vacuum inviting the vast Red Army, and Washington officials compounded that error by too rapidly dismantling the American military establishment (a point, incidentally, which Horowitz vigorously disputes, for he believes the Western nations dismantled their armies more slowly than did the Soviets during the 1945–1948 period).

The monopoly of the atomic bomb, Halle continues, meant little, for in the immediate postwar period it was a paper tiger in the sense that it could not be used to correct the balance of power unless the Soviets actually invaded Western Europe.

Horowitz has most directly rejected Halle's thesis: "For the point which I have tried to establish beyond all others, and which has been virtually ignored in previous cold war studies, is that the early post-war power situation was such as to give the United States a near monopoly on the *strategic* decisions which would affect the basic structure of international relations in the post-war period. Conversely, the Kremlin rulers, *whatever their long-range intentions,* were bound by the same imbalance of power to make moves of primarily tactical significance."

In explaining more fully Stalin's responses, revisionists accept an argument first made by Isaac Deutscher. In Oglesby's words: "Stalin's record in the early Cold War is less that of a fairy-tale monster on the prowl . . . than that of a small, cold, very practical nationalist in a tight, dangerous situation. Stalin accepted the Cold War. He seems to have had little choice. . . . But that does not prove that he *created* it. The terms of that eerie battle were mainly set by the power that held the initiative and commanded the heights, and those powers were England in the rear and the United States far out in front."

Oglesby summarizes why the United States was in the vanguard: "The uniformly powerful West wanted—and believed . . . that it had to obtain—a guarantee against the spread of revolution and . . . a guarantee of economic and political access to all of Europe. The unevenly powerful Soviet Union wanted development capital without strings, heavy German machinery, and some reprieve from militant Wagnerism."

Oglesby's words summarize several revisionist assumptions about the origins of the Cold War: the United States was determined to enter a sphere of interest (Eastern Europe) which was Russia's by reason of both historical factors and military occupation; the United States attempted to use its overwhelming power to force Russia's hand in Eastern Europe, thus putting Stalin in a defensive position; and, finally, that in making such an assessment of the situation Stalin was sane and knowledgeable. (One revisionist has suggested that if Liberal historians continue to psychoanalyze Stalin, equal time should be given to Harry Truman, particularly his early insecurity in the White House, his intense jealousy of his presidential powers, and his long-time dislike for the Soviet Union.) . . .

A faith in history is perhaps the most important and far-reaching of the revisionist views. In one of the most significant articles on American historical writing, Warren Susman commented in a 1964 issue of *American Quarterly* that "in that great era of historical awareness beginning roughly in the 1890s, American intellectuals *did* care. They cared because they realized the vital ideological importance in a society like ours of history and the 'proper' attitudes toward it. They cared because they realized that views held about the past generally had consequences for the present. . . . It was precisely because in our kind of social order history becomes a key to ideology, a key to the world view that shapes programs and actions in the present and future."

This view remained until about 1940, Susman observed, when "a singularly anti-historical spirit" appeared "among the leading figures of our intellectual life. . . . Many of our newer literary vogues—some of them brilliantly evocative of major moral dilemmas of our time to be sure—are deliberately wedded to the present moment alone." In this vein Susman mentioned the works of Nevins and Schlesinger Jr., noting Schlesinger's words that "history is a constant tragedy in which we are all involved, whose keynote is anxiety and frustration, not progress and fulfillment."

Susman commented that in such history written recently "we look in vain for a vision of the past which will enable us to remake the present and the future. Here ideology is specifically rejected. Here we find a history which offers a reinforcement of current moral values and no effective challenge to the decision makers within the social order who do most frequently operate in terms of some view of history, some ideology."

The revisionists are posing fundamental objections to the past quarter-century of American diplomacy, but more generally they are challenging the predominant tendencies of a historiography and the way this historiography has been used to buttress policy. American diplomatic historians have been reluctant to acknowledge the inter-relationship over a long period of time between their history and national policy. When debates on the subject did begin, they too often terminated with the Liberals invoking "scientific" history, and "scientific" research.

It is past time, the revisionists believe, for the admission that for American historians history begins and ends with ideology. Between is the honest and systematic research which both revisionist and Liberal historians can do, should do, and have done. The issue of "scientific" history is no longer interesting. It is simply irrelevant. The problem is not whether the research will be as thorough as possible (that should be assumed), but the questions which the historian will ask when he undertakes his research.

For the foreseeable future it now seems very likely that throughout the American diplomatic history profession such questions will be increasingly revisionist and radical in tone, and will construct a picture of American history that will move so far away from the Liberals that the present revisionists will be revised. One push in this direction is the horror of the Vietnam War and the realization that revisionist history, rather than Liberal history, better explains—and even forecasts—such a tragedy.

Another push is the growing realization that the war, racism, domestic violence, and sundry economic ills pose a fundamental challenge to the whole system, and that revisionists have constructed the best matrix within which to study that challenge in its entirety.

A third push is the number of diplomatic historians who will receive their

PhDs in the 1970s, having matured in a period when the Tragic Sixties, the New Left movements, and the early fundamental works of revisionists will be accepted as fact and as a logical result rather than as the result of a great aberration.

And finally, this historiography will move into and beyond revisionism as present middle-of-the-roaders accept revisionism in many of its parts, thus allowing the present revisionists (who will believe that they have made their points) to become more revisionist in their view of history; this might result both as a reaction to the Liberals' move toward revisionism and the impetus caused by new, young scholars. There seems considerably less likelihood now that there will be a swing against revisionism, as occurred after the revisionists of World War I made their appearance.

Whatever the outcome of the present turmoil among American diplomatic historians, two results are already apparent. First, whether the revisionists are proven wrong, right, or somewhere in-between, the profession has been stirred and the resulting debate is enlivening and broadening the writing of diplomatic history in a manner unmatched since such men as Samuel Flagg Bemis, Thomas A. Bailey, and Julius Pratt built the foundation-stones of the profession—and touched off magnificent controversies of their own. And second, whatever else the revisionists accomplish, perhaps their greatest contribution will be a reaffirmation of the faith that the study of history is the necessary means through which the promise of the past can be transformed into fulfillment. Even if, at times, this requires thinking otherwise.

SUGGESTIONS FOR ADDITIONAL READING

Any investigation of the origins of the Cold War must ground itself in pre-1945 relations between the United States and Russia. William A. Williams, *American-Russian Relations, 1781–1947* (New York, 1952), Thomas A. Bailey, *America Faces Russia* (Ithaca, 1950), Desmond Donnelly, *Struggle for the World: The Cold War, 1917–1965* (New York, 1965), and B. Ponomaryov *et al.*, eds., *History of Soviet Foreign Policy, 1917–1945* (Moscow, 1969) provide varying points of view. For the American response to the Bolshevik Revolution of 1917, see the representative collection of studies and the bibliography in Betty Miller Unterberger, ed., *American Intervention in the Russian Civil War* (Lexington, Mass., 1969). Peter G. Filene, *Americans and the Soviet Experiment, 1917–1933* (Cambridge, Mass., 1967) discusses the ambivalent reaction to Soviet Russia. Robert Browder, *The Origins of Soviet-American Diplomacy* (Princeton, 1953) and Edward M. Bennett, *Recognition of Russia: An American Foreign Policy Dilemma* (Waltham, Mass., 1970) study the hopes and anxieties of recognition in 1933 and the aftermath.

Indispensable for World War II diplomacy are Herbert Feis, *Churchill, Roosevelt, Stalin: The War They Waged and the Peace They Sought* (Princeton, 1957), and *Between War and Peace: The Potsdam Conference* (Princeton, 1960), Gabriel Kolko, *The Politics of War: The World and United States Foreign Policy, 1943–1945* (New York, 1968), and William H. McNeill, *America, Britain, and Russia: Their Cooperation and Conflict, 1941–1946* (London, 1953). Also useful are Robert A. Divine, ed., *Causes and Consequences of World War II* (Chicago, 1969), *Roosevelt and World War II* (Baltimore, 1969), and *Second Chance: The Triumph of Internationalism in America During World War II* (New York, 1967), John L. Snell, *Illusion and Necessity: The Diplomacy of Global War, 1939–1945* (Boston, 1963), and Gaddis Smith, *American Diplomacy During the Second World War, 1941–1945* (New York, 1965).

The literature on the origins of the Cold War and American relations with Russia after 1945 is extensive, and for a more complete bibliography, one should consult Walter LaFeber's *America, Russia, and the Cold War* (New York, 1967), Thomas T. Hammond, ed., *Soviet Foreign Relations and World Communism*, Henry L. Roberts, ed., *Foreign Affairs Bibliography* (New York, 1955), and issues of *Foreign Affairs* (published by the Council on Foreign Relations). The works mentioned above in the headnotes and below contain bibliographies on their special topics.

General traditional studies include John Spanier, *American Foreign Policy Since World War II* (New York, 1965), Seyom Brown, *The Faces of Power* (New York, 1968), Wilfrid Knapp, *A History of War and Peace, 1939–1965* (London, 1967), Dexter Perkins, *The Diplomacy of a New Age* (Bloomington, 1967), G. F. Hudson, *The Hard and Bitter Peace* (New York, 1967), George F. Kennan, *Russia and the West Under Lenin and Stalin* (Boston, 1969), Paul Y. Hammond, *The Cold War Years* (New York, 1969), and Herbert Druks, *Harry S Truman and the Russians, 1945–1953* (New York, 1966).

General works which can be considered "revisionist" include Dana F. Fleming, *The Cold War and Its Origins* (Garden City, 1961; 2 vols.), David Horowitz, *The Free World Colossus* (New York, 1965) and ed., *Containment and Revolution* (Boston, 1967), Kenneth Ingram, *History of the Cold War* (New York, 1955), Frederick L. Schuman, *The Cold War: Retrospect and Prospect* (Baton Rouge, 1967), N. D. Houghton, ed., *Struggle Against History* (New York, 1968), Thomas G. Paterson, ed., *Cold War Critics: Alternatives to American Foreign Policy in the Truman Period* (Chicago, 1971), Lloyd C. Gardner, *Architects of Illusion: Men and Ideas in American Foreign Policy, 1941–1949*

(Chicago, 1970), Richard J. Barnet and Marcus G. Raskin, *After 20 Years: Alternatives to the Cold War in Europe* (New York, 1965), Carl Oglesby and Richard Shaull, *Containment and Change* (New York, 1967), William A. Williams, *The Tragedy of American Diplomacy* (New York, 1962), Joseph P. Morray, *From Yalta to Disarmament: Cold War Debate* (New York, 1961), and Rexford Tugwell, *A Chronicle of Jeopardy, 1945–1955* (Chicago, 1955).

Other general books include William G. Carleton, *The Revolution in American Foreign Policy* (New York, 1967), Charles L. Robertson, *International Politics Since World War II* (New York, 1966), John Lukacs, *A New History of the Cold War* (Garden City, 1966), Paul Seabury, *The Rise and Fall of the Cold War* (New York, 1967), Andre Fontaine, *History of the Cold War: From the October Revolution to the Korean War, 1917–1950* (New York, 1968), H. Bradford Westerfield, *Foreign Policy and Party Politics: Pearl Harbor to Korea* (New Haven, 1955), William L. Neumann, *After Victory* (New York, 1967), Robert E. Osgood, *et al.*, *America and the World: From the Truman Doctrine to Vietnam* (Baltimore, 1970), Edmund Stillman and William Pfaff, *The New Politics: America and the End of the Postwar World* (New York, 1961), Marshall D. Shulman, *Stalin's Foreign Policy Reappraised* (Cambridge, Mass., 1963), Robert D. Warth, *Soviet Russia in World Politics* (New York, 1963), and J. M. Mackintosh, *Strategy and Tactics of Soviet Foreign Policy* (London, 1962). Especially useful for information and chronology are John C. Campbell, *The United States in World Affairs, 1945–1947* (New York, 1947), and succeeding volumes.

For interpretive essays of some of this general literature and of the origins of the Cold War, see Norman A. Graebner, "Cold War Origins and the Contemporary Debate: A Review of Recent Literature," *Journal of Conflict Resolution*, XIII (March, 1969), 123–132; H. Stuart Hughes, "The Second Year of the Cold War: A Memoir and an Anticipation," *Commentary*, XLVIII (August, 1969), 27–32; Christopher Lasch, "The Cold War: Revisited and Re-Visioned," *New York Times Magazine*, January 14, 1968, pp. 26 ff.; Staughton Lynd, "How the Cold War Began," *Commentary*, XXX (November, 1960), 379–389; and John L. Snell, "The Cold War: Four Contemporary Appraisals," *American Historical Review*, LXVIII (October, 1962), 69–75.

Herbert Feis, *The Atomic Bomb and the End of World War II* (Princeton, 1966), disagrees with Alperovitz and argues that the bomb was used simply to end the war quickly in order to save lives. P. M. S. Blackett gives an earlier suggestive account paralleling Alperovitz in *Fear, War, and the Bomb* (New York, 1948). Henry L. Stimson explains his reasons for questioning the American diplomatic use of the bomb in Stimson and McGeorge Bundy, *On Active Service in Peace and War* (New York, 1948). The place of the scientists in the debate is treated in Alice K. Smith, *A Peril and a Hope: The Scientists' Movement in America, 1945–1947* (Chicago, 1965). Subsequent negotiations on atomic disarmament can be followed in Berhard G. Bechhoefer, *Postwar Negotiations for Arms Control* (Washington, 1961), John W. Spanier and Joseph L. Nogee, *The Politics of Disarmament* (New York, 1962), and David E. Lilienthal, Vol. III of *Journals: Atomic Energy Years, 1945–1950* (New York, 1964). Two volumes of the official history of the Atomic Energy Commission have been published thus far by The Pennsylvania State University Press, titled *The New World* (1962) and *Atomic Shield* (1969).

There are few comprehensive studies of postwar American economic foreign policy. For background, see Lloyd C. Gardner, *Economic Aspects of New Deal Diplomacy* (Madison, 1964). Useful for loan, aid and trade policy are Richard Gardner, *Sterling-Dollar Diplomacy*, rev. ed. (London, 1969), David A. Baldwin, *Economic Development and American Foreign Policy, 1943–62* (Chicago, 1966), which concentrates on the Third World, Raymond F. Mikesell, *U.S. Private and Government Investment Abroad* (Corvallis, 1962), George Lenczowski, *Oil and State in the Middle East* (Ithaca,

1960), Leonard M. Fanning, *American Oil Operations Abroad* (New York, 1947), C. Addison Hickman, *Our Farm Program and Foreign Trade* (New York, 1949), William A. Brown, Jr., *The United States and the Restoration of World Trade* (Washington, 1950), and William A. Brown, Jr. and Redvers Opie, *American Foreign Assistance* (Washington, 1953). Helpful for data are the Department of the Treasury, *Census of American-Owned Assets in Foreign Countries* (Washington, 1947) and Department of Commerce, *Foreign Aid, 1940–1951* (Washington, 1952). An important article is Herbert Feis, "The Conflict over Trade Ideologies," *Foreign Affairs,* 25 (October, 1946), 217–228. The question of relief is discussed in George Woodbridge *et al., UNRRA* (New York, 1950; 3 vols.). The Marshall Plan is given standard treatment in Harry Price, *The Marshall Plan and Its Meaning* (Ithaca, 1955) and a revisionist interpretation in Warren L. Hickman, *Genesis of the European Recovery Program* (Geneva, 1949). David Wightman, *Economic Co-operation in Europe* (New York, 1956) studies the ECE. Paterson is completing a general study of economic foreign policy, 1940's–1950's.

Issues over and in Eastern Europe are specifically discussed in Martin Herz, *Beginnings of the Cold War* (Bloomington, 1966), which studies the period from Yalta to Potsdam and emphasizes Poland, Hugh Seton-Watson, *The East European Revolution* (New York, 1956), Stephen Kertesz, ed., *The Fate of East Central Europe* (Notre Dame, 1956), R. R. Betts, ed., *Central and South East Europe, 1945–1948* (London, 1950), Margaret Dewar, *Soviet Trade with Eastern Europe, 1945–49* (London, 1951), Paul E. Zinner, *Communist Strategy and Tactics in Czechoslovakia, 1918–1948* (New York, 1963), Joseph Korbel, *The Communist Subversion of Czechoslovakia, 1938–1948* (Princeton, 1959), James P. Warburg, *Last Call for Common Sense* (New York, 1949), William Diamond, *Czechoslovakia Between East and West* (London, 1947), Andrew Gyorgy, *Governments of Danubian Europe* (New York, 1949), and Ygael Gluckstein, *Stalin's Satellites in Europe* (Boston, 1952). Important memoirs include Ambassador to Poland Arthur Bliss Lane, *I Saw Poland Betrayed* (Indianapolis, 1948), Polish leader Stanislaw Mikolajczyk, *The Rape of Poland: Pattern of Soviet Aggression* (New York, 1948), and Czech Foreign Trade Minister Hubert Ripka, *Czechoslovakia Enslaved* (London, 1950).

The international squabble over Germany is treated by John Gimbel, *The American Occupation of Germany* (Stanford, 1968), Harold Zink, *United States in Germany* (New York, 1957), Manuel Gottlieb, *The German Peace Settlement and the Berlin Crisis* (New York, 1960), James P. Warburg, *Germany—Bridge or Battleground* (New York, 1947), and *Germany: Key to Peace* (Cambridge, Mass., 1953), Eugene Davidson, *The Death and Life of Germany: An Account of the American Occupation* (New York, 1959), Michael Balfour and John Mair, *Four Power Control in Germany and Austria 1945–1946* (London, 1956), Philip E. Mosely, *The Kremlin and World Politics* (New York, 1960), Alfred Grosser, *The Collossus Again: Western Germany From Defeat to Rearmament* (New York, 1955), and J. P. Nettl, *The Eastern Zone and Soviet Policy in Germany, 1945–50* (London, 1951). Two essays in Harold Stein, ed., *American Civil-Military Decisions: A Book of Case Studies* (Birmingham, Ala., 1963) are important: Paul Y. Hammond, "Directives for the Occupation of Germany: The Washington Controversy," pp. 311–460 and Laurence W. Martin, "The American Decision to Rearm Germany," pp. 643–663. See also William M. Franklin, "Zonal Boundaries and Access to Berlin," *World Politics,* XVI (October, 1963), 1–31, and Walter L. Dorn, "The Debate over American Occupation in Germany in 1944–1945," *Political Science Quarterly,* LXXII (December, 1957), 481–501. French policy is discussed in A. W. Porte, *De Gaulle's Foreign Policy, 1944–1946* (Cambridge, Mass., 1968). Henry Morgenthau, Jr., explains the so-called Morgenthau Plan in *Germany Is Our Problem* (New York, 1945), and in John Blum, *From the Mor-*

genthau Diaries: Years of War, 1941–1945 (Boston, 1967; Vol. III of 3 vols.). Provocative memoirs by people associated with American policy include Lewis H. Brown, *A Report on Germany* (New York, 1947), Gustav Stolper, *German Realities* (New York, 1948), James S. Martin, *All Honorable Men* (Boston, 1950), and Military Governor Lucius Clay, *Decision in Germany* (Garden City, 1950). See also United States Department of State, *Germany, 1947–1949: The Story in Documents* (Washington, 1950).

For events leading to and from the Truman Doctrine, see, besides Jones and Barnet, Stephen G. Xydis, *Greece and the Great Powers, 1944–1947* (Thessaloniki, 1963), Edgar O'Ballance, *The Greek Civil War* (New York, 1966), Theodore A. Couloumbis, *Greek Political Reaction to American and NATO Influences* (New Haven, 1966), Stephen Rousseas, *The Death of a Democracy: Greece and the American Conscience* (New York, 1967), and Leften Stavros Stavrianos, *Greece: American Dilemma and Opportunity* (Chicago, 1952). The problems of British policy are discussed in Michael R. Gordon, *Conflict and Consensus in Labour's Foreign Policy, 1914–1965* (Stanford, 1969), F. S. Northedge, *British Foreign Policy: The Process of Readjustment, 1945–1961* (New York, 1962), and M. A. Fitzsimons, *The Foreign Policy of the British Labour Government: 1945–1951* (Notre Dame, 1953).

For the Far East in the early Cold War, see John K. Fairbank, *The United States and China* (Cambridge, Mass., 1958), Tang Tsou, *America's Failure in China, 1941–1950* (Chicago, 1963), Herbert Feis, *The China Tangle* (Princeton, 1953) and *Contest Over Japan* (New York, 1967), George Kahin and John W. Lewis, *The United States in Vietnam* (New York, 1967), Joseph Buttinger, *Vietnam: A Political History* (New York, 1968), and William L. Neumann, *America Encounters Japan* (Baltimore, 1963).

Other topics of the early Cold War period have received historical interpretation. For competition in the Middle East and Iran, consult George Kirk, *The Middle East, 1945–1950* (London, 1954) and George Lenczowski, *Russia and the West in Iran, 1918–1948: A Study in Big Power Rivalry* (Ithaca, 1949). General studies of relations with Latin America include Donald Dozer, *Are We Good Neighbors?* (Gainesville, 1959) and J. Lloyd Mechan, *A Survey of United States–Latin American Relations* (New York, 1965). For the peace movement in the United States, see Lawrence S. Wittner, *Rebels Against War: The American Peace Movement,* 1941–1960 (New York, 1969). Useful is Robert E. Asher, *et al., The United Nations and Economic and Social Co-operation* (Washington, 1957).

Some of the leading characters of the early Cold War period can be studied through their own accounts, collected speeches, or secondary works. Truman has written *Memoirs* (Garden City, 1955–56; 2 vols.). The *Public Papers of the Presidents, Truman* (Washington, 1961–66; 8 vols.) contain his formal statements as well as transcripts of press conferences. Fruitful, but fragmentary, readings are Cabell Phillips, *The Truman Presidency: The History of a Triumphant Succession* (New York, 1966), Richard E. Neustadt, *Presidential Power: The Politics of Leadership* (New York, 1960), and Jonathan Daniels, *The Man of Independence* (Philadelphia, 1950). Secretary of State James F. Byrnes has written *Speaking Frankly* (New York, 1947) and Dean Acheson has added *Present at the Creation: My Years in the State Department* (New York, 1969) to his many publications. All of the Cold War Secretaries of State are discussed in Norman A. Graebner, ed., *An Uncertain Tradition* (New York, 1961). Winston S. Churchill reveals himself carefully in *Triumph and Tragedy* (Boston, 1953). Other leading foreign policy figures include George F. Kennan, *Memoirs, 1925–1950* (Boston, 1967), John Foster Dulles, *War or Peace* (New York, 1950), William D. Leahy, *I Was There* (New York, 1950), Robert Murphy, *Diplomat Among Warriors* (Garden City, 1964), Walter Bedell Smith, *My Three Years in Moscow* (Philadelphia, 1950), and Henry A. Wallace, *Toward World Peace* (Boston, 1948).

James Forrestal, Secretary of Navy and of Defense, is frank in Walter Millis, ed., *The Forrestal Diaries* (New York, 1951), and the foreign policy positions of the most influential Republican senator are in Arthur H. Vandenberg, Jr., ed., *The Private Papers of Senator Vandenberg* (Boston, 1952). For other viewpoints, see Andrew W. Cordier and Wilder Foote, eds., *Public Papers of the Secretaries—General of the United Nations*, Vol. I, *Trygve Lie, 1946–1953* (New York, 1969), and Charles de Gaulle, *The War Memoirs of Charles de Gaulle: Salvation, 1944–1946* (New York, 1960).

Russian sources are extremely limited. Some statements are located in *J. V. Stalin on Post-War International Relations* (London, 1947) and V. M. Molotov, *Problems of Foreign Policy: Speeches and Statements, April, 1945–November, 1948* (Moscow, 1949). Somewhat useful are Harrison Salisbury, ed., *Marshal Zhukov's Greatest Battles by Georgi K. Zhukov* (New York, 1969) and Andrei Y. Vyshinsky, *On Eliminating the Dangers of a New War and Strengthening the Peace and Security of Nations* (Moscow, 1951). Also consult Milovan Djilas, *Conversations with Stalin* (New York, 1962) and Isaac Deutscher, *Stalin: A Political Biography* (New York, 1966). *New Times* (periodical) and *Soviet Press Translations* (Seattle, University of Washington, 1946–1948) provide Soviet commentary on a wide range of issues. Helpful is Robert M. Slusser and Jan F. Triska, eds., *A Calendar of Soviet Treaties, 1917–1957* (Stanford, 1959).

Cold War documents—diplomatic correspondence, agreements, press releases, State Department reports—are available in the Department of State's *Foreign Relations of the United States* (multiple volumes for each year and special volumes on some conferences) and the *Department of State Bulletin*. The Ministry of Foreign Affairs of the U.S.S.R. has published *Correspondence Between the Chairman of the Council of Ministers of the U.S.S.R. and the Presidents of the U.S.A. and the Prime Ministers of Great Britain During the Great Patriotic War of 1941–1945* (Moscow, 1957; 2 vols.). A handy collection for the Truman Administration as a whole is Barton J. Bernstein and Allen J. Matusow, *The Truman Administration: A Documentary History* (New York, 1966).

345678910